Der Tatort Mauthausen
The Crime Scenes of Mauthausen

Eine Spurensuche
Searching for Traces

Der Tatort Mauthausen
The Crime Scenes of Mauthausen

Eine Spurensuche
Searching for Traces

Finanziert aus Mitteln des Bundesministeriums für Inneres und des Zukunftsfonds der Republik Österreich

Bibliografische Information der Deutschen Nationalbibliothek
Die Deutsche Nationalbibliothek verzeichnet diese Publikation in der Deutschen Nationalbibliografie; detaillierte bibliografische Daten sind im Internet über http://dnb.d-nb.de abrufbar.

Alle Rechte, insbesondere das Recht der Vervielfältigung und Verbreitung sowie der Übersetzung, vorbehalten. Kein Teil des Werkes darf in irgendeiner Form (durch Photokopie, Mikrofilm oder ein anderes Verfahren) ohne schriftliche Genehmigung des Verlages reproduziert oder unter Verwendung elektronischer Systeme gespeichert, verarbeitet, vervielfältigt oder verbreitet werden.

Der Tatort Mauthausen – Eine Spurensuche
Katalog zur Ausstellung in der KZ-Gedenkstätte Mauthausen

Herausgeber: Verein für Gedenken und Geschichtsforschung in österreichischen KZ-Gedenkstätten (Gesamtleitung: Barbara Glück, Projektkoordination: Wilhelm Stadler)

Redaktion: Gregor Holzinger, Andreas Kranebitter

Wissenschaftliche Betreuung: Bertrand Perz

Layout und Grafik: Peter Sachartschenko

Coverfoto: Aufnahme der Gedenkplaketten, die von Überlebenden des KZ Mauthausen und Angehörigen der Verstorbenen im Bereich des ehemaligen Krematoriums angebracht wurden (Foto: Tal Adler).

Copyright © 2014 by new academic press
A-1160 Wien
www.newacademicpress.at
ISBN 978-3-7003-1899-6

Druck: Rema-Print-Littera Druck- und VerlagsgmbH

Financed by the Federal Ministry of the Interior and the Future Fund of the Republic of Austria

Bibliographic information published by the Deutsche Nationalbibliothek.
The Deutsche Nationalbibliothek lists this publication in the Deutsche Nationalbibliografie; detailed bibliographic data are available on the Internet at http://dnb.dnb.de

All rights reserved, including those of reproduction, transmission and translation into foreign languages. No part of this publication may be reproduced in any form or by any means (photocopying, microfilm or otherwise) or stored in an electronic retrieval system, reworked, reproduced or transmitted without prior written permission from the publishers.

The Crimes Scenes of Mauthausen – Searching for Traces
Catalogue to the exhibition at the Mauthausen Memorial

Editor: Association for Remembrance and Historical Research in Austrian Concentration Camp Memorials (Director: Barbara Glück, Co-ordinator: Wilhelm Stadler)

Editing: Gregor Holzinger, Andreas Kranebitter

Academic Supervision: Bertrand Perz

Translation into English: Joanna White

Layout and graphic design: Peter Sachartschenko

Cover: Photograph of the memorial plaques erected in the area of the former crematorium by survivors of the Mauthausen concentration camp and the relatives of those who died (Photograph: Tal Adler).

Copyright © 2014 by new academic press
A-1160 Vienna
www.newacademicpress.at
ISBN 978-3-7003-1899-6

Printed by: Rema-Print-Littera Druck und VerlagsGmbH

Inhalt

I./ Einleitungen — 6

II./ Die Ausstellung

Alltägliche Gewalt
Everyday Violence — 17

Hinrichtungen
Executions — 29

Todesort Lagergrenze
Death at the Camp Perimeter — 43

Tod im Steinbruch
Death in the Quarry — 57

Tödliche Medizin
Deadly Medicine — 69

Mord durch Giftgas
Murder by Poison Gas — 85

Die Beseitigung der Leichen
The Disposal of the Corpses — 99

III./ Der Hintergrund

Bertrand Perz/Jörg Skriebeleit — 117
Den Tod ausstellen
Exhibiting Death

Christian Dürr/Ralf Lechner/Niko Wahl/Johanna Wensch — 134
„Der Tatort Mauthausen – Eine Spurensuche".
Zum Konzept der Ausstellung
'The Crime Scenes of Mauthausen – Searching for Traces'.
On the concept behind the exhibition

Paul Mitchell — 145
Bauarchäologie in der KZ-Gedenkstätte Mauthausen
Building Archaeology at the Mauthausen Memorial

Robert Vorberg — 157
Vom Reviergebäude zum Museum.
Zur Nutzungsgeschichte eines Gebäudes
From Infirmary to Museum.
On the history of a building and its uses

Manuel Schilcher — 166
Die architektonische Gestaltung der Ausstellung
The Exhibition's Architectural Design

Zum Geleit

Im Jahr 2015 feiert die KZ-Gedenkstätte Mauthausen den 70. Jahrestag der Befreiung des Konzentrationslagers Mauthausen. Oft wird von verschiedenen gesellschaftlichen Gruppierungen darauf hingewiesen, dass man die Vergangenheit doch nun endlich ruhen lassen sollte. Nicht nur in Anbetracht des bevorstehenden Jubiläums ist es mir ein Anliegen, diese Forderung entschieden zurückzuweisen.

Die Befreiungsfeiern 2014 an der KZ-Gedenkstätte Mauthausen wurden von neonazistischen Beschmierungen an der Außenmauer des ehemaligen KZs überschattet. Es handelt sich hierbei bereits um die dritte Schändung der KZ-Gedenkstätte Mauthausen innerhalb von wenigen Jahren.

Diese Vorkommnisse sind der beste Beweis dafür, dass wir immer weiter und immer intensiver an der Vermittlung von Menschenrechten arbeiten müssen und der Kampf gegen Rassismus und Antisemitismus weiterhin aktuell ist. Mit zunehmender zeitlicher Distanz zu den Ereignissen wird es immer wichtiger, Mauthausen als einen Lernort zu etablieren. Besonders die junge Generation, der jene Ereignisse „fremd" und „aus einer fernen Zeit" erscheinen mögen, muss über die Geschichte dieses Ortes und die Bedingungen aufgeklärt werden, die den Terror erst möglich machten.

Die Ausstellung „Der Tatort Mauthausen – Eine Spurensuche" wird in dem vorliegenden Katalog abgebildet und thematisiert die gezielten Tötungsaktionen im Zusammenhang mit der grundlegenden Vernichtungslogik des Konzentrationslagers. Bei vielen BesucherInnen der Gedenkstätte stehen die Krematorien, Gaskammer und Hinrichtungsstätte im Zentrum des Interesses. Diese Orte sind bedeutende Gedenkbereiche, gleichzeitig aber auch zentrale Bezugspunkte revisionistischer Geschichtsleugnungen.

Diesen Leugnungen wollen wir bewusst entgegentreten, indem die Ausstellung eine forensische „Spurensuche" nach den historischen Zeugnissen des Massenmords unternimmt.

Ich möchte hiermit allen danken, die direkt oder indirekt zum Gelingen der Ausstellung und des Ausstellungskataloges beigetragen haben insbesondere dem Zukunftsfonds der Republik Österreich und dem Verein für Gedenken und Geschichtsforschung in österreichischen KZ-Gedenkstätten.

Johanna Mikl-Leitner
Bundesministerin für Inneres

Preface

In 2015 the Mauthausen Memorial will commemorate the 70th anniversary of the liberation of the Mauthausen concentration camp. Different groups within society often remark that it is high time to lay the past to rest. It is a matter of personal concern, and not only in view of the approaching anniversary, to repudiate these calls firmly and decisively.

The commemorations held in 2014 at the Mauthausen Memorial to mark the liberation were overshadowed by neo-Nazi graffiti scrawled on the external wall of the former concentration camp. This is already the third time that the Mauthausen Memorial has been defaced in recent years.

These incidents are the best argument for continuing with and intensifying our work on human rights education and that the fight against racism and anti-Semitism is as relevant today as ever. With the increasing temporal distance to the events themselves it becomes ever more important to establish Mauthausen as a place of learning. Younger generations in particular, to whom these events might appear 'foreign' or 'from a distant past', must be educated about the history of this place and the conditions that made terror possible in the first place.

The exhibition 'The Crime Scenes of Mauthausen – Searching for Traces', which is reproduced in this catalogue, thematises the targeted killing actions in relation to the underlying logic of extermination of the concentration camp. For many visitors to the memorial museum, their main interest lies in the crematoria, the gas chamber and the execution room. These places are important memorial sites, whilst at the same time they serve as central points of reference for historical revisionism and denial.

In undertaking a forensic search for the traces of historical evidence of mass murder, the exhibition deliberately seeks to confront these denials.

I would like to take this opportunity to thank all those who, directly or indirectly, contributed to the success of the exhibition and the catalogue, in particular the Future Fund of the Republic of Austria and the Association for Remembrance and Historical Research in Austrian Concentration Camp Memorials.

Johanna Mikl-Leitner
Federal Minister of the Interior

Gedenken und Lernen

Am 5. Mai 1945 – wenige Tage vor Ende des 2. Weltkrieges in Europa und der endgültigen Befreiung Österreichs vom NS-Terrorregime – wurde das KZ Mauthausen durch Einheiten der US Army befreit. Mauthausen war mit seinen Außenlagern das größte Vernichtungslager auf dem Boden des heutigen Österreich, in dem zehntausende Menschen zu Tode kamen und unermessliches Leid ertragen mussten.

Heute ist das ehemalige Konzentrationslager die größte KZ-Gedenkstätte in Österreich, die in den letzten Jahren in wesentlichen Teilen neugestaltet wurde. Diese Neugestaltung spiegelt auch den Wandel wider, der sich in unserer Gesellschaft vollzogen hat: Von der Geschichtsverdrängung über ein zaghaftes Hinschauen zur aktiven Auseinandersetzung mit den schmerzvollsten und unbequemsten Wahrheiten unserer Geschichte.

Dieser Wandel erfordert neue Formen der Wissensvermittlung. Die Jugend von heute stellt andere Fragen, als wir dies vor vierzig oder fünfzig Jahren getan haben. Darauf sind Antworten umso dringender notwendig, als die Anzahl jener Zeitzeugen, die noch aus eigenem Erinnern ihr Überleben im Konzentrationslager beschreiben können, immer kleiner wird. Der Zeitpunkt naht, an dem die Jüngeren überhaupt nur noch Ausstellungen, Filme und Tondokumente haben werden, um die Berichte von Augenzeugen und Überlebenden kennen zu lernen.

Warum ist Mauthausen so wichtig? Weil es ein Ort kaum beschreibbaren Leids ist, ein Ort des Gedenkens, ein Ort der Mahnung und des Lernens, ein Ort, an dem die Mitverantwortung vieler Österreicherinnen und Österreicher für die nationalsozialistischen Verbrechen evident wird, aber auch ein Tiefpunkt in der Geschichte eines seiner staatlichen Freiheit beraubten Landes. Die Ausstellung in der Gedenkstätte Mauthausen gibt den Überlebenden eine Stimme, erweist den Opfern Ehre und nennt die Täter. Sie zeigt aber auch, dass selbst die brutalste Diktatur den Wunsch nach Freiheit, Menschenwürde, Rechtsstaatlichkeit und Demokratie nicht auszurotten vermochte. Tausende gaben dafür im Konzentrationslager Mauthausen und den Außenlagern ihr Leben. Die Ausstellung und der Katalog versuchen, dem Erbe dieser Opfer gerecht zu werden.

Es ist gesetzlicher Auftrag des Zukunftsfonds der Republik Österreich, Projekte und Initiativen zu unterstützen und zu ermöglichen, „die den Interessen und dem Gedenken der Opfer des nationalsozialistischen Regimes, der Erinnerung an die Bedrohung durch totalitäre Systeme und Gewaltherrschaft sowie der internationalen Zusammenarbeit dienen und zu einer Förderung der Achtung der Menschenrechte und der gegenseitigen Toleranz auf diesen Gebieten beitragen".

Eines der wesentlichen Ergebnisse einer vom Zukunftsfonds geförderten und 2014 präsentierten Studie „NS-Geschichtsbewusstsein und autoritäre Einstellungen in Österreich" lautet, dass die Auseinandersetzung mit der Geschichte, mit dem Nationalsozialismus und dem Zweiten Weltkrieg eine wichtige Orientierungshilfe ist, um die aktuellen politischen Herausforderungen der modernen globalisierten Gesellschaft zu verstehen und gegenüber autoritären, nationalistischen, antisemitischen, fremdenfeindlichen und rassistischen Tendenzen und Versuchungen immunisiert zu sein. Intensive politische Bildungsarbeit in allen Bereichen und die Förderung der Auseinandersetzung mit der Geschichte des Nationalsozialismus mit Kooperationspartnern, die möglichst alle Schichten der Bevölkerung erreichen, sind daher das Gebot der Zeit.

Alljährlich besuchen weit über 170.000 Menschen, darunter fast die Hälfte Schülerinnen und Schüler, die Gedenkstätte Mauthausen. Die neugestalteten Ausstellungen und die Kataloge leisten daher wesentliche Beiträge zur notwendigen Bewusstseinsbildung. Deren Unterstützung ist daher für den Zukunftsfonds ein besonders wichtiges Projekt.

Unser Dank gilt vor allem Prof. Dr. Bertrand Perz und allen Mitarbeiterinnen und Mitarbeitern für die Gestaltung der Ausstellungen. Vor allem aber gebührt er allen Besucherinnen und Besuchern.

Wir danken für Ihr Interesse und Ihre Nachdenklichkeit.

Kurt Scholz
Vorsitzender des Kuratoriums
des Zukunftsfonds der Republik Österreich

Herwig Hösele
Generalsekretär des
Zukunftsfonds der Republik Österreich

Remembering and Learning

On 5 May 1945 – a few days before the end of the Second World War in Europe and Austria's final liberation from the National Socialist regime of terror – the Mauthausen concentration camp was liberated by units of the US army. Together with its subcamps, Mauthausen was the largest extermination camp on Austrian soil; tens of thousands of people died there and were subjected to immeasurable suffering. Today the former concentration camp is the largest concentration camp memorial museum in Austria and large parts of it have been redesigned over recent years. This redesign also reflects the changes that have taken place in our society: from the suppression of history to a hesitant nod in its direction to active engagement with the most painful and uncomfortable truths of our history.

This change also calls for new forms of communicating knowledge. The questions asked by young people today are different to those we asked forty or fifty years ago. The need for answers to them is becoming all the more urgent as the number of eyewitnesses who can still describe their survival of the concentration camp based on their own experience of it continues to decrease. The time is approaching when young people will have access to the memories of eyewitnesses and survivors only through exhibitions, films and audio recordings.

Why is Mauthausen so important? Because it is a place of almost indescribable suffering, a place of remembrance, a place of warning and of learning, a place where the responsibility many Austrians bear for the crimes of National Socialism becomes clear, but also a low point in the history of a country robbed of its national freedom. The exhibition at the Mauthausen Memorial gives the survivors a voice, honours the victims, and names the perpetrators. But it also shows that even the most brutal of dictatorships was not able to stamp out the wish for freedom, human dignity, the rule of law, and democracy. Thousands gave their lives for this in the Mauthausen concentration camp and its subcamps. The exhibition and the catalogue are an attempt to do justice to the legacy of these victims.

The Future Fund of the Republic of Austria has a mandate to support and enable projects and initiatives 'that further the commemoration of the victims of the National Socialist regime, the remembrance of the threat posed by totalitarian systems and tyranny, and international cooperation and, on the basis of this, that foster human rights education and mutual tolerance.'

One important finding of a study supported by the Future Fund – 'Historical Consciousness of National Socialism and Authoritarian Attitudes in Austria', published in 2014 – was that a critical engagement with history, with National Socialism and the Second World War provides important guidance for understanding the contemporary political challenges facing a modern, globalised society and for protecting against authoritarian, nationalist, anti-Semitic, xenophobic, and racist tendencies and temptations. Intensive political education across all fields and the promotion of a critical engagement with the history of National Socialism, with cooperation partners who can reach as many sections of the population as possible, are therefore the order of the day.

Every year well over 170,000 people, almost half of whom are school pupils, visit the Mauthausen Memorial. The redesigned exhibitions and catalogues thus make a significant contribution to the consciousness-raising that is needed. Supporting them is therefore a particularly important project for the Future Fund.

Our thanks go, first and foremost, to Prof. Dr. Bertrand Perz and to all those who worked on creating the exhibitions. But above all, we owe thanks to all those who visit them.

We are grateful for their interest and their thoughtful reflection.

Kurt Scholz
President of the Board of Trustees
of the Future Fund of the Republic of Austria

Herwig Hösele
Secretary General of the
Future Fund of the Republic of Austria

Vorwort

In den Wochen und Monaten, in denen wir den vorliegenden Katalog fertig gestellt haben, sind unerwartete und unglaubliche Dinge passiert – Dinge, von denen viele von uns gehofft hatten, wir hätten sie überstanden. Erneut prangten menschenverachtende Beschmierungen auf den Mauern der KZ-Gedenkstätte Mauthausen – gleich Wunden, geschlagen in jenen Ort, der ohnehin für die unendliche Verletzung steht. Erneut beschädigten Vandalen Holocaust-Denkmäler in Salzburg.

Soweit das Sichtbare. Aber betrachten wir das „Bigger Picture": Das Wall Street Journal berichtet über eine von der Anti Defamation League initiierte Umfrage, wonach weltweit nur knapp jeder zweite unter 35-Jährige über den Holocaust Bescheid weiß. Ähnliche Studien für Europa zeichnen kein wesentlich besseres Bild.

Antisemitismus und Rassismus scheinen sich, quasi auf Schleichwegen, den Weg in die Mitte unserer modernen und liberalen Gesellschaft zurückzuerobern. Trotzdem werde ich häufig gefragt, ob es nun, 70 Jahre nach dem Ende des Holocaust, nicht langsam „genug" wäre. Die Gräuel des Zweiten Weltkriegs und die Schuld, die sich einige europäische Staaten, allen voran natürlich Deutschland und Österreich, aufgeladen haben, scheinen nicht mehr „zu ziehen". In den USA, wo ich nun sechs Monate am United States Holocaust Memorial Museum forschen durfte, heißt das: „it doesn´t resonate with people" – es bringt keine Saite mehr zum Schwingen.

An diesem Punkt entstehen Selbstzweifel: sind wir zu wenig aktiv? Kennen wir unser Zielpublikum? Erreichen wir die Menschen, die wir erreichen wollen, oder müssen wir unsere Konzepte überarbeiten? Wie muss unsere Kommunikation und Vermittlung aufgebaut sein?

Eines weiß ich bestimmt: mir gibt Hoffnung, dass sich so viele junge Menschen, besonders auch in meinem Team, engagieren und nicht müde werden, neue Ideen und Aspekte einzubringen. Tag für Tag.

Wollen wir in unserer Arbeit, mit unserem Anliegen erfolgreich sein, braucht es Zusammenarbeit auf breiter Basis: Die Wissenschaft muss die Wissenslücken schließen, die PädagogInnen, die bei uns in der Gedenkstätte Mauthausen und an so vielen bedeutenden Orten Tag für Tag tätig sind, müssen zur Menschen- und Herzensbildung der BesucherInnen beitragen, die Politik muss die ultimative und nicht bloß die „übergeordnete" Verantwortung tragen und jeder von uns jeden Tag Courage als Grundhaltung seines/ihres Handelns beweisen. Denn, von einer Sache bin ich überzeugt: Vergessen dürfen wir uns nicht leisten. „Never Again" ist heute wichtiger denn je.

Barbara Glück
Leiterin der KZ-Gedenkstätte Mauthausen

Foreword

In the weeks and months spent working on this catalogue, unexpected and unthinkable things have occurred – things which many of us hoped we had seen the last of. Once again the walls of the Mauthausen Memorial were emblazoned with racist graffiti – like wounds, inflicted on the very place which stands for everlasting injury. Once again vandals damaged Holocaust memorials in Salzburg.

So much for the visible. But let us take a look at the bigger picture: The Wall Street Journal reported on a survey commissioned by the Anti-Defamation League, according to which only just over half of those under 35 worldwide know about the Holocaust. The picture painted by similar studies in Europe is not a great deal better.

Anti-Semitism and racism seem, by some back route, to be gaining ground at the centre of our modern and liberal society. In spite of this I am often asked whether now, 70 years after the end of the Holocaust, it isn't time to say 'enough'. The atrocities of the Second World War and the guilt that several European states, first and foremost of course Germany and Austria, have brought upon themselves no longer have 'traction'. In the USA, where I recently spent six months researching at the United States Holocaust Memorial Museum, they say that 'it doesn't resonate with people'.

At this point self-doubt creeps in: Are we not being active enough? Do we know our target audience? Are we reaching the people we want to reach, or do we need to rethink our concepts? How should our outreach and education programmes be structured?

One thing I do know for certain: I am given hope by the many young people, especially in my team, who are engaged with the topic and do not tire of contributing new ideas and angles. Day after day.

If we want to be successful in our work, in our aims, we need cooperation on a broad basis: academic research must fill the gaps in our knowledge; the guides who, day in, day out, are active at the Mauthausen Memorial and at so many other important sites must reach out to visitors' hearts and humanity; politicians must bear an ultimate responsibility, not merely a 'higher' one; and every day each one of us must demonstrate that our actions are based on courage. For there is one thing I am certain of: we cannot afford to forget. 'Never again' is more important today than ever.

Barbara Glück
Director of the Mauthausen Memorial

Gregor Holzinger/Andreas Kranebitter

Editorial

Die Ausstellung *Der Tatort Mauthausen – Eine Spurensuche* wurde im Mai 2013 – gemeinsam mit der Ausstellung *Das Konzentrationslager Mauthausen 1938–1945* und dem *Raum der Namen* – eröffnet. Sie thematisiert, als erste von fünf geplanten Themenausstellungen, den Massenmord im KZ Mauthausen – und geht den unterschiedlichen Methoden des Tötens an den unterschiedlichen Tatorten des Konzentrationslagers nach. Einer forensischen Analyse gleich werden die Spuren der Verbrechen rekonstruiert und kontextualisiert, historische Details vermittelt und der Umgang mit den Relikten der Massentötungen nach 1945 dargestellt.

Der vorliegende Katalog bildet die sieben Themenstationen der Ausstellung in sieben Kapiteln ab. Die einzelnen Stationen werden – analog zu den Baukörpern der Ausstellung – von großformatigen Fotogra-

Gregor Holzinger/Andreas Kranebitter

Editorial

The exhibition *The Crime Scenes of Mauthausen – Searching for Traces* opened in May 2013 together with the exhibition *The Mauthausen Concentration Camp 1938-1945* and the *Room of Names*. As the first of five planned thematic exhibitions, it focuses on mass murder in the Mauthausen concentration camp – and examines the different killing methods used at the different crime scenes around the concentration camp. As in a forensic analysis, the traces of the crimes are reconstructed and contextualised, historical details are presented, and an account is given of how these relics of the mass killings were dealt with after 1945.

This catalogue presents the exhibition's seven thematic stations in seven chapters. In analogy to the display cases in the exhibition, each individual chapter is introduced by a large-format photograph.

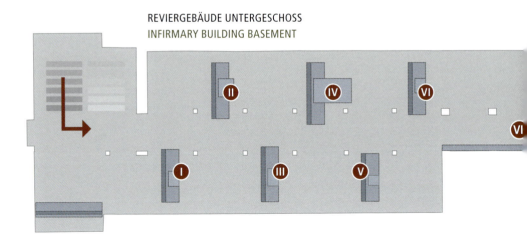

Graphics: Eva Schwingenschlögl

fien eingeleitet. Sie zeigen die jeweiligen „Tatorte" in ihrer heutigen Form, wie sie beim vorangehenden Besuch des Gedenkstättengeländes zu sehen sind. Die Ausstellung bildet damit gewissermaßen zugleich eine Nachbereitung des Gedenkstättenrundgangs und Vorbereitung für die Besichtigung der Tötungsbereiche der Gaskammer und der Exekutionsstätte.

In jeder Themenstation der Ausstellung findet sich ein Leitobjekt, das im Katalog den eigentlichen Inhalten der Station vorangestellt wird. Die Inhalte der Stationen gliedern sich wiederum in zwei Unterkapitel. Während im ersten Teil die historischen Relikte präsentiert werden, thematisiert der zweite Teil den Umgang mit den Relikten in der Nachkriegszeit. Diese Unterkapitel sind im Katalog durch Überschiften und einleitende Absätze getrennt.

This shows the 'crime scene' in question in its current state, as it would just have been seen by visitors on their preceding tour of the memorial complex. Thus to a certain extent, the exhibition provides both a follow-up to the tour of the memorial site and a preparation for viewing the killing areas, comprising gas chamber and execution room.

Each thematic station in the exhibition has a central object that, in the catalogue, is placed before the actual content for that station. In turn, this content is divided into two subchapters for each station: whilst the first part presents the historical relics, the second part thematises how these relics have been dealt with in the post-war era. In the catalogue these subchapters are separated by headings and introductory paragraphs.

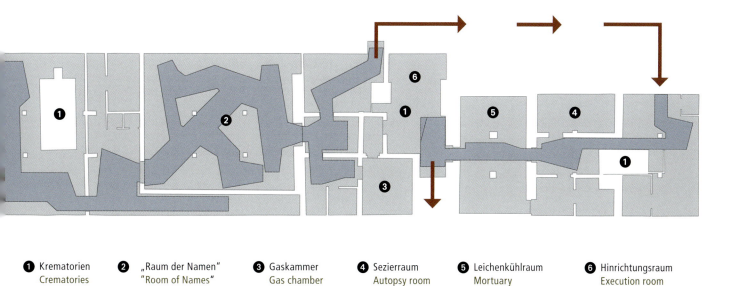

❶ Krematorien / Crematories ❷ „Raum der Namen" / "Room of Names" ❸ Gaskammer / Gas chamber ❹ Sezierraum / Autopsy room ❺ Leichenkühlraum / Mortuary ❻ Hinrichtungsraum / Execution room

Der vorliegende Katalog bildet die Ausstellung *Der Tatort Mauthausen – Eine Spurensuche* vollständig ab. Das bereits für den 2013 publizierten Ausstellungskatalog *Das Konzentrationslager Mauthausen 1938–1945* verfolgte Ziel, neben den Fotografien, Dokumenten, Objekten und Texten der Ausstellung auch alle Audioinhalte im Katalog zu veröffentlichen, konnte für den vorliegenden Katalog ausnahmslos umgesetzt werden. Die Transkripte der Audiostationen finden sich in grafisch abgehobenen Kästen.

Im letzten Teil des Katalogs finden sich vier vertiefende Texte, die die Hintergründe und Ausstellungsideen beleuchten. Betrand Perz und Jörg Skriebeleit gehen auf die grundlegende Idee der Ausstellung ein – eine archäologische bzw. forensische „Spurensuche" nach den historischen Zeugnissen des Massenmords, der die BesucherInnen in den Ausstellungsstationen nachgehen. Christian Dürr, Ralf Lechner, Niko Wahl und Johanna Wensch erläutern das kuratorische Feinkonzept der Ausstellung und erklären Aufbau und Inhalt der Stationen anhand ausgewählter Beispiele. Paul Mitchell stellt in seinem Artikel die Ergebnisse seiner bauarchäologischen Forschungen vor, die in den letzten Jahren vor und während der Umbauten des historischen Ausstellungsgebäudes durchgeführt wurden und an vielen Stellen in die Ausstellung eingeflossen sind. Diese Beschäftigung mit dem Ausstellungsort, die einen wesentlicher Bestandteil der „Spurensuche"

The catalogue reproduces the exhibition *The Crime Scenes of Mauthausen – Searching for Traces* in full. The intention already pursued in the 2013 catalogue to the exhibition *The Mauthausen Concentration Camp 1938-1945* – namely, of including the audio content in the catalogue alongside the photographs, documents, objects and texts used in the exhibition – could also be carried out here without exception. The transcripts of the audio exhibits are to be found in the visually distinctive boxed texts.

The final section of the catalogue contains four in-depth articles which shed light on the background to and ideas for the exhibition. Bertrand Perz and Jörg Skriebeleit explore the basic idea behind the exhibition – an archaeological or forensic 'searching for traces' of the historical evidence of mass murder, which visitors undertake as they make their way around the exhibition. The curators Christian Dürr, Ralf Lechner, Niko Wahl and Johanna Wensch explain their detailed concept for the exhibition and illustrate the composition and content of each thematic station through selected examples. Paul Mitchell outlines the results of his building archaeological investigations in his article, which were carried out over the past few years both before and during the remodelling of the exhibition building, and which have been incorporated into the exhibition in several places. This engagement with the site of the exhibition itself, which constitutes a

bildet, setzt Robert Vorberg in seiner Darstellung der baulichen Maßnahmen während der Sanierung und Adaption des ehemaligen Reviergebäudes fort. Manuel Schilcher gibt hier schließlich einen kurzen Überblick über die ausstellungsarchitektonischen Grundüberlegungen.

Wir danken allen an der Erstellung dieses Katalogs Beteiligten, insbesondere den AutorInnen der Beiträge, dem Zukunftsfonds der Republik Österreich sowie dem Bundesministeriums für Inneres für die Finanzierung, und dem Verein für Gedenken und Geschichtsforschung in österreichischen KZ-Gedenkstätten und Willi Stadler für die professionelle Umsetzung dieses Projektes. Joanna White gilt unser Dank für die umsichtigen Übersetzungen, Tal Adler für die Fotografie der Ausstellungsobjekte und Harald Knill und Peter Sachartschenko von der new academic press für die produktive Zusammenarbeit.

Abschließend gilt unser Dank allen Leihgebenden, die uns mit der Ausstellungsproduktion auch die Genehmigung zur Reproduktion im ausstellungsbegleitenden Katalog erteilt haben. In allen anderen Fällen haben wir uns um nochmalige Genehmigung zur Reproduktion bemüht. Sollte uns das in Ausnahmefällen nicht gelungen sein, bitten wir um Nachsicht und entsprechende Rückmeldung.

significant feature of the 'search for traces', is taken up by Robert Vorberg in his description of the construction measures carried out during the renovation and adaptation of the former infirmary building. Finally, Manuel Schilcher gives a short overview of rationale behind the exhibition architecture.

We would like to thank all those involved in the creation of this catalogue, in particular the authors of the articles, the Future Fund of the Republic of Austria and the Federal Ministry of the Interior for providing the funding, and the Association for Remembrance and Historical Research in Austrian Concentration Camp Memorial Sites and Willi Stadler for their professional project management. Our thanks to Joanna White for her thoughtful translations, Tal Adler for his photographs of the exhibits, and Harald Knill and Peter Schartschenko of the *new academic press* for a productive collaboration.

Finally, we would like to thank all those who loaned objects and who, when giving us permission for the exhibition, also granted us reproduction rights for the accompanying catalogue. In all other cases we have endeavoured to obtain separate permission for the reproduction. In the few exceptional cases where this has not been possible, we ask for the understanding of the parties concerned and that they contact us.

Alltägliche Gewalt
Everyday Violence

Ehemaliger Appellplatz, 2012
Foto: Tal Adler

Former roll call area, 2012
Photograph: Tal Adler

Alltägliche Gewalt

Die SS ahndet bestimmte Verstöße gegen die Lagerordnung offiziell mit körperlichen Strafen. Viele Häftlinge sterben an deren Folgen. Darüber hinaus kann jeder Gefangene stets Opfer willkürlicher Gewaltexzesse von SS-Angehörigen und Funktionshäftlingen werden. In heimlichen Aufzeichnungen dokumentieren Gefangene diese Verbrechen.

Everyday Violence

The SS officially punishes certain violations of the *Lagerordnung* (camp regulations) with corporal punishment. Many prisoners die from the consequences of this. What is more, any inmate may fall victim to the arbitrary violent excesses of SS members and prisoner functionaries at any time. Inmates keep secret records documenting these crimes.

Ochsenziemer aus Mauthausen
KZ-Gedenkstätte Mauthausen, OS450
Foto: Tal Adler

SS-Angehörige sowie Funktionshäftlinge mit Bewachungsaufgaben tragen meist eine Peitsche oder einen Schlagstock bei sich. Die in der Lagerordnung als Strafe vorgesehenen Stockhiebe werden in Mauthausen mit einem Ochsenziemer ausgeführt.
Den hier gezeigten Ochsenziemer nehmen tschechische Häftling kurz nach der Befreiung als Beweis- und Erinnerungsstück mit in die Heimat. 1967 wird er der Sammlung der KZ-Gedenkstätte Mauthausen übergeben.

Ochsenziemer (leather whip) from Mauthausen
KZ-Gedenkstätte Mauthausen, OS450
Photograph: Tal Adler

Members of the SS as well as prisoner functionaries with guard duties usually carry a whip or truncheon. The lashes laid down as punishment in the camp regulations are carried out in Mauthausen using an *Ochsenziemer* (leather whip).
Shortly after liberation, Czech prisoners take the whip shown here back to their home country as both evidence and a memento. In 1967 it is presented to the collection of the Mauthausen Memorial.

Pfahlhängen, Zeichnung eines unbekannten Häftlings, vermutlich vor 1943
Dokumentationsarchiv des österreichischen Widerstandes, Wien, 10457

Die Skizze wird als Beleg für die Vorgänge im Lager heimlich aus Mauthausen herausgeschmuggelt. Das mindestens halbstündige Pfahlhängen ist bis 1943 eine regulär angewandte Bestrafungsform und eine häufig eingesetzte Foltermethode.

Post hanging, sketch by an unknown prisoner, probably before 1943
Dokumentationsarchiv des österreichischen Widerstandes, Vienna, 10457

The sketch is secretly smuggled out of Mauthausen as evidence of what goes on in the camp. Post hanging, which lasts for at least half an hour, is used as a standard form of punishment until 1943 and is frequently employed as a method of torture.

Meldung der Todesfälle im Außenlager Ebensee an das Hauptlager, 15. Mai 1944
Hrvatski povijesni muzej, Zagreb, ur. broj: 3-18-1/13

Etliche Gefangene erleben mit, wie der Lagerführer von Ebensee einen Hund solange auf den Italiener Danilo Veronesi hetzt, bis dieser tot ist. In der Meldung der Todesfälle aus Ebensee nennt die SS als Ursache für Veronesis Tod Selbstmord am elektrisch geladenen Lagerzaun. Beim Todesdatum liegt ein Schreibfehler vor.

Notification of deaths in the Ebensee subcamp sent to the main camp, 15 May 1944
Hrvatski povijesni muzej, Zagreb, ur. broj: 3-18-1/13

A number of prisoners witness how the head of the Ebensee camp sets a dog on the Italian Danilo Veronesi and lets it maul him to death. In the Ebensee death reports, the SS gives Veronesi's cause of death as suicide on the electrically charged camp fence. There is a clerical error regarding the date of death.

K. L. M a u t h a u s e n   O. U. den 15. Mai 1944
Arbeitslager 3.- Kalksteinbergwerk

Betrifft : Todesfälle von Häftlingen
Bezug   : ohne
Anlagen : keine

An das
Schutzhaftlager
K. L. M a u t h a u s e n / Oberdonau

Jm hiesigen Lager starben nachstehende Häftlinge :

1. Sch. Pole P i s k o r z Wawrzynice, Nr. 33495 geb. 30.8.00 in Rosa-Podgorna, verstorben am 12.5.44 um 6.15 Uhr.
2. Sch. Jugo V u k o s a v l j e v i c Milutan, Nr. 38654 geb. 15.3.08 in Rogaca, verstorben am 12.5.44 um 6.30 Uhr.
3. Sch. Pole O l s z e w s k i Stanislaw, Nr. 58437 geb. 10.10.99 in Bronowo, verstorben am 12.5.44 um 9 Uhr.
4. Sch. Pole U r b a n o w s k i Josef, Nr. 58603 geb. 11.5.26, in Warschau, verstorben am 12.5.44 um 9.10 Uhr.
5. Sch. Pole K r z e m i n s k i Stanislaw, Nr. 52813 geb. -.-.09 in Poddebice, am 12.5.44 um 11.45 Uhr auf der Flucht erschossen.
6. Sch. Jugo J o v i c i c Mijajlo, Nr. 38478 geb. 22.2.22 in Grab, am 12.5.44 um 13.30 Uhr auf der Flucht erschossen.
7. Ziv. Russe S c h u l y k Pawel, Nr. 41382 geb. 5.11.05 in Kusmin, verstorben am 12.5.44 um 18.15 Uhr.
8. Sch. Pole G o r s k i Wladyslaw, Nr. 41482 geb. 21.5.03 in Nosalewo, verstorben am 12.5.44 um 20 Uhr.
9. Sch. Pole P i e t k o w s k i Josef, Nr. 58459 geb. 14.10.18 in Kodesko, verstorben am 13.5.44 um 7.30 Uhr.
10. Sch. Ital. C a c i a l l i Tommaso, Nr. 56998 geb. 7.5.90. in Monte-Lupo, verstorben am 13.5.44 um 20 Uhr.
11. Sch. Ital. V e r o n e s i Danilo, Nr. 57467 geb. 7.3.26 in Caprino-Veronese, verstorben am 13.4.55 um 24 Uhr durch Freitod (Elektrizität).
12. Krgf. SU K o s b u s c h k o Wassilij, Nr. 39692 geb. 12.4.96 in Chabinskaja, verstorben am 14.5.44 um 7.30 Uhr.
13. Sch. Pole K r z y w i c k i Tadeusz, Nr. 57804 geb. 6.6.18 in Kleszawa verstorben am 14.5.44 um 10 Uhr.
14. Sch. Pole S a w i c k i Stefan, Nr. 57711 geb. 9.10.16. in Jaroszewo, verstorben am 14.5.44 um 11.15 Uhr
15. Sch. Ital. G u a r n i e r i Guiseppe, Nr. 57194 geb. 24.3.87 in Pistoia verstorben am 14.5.44 um 12.30 Uhr.

SS-Obersturmführer und

Auszüge aus den Notizen von Drahomír Bárta, zwischen 1943 und 1945
Privatbesitz Vít Bárta

Extracts from the notes of Drahomír Bárta, between 1943 and 1945
Owned by Vít Bárta

Tagebucheintrag von Drahomír Bárta über den Mord an Danilo Veronesi im Außenlager Ebensee, 14. Mai 1944
Drahomír Bárta: Tagebuch aus dem KZ Ebensee, hg. v. Florian Freund und Verena Pawlowsky, Wien: Verlag Turia + Kant 2005

Der tschechische Häftling Drahomír Bárta ist Zeuge des Mordes an Danilo Veronesi. Da Bárta in der Lagerschreibstube eingesetzt ist, bekommt er zudem mit, dass die Todesursache in den SS-Dokumenten bewusst gefälscht wird. In seinem heimlich geführten Tagebuch hält er den Vorfall fest.

14.5.44

Schreckliche Nacht. Ein junger Italiener, Veronesi Danilo, Nr. 57467, geb. 7.5.26 in Caprino Veronese, versuchte zu fliehen. Er wurde zwei oder drei Tage von der Polizei und speziellen SS-Einheiten gesucht, bis er von einem Waldarbeiter in den Bergen ca. 15 km vom Lager entfernt gefasst wurde. Am 13. Mai wurde er in der Nacht zurückgebracht. Verhör, Lagerführer Otto Riemer und Blockführer Hans Büchner. Er wurde gefoltert und geschlagen. Schließlich ließen sie eine Dogge, Lord genannt, der Schrecken aller Häftlinge, auf ihn los. Lord wurde von Riemer angetrieben, er griff ihn fast ein Stunde an, bis er ihn tot biss. Ein schrecklicher Anblick. Der arme achtzehnjährige Danilo versuchte sich die ganze Zeit zu wehren, und er rief die ganze Zeit flehend: „Pietà Commandante. Pietà Commandante. Aiuto Mamma mia! Nach Mitternacht ging es zu Ende. Die SS warf den zerrissenen Körper in die elektrischen Drähte. Nach Mauthausen wurde gemeldet: Freitod durch Elektrizität.

Diary entry by Drahomír Bárta on the murder of Danilo Veronesi in the Ebensee subcamp, 14 May 1944
Drahomír Bárta: Tagebuch aus dem KZ Ebensee, eds. Florian Freund and Verena Pawlowsky, Vienna: Turia + Kant 2005

The Czech prisoner Drahomír Bárta is a witness to Danilo Veronesi's murder. Since Bárta is assigned to the camp clerk's office, he also sees that the cause of death has been deliberately falsified in SS documents. He records the incident in his diary, which he writes in secret.

14.5.44

A terrible night. A young Italian, Veronesi Danilo, No. 57467, born 7.5.26 in Caprino Veronese, tried to escape. He was hunted by the police and special SS units for two or three days before being caught by a woodsman in the mountains about 15 km from the camp. On 13 May he was brought back in the night. Interrogation, Lagerführer Otto Riemer and Blockführer Hans Büchner. He was tortured and beaten. Finally they let a mastiff, called Lord, the terror of all the prisoners, loose on him. Lord was spurred on by Riemer, he attacked him for nearly an hour before biting him to death. A terrible sight. The poor eighteen-year old Danilo was trying to defend himself the entire time, and he kept calling out, pleading: "Pietà Commandante. Pietà Commandante. Aiuto Mamma mia!" After midnight it came to an end. The SS threw his mauled body onto the electric fence. The report sent to Mauthausen was: Suicide by electrocution.

Erinnerte Gewalt

Exekutionen oder Tötungsaktionen finden meist im Verborgenen oder in Anwesenheit nur weniger Häftlinge statt. Die alltäglichen Gewaltexzesse im Lager haben dagegen viele Augenzeugen. Sie brennen sich in das Gedächtnis der überlebenden Gefangenen ein. Einige halten ihre Erinnerungen in Zeichnungen fest.

Remembered Violence

Executions and killing actions mainly take place out of sight or with only a few prisoners present. In contrast, the everyday acts of excessive violence in the camp have a great many eye-witnesses. These acts are burned into the memories of the survivors. Some turn their recollections into drawings.

Eo Baussano: „Il capo baracca si diverte"
(Der Blockführer vergnügt sich), um 1946
Istituto per la Storia della Resistenza e della Società
Contemporanea in Provincia di Asti (ISRAT), Fondo Spada,
scheda n. 640

Eo Baussano: 'Il capo baracca si diverte'
(The block leader amuses himself), around 1946
Istituto per la Storia della Resistenza e della Società
Contemporanea in Provincia di Asti (ISRAT), Fondo Spada,
scheda n. 640

Der italienische Dekorationsmaler Eo Baussano ist ab 1944 in Mauthausen, später in Gusen inhaftiert. Nach seiner Befreiung verfasst er einen langen Erinnerungsbericht und zeichnet zur Illustration einige Szenen aus Mauthausen.

The Italian decorator Eo Baussano is imprisoned in Mauthausen, later in Gusen, from 1944. Following his liberation he writes a long account of his experiences and draws some scenes from Mauthausen as illustrations.

David Olère: „à Melk Capo Paulus" (in Melk Kapo Paulus), 1950
Ghetto Fighters' House archives, Art Collection, Westgaliläa, Catalog No. 2685

Der als Jude verfolgte David Olère wird 1943 aus Frankreich nach Auschwitz deportiert. 1945 kommt er zunächst in das Mauthausener Außenlager Melk und schließlich nach Ebensee. Nach seiner Befreiung widmet sich der Maler und Bildhauer in seiner künstlerischen Arbeit ganz der Erinnerung an das Erlebte.

David Olère: 'à Melk Capo Paulus' (in Melk Kapo Paulus), 1950
Ghetto Fighters' House archives, Art Collection, Western Galilee, Catalog No. 2685

David Olère, persecuted as a Jew, is deported to Auschwitz from France in 1943. In 1945 he is sent first to the Mauthausen subcamp in Melk and later to Ebensee. After liberation the painter and sculptor devotes his artistic work wholly to the memory of what he has lived through.

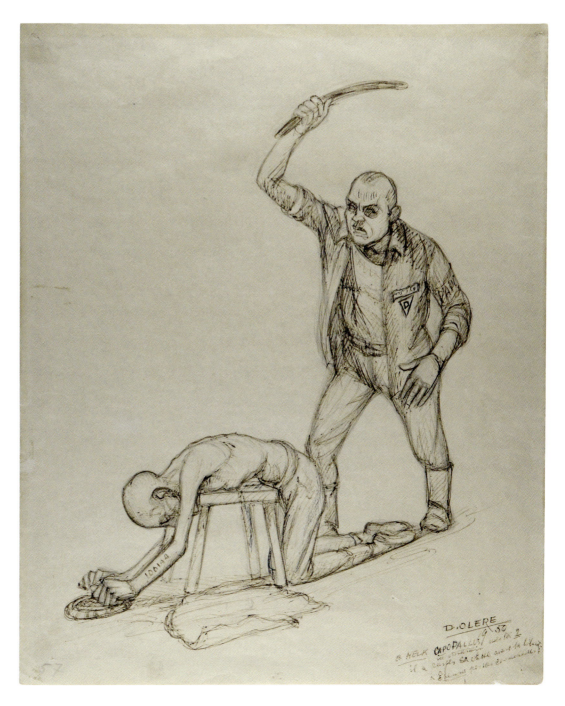

Bernard Aldebert: „Gusen II – Un detenu arrive en retard au Rassemblement" (Gusen II - Ein Häftling kommt beim Antreten zu spät), 1945
KZ-Gedenkstätte Mauthausen, F/9b/3/8/23

Bernard Aldebert, ein französischer Grafiker, verarbeitet seine Erlebnisse in den Konzentrationslagern Buchenwald, Mauthausen und Gusen nach seiner Befreiung künstlerisch. Er veröffentlicht seine Zeichnungen 1946 zusammen mit eigenen Texten unter dem Titel „Chemin de la croix en 50 stations" (Kreuzweg in 50 Stationen).

Bernard Aldebert: 'Gusen II – Un detenu arrive en retard au Rassemblement' (Gusen II - A prisoner arrives late for roll call), 1945
KZ-Gedenkstätte Mauthausen, F/9b/3/8/23

After his liberation, the French graphic artist Bernard Aldebert works through his experiences in the Buchenwald, Mauthausen and Gusen concentration camps in his art. In 1946 he publishes his drawings, together with his own texts, under the title 'Chemin de la croix en 50 stations' (The way of the cross in 50 stations).

Tomás Jiménez Santos, ohne Titel, zwischen 1946 und 1948
Privatbesitz Paul Jiménez, Eggersdorf

Der Spanier Tomás Jiménez Santos studiert Kunst in Madrid, ehe er vor den spanischen Faschisten nach Frankreich flieht. Von dort wird er nach Mauthausen deportiert. Nach fünf Jahren Haft in Mauthausen und Gusen fertigt er ein umfassendes Bilder-Tagebuch an, das die Zeit seiner Verfolung dokumentiert.

Tomás Jiménez Santos, untitled, between 1946 and 1948
Owned by Paul Jiménez, Eggersdorf

The Spaniard Tomás Jiménez Santos studies art in Madrid before fleeing the Spanish fascists to France. From there he is deported to Mauthausen. After five years' imprisonment in Mauthausen and Gusen he creates a comprehensive picture diary that documents the period of his persecution.

Hinrichtungen
Executions

Ort der ehemaligen Hinrichtungsstätte nördlich des
Häftlingslagers, 2012
Foto: Tal Adler

Area of the former execution site to the north of the
prisoner camp, 2012
Photograph: Tal Adler

Hinrichtungen

Tausende Menschen werden im KZ Mauthausen durch Erhängen oder Erschießen hingerichtet. Von Beginn an ahndet die SS schwerwiegende Verstöße gegen die Lagerordnung mit der Todesstrafe.

Nach Kriegsbeginn nutzen SS-Behörden und Polizei die Konzentrationslager zunehmend, um dort politische Gegner ohne gerichtliches Urteil oder nach standrechtlicher Verurteilung ohne Zeugen töten zu lassen.

Executions

Thousands of people are executed in the Mauthausen concentration camp by hanging or shooting. From the beginning the SS punishes serious violations of the camp regulations with the death penalty.

After the outbreak of war, the SS authorities and the police increasingly make use of the concentration camps to have political opponents killed out of sight, either without judicial sentencing or following conviction by a court-martial.

Klapptisch des Galgens im Hinrichtungsraum
Památník Terezín, 216
Foto: Tal Adler

Collapsible table for the gallows in the execution room
Památník Terezín, 216
Photograph: Tal Adler

Eine Form der Exekution ist die Tötung durch den Strang. Im Hinrichtungsraum müssen die Opfer auf den Klapptisch steigen. Sie werden an einer Eisentraverse festgebunden. Durch die Betätigung des Klappmechanismus vollzieht ein SS-Angehöriger die Exekution.
Kurz vor der Befreiung des Lagers lässt die SS die Eisentraverse entfernen. Tschechische Häftlinge sichern den Klapptisch und nehmen ihn in ihre Heimat mit.

One form of execution is death by hanging. In the execution room the victims are forced to climb onto the collapsible table. They are strung up to an iron cross-beam. By activating the collapse mechanism, a member of the SS carries out the execution.
Shortly before the camp is liberated the SS has the iron cross-beam removed. Czech prisoners save the collapsible table and take it home with them.

SS-Wachposten niedergeschlagen

Der Reichsführer SS und Chef der deutschen Polizei teilt mit: Am 25. November überfielen die vorbestraften Schutzhäftlinge Franz Brönner und Anton Kropf in einem Konzentrationslager nach einem vorgefaßten Plan einen SS-Wachposten und schlugen ihn nieder. Sie ergriffen darauf die Flucht, wurden jedoch nach kurzer Zeit wieder gestellt und festgenommen. Die beiden Verbrecher wurden am 9. Dezember im Konzentrationslager erhängt.

„SS-Wachposten niedergeschlagen", Wiener Neueste Nachrichten, 11. Dezember 1939, S. 4
KZ-Gedenkstätte Mauthausen, 1.8.1.0005

Fluchtversuche und Angriffe auf das Wachpersonal gelten als die gröbsten Verstöße gegen die Lagerordnung. Sie werden mit der Tötung durch den Strang geahndet. Eigentlich sollen diese Hinrichtungen außerhalb des KZ Mauthausen nicht bekannt werden. Reichsführer-SS Heinrich Himmler macht diesen Fall kurz nach Kriegsbeginn aber öffentlich, um unerbittliches Durchgreifen zu demonstrieren.

SS guard beaten down

The Reich Chief of the SS and the Head of the German Police reports: On 25 November the protective custody prisoners Franz Brönner and Anton Kropf, both with previous convictions, acted on a premeditated plan and attacked an SS guard at a concentration camp, beating him to the ground. They then took flight but were apprehended a short time later and arrested. Both criminals were hanged on 9 December at the concentration camp.

'SS guard beaten down', Wiener Neueste Nachrichten newspaper, 10 December 1939, p.4
KZ-Gedenkstätte Mauthausen, 1.8.1.0005

Escape attempts and attacks on guards are considered to be the most offensive violations of the camp regulations. They are punished with death by hanging. In actual fact, no one outside the Mauthausen concentration camp is supposed to know about these executions. However, Reich Chief of the SS Heinrich Himmler publicises this case shortly after the outbreak of war in order to demonstrate the merciless crackdown on prisoners.

1022	Pawljutschenko	Egor	R.Z.A.	20.7.44	Auf Befehl RF SS erschossen
1023	Agarejew	Alekej	"	"	" " " " erhängt
1024	Fridrich	Anatolij	"	"	" " " " "
1025	Lagoda	Konstantin	"	"	" " " " "
1026	Kuriloschenko	Alexander	"	"	" " " " "
1027	Lenin	Iwan	"	"	" " " " "
1028	Vilschenko	Wladimir	"	"	" " " " "
1029	Bibinski	Marian	"	"	" " " " erschossen
1030	Lewendel	Mor	ung. Jude	21.7.44	Auf der Flucht erschossen
1031	Preler	Anton	Jsl. Sch.	"	Verletzg. durch Fliegerangriff 26.6.44.
1032	Mrsnik	Iwan	"	"	"
1033	Alzien	Jules	Frz. Sch.	"	
1034	Bron	Zsigmond	ung. Jude	"	Freitod
1035	Firsow	Pawel	R.Z.A.	"	Auf der Flucht erschossen
1036	Nasarow	Ilja	"	"	Auf Befehl RF SS erhängt
1037	Petrovic	Antonije	Jugo. Sch.	22.7.44	
1038	Mandi	Jenö	ung. Jude	"	Verletzg. durch Fliegerangriff 26.6.44
1039	Gorce	Bernard	Frz. Sch.	"	
1040	Krek	Andrej	Jugo. Sch.	"	Auf der Flucht erschossen
1041	Saridakis	Dionissios	Griech. Sch.	"	Durch Fliegerangriff getötet
1042	Franzel	Iwan	Jugo. Sch.	"	"
1043	Genzes	Georges	Franz.	"	"

Auszug aus dem Verzeichnis „unnatürlicher Todesfälle", Eintrag zum 20. Juli 1944
Národní archiv, Prag, OVS, inv. č. 39, karton 29

Excerpt from the register of 'unnatural deaths', entry for 20 July 1944
Národní archiv, Prague, OVS, inv. č. 39, karton 29

Die Mauthausener SS vollstreckt auch von externen Polizei- oder SS-Behörden offiziell angeordnete Todesurteile gegen Personen, die nicht im KZ inhaftiert sind. Sie müssen vom Reichsführer-SS Heinrich Himmler genehmigt werden. Über diese Hinrichtungen führt die SS genau Buch.

The Mauthausen SS also carry out death sentences officially handed down by external police or SS authorities against persons not imprisoned in the concentration camp. These must be authorised by Reich Chief of the SS Heinrich Himmler. The SS keeps exact records of these executions.

Nachgestellter Tathergang in der Genickschussecke,
Mai 1945
Foto: U.S. Signal Corps, Fotograf unbekannt
United States National Archives and Records Administration,
RG 549, Box 345, Folder 2, p. 62

Erschießungen werden anfangs von einem SS-Kommando nordöstlich des Lagers durchgeführt.
1941 baut die SS im Keller zwischen Reviergebäude und Lagergefängnis eine Genickschussanlage. Mit Schüssen durch einen Mauerschlitz kann ein einzelner SS-Angehöriger ein Opfer nach dem anderen ermorden.
Nach dem Abbau der Genickschussanlage richtet die SS 1942 im selben Raum eine Genickschussecke ein.

Reconstruction of a shooting in the *Genickschussecke*,
May 1945
Photograph: U.S. Signal Corps, unknown photographer
United States National Archives and Records Administration,
RG 549, Box 345, Folder 2, p. 62

At first shootings are carried out by an SS firing squad to the northeast of the camp.
In 1941 the SS builds a *Genickschussanlage* (an apparatus for shooting people in the back of the neck) in the cellar between the infirmary building and the camp prison. By firing through a slit in the wall, a single member of the SS can murder one victim after another.
After dismantling the *Genickschussanlage* the SS sets up a *Genickschussecke* (a corner where people are shot in the back of the neck) in the same room in 1942.

Auszug aus der Befragung von Wilhelm Ornstein durch die Staatsanwaltschaft Köln, New York 1969
KZ-Gedenkstätte Mauthausen, M/5/14

Der polnische Häftling Wilhelm Ornstein muss ab 1944 unter dem Kommando des SS-Angehörigen Martin Roth im Krematorium arbeiten. Bei seiner Befragung beschreibt er den Ablauf der Erschießungen im Hinrichtungsraum. Die Genickschussecke nennt Ornstein Genickschussanlage.

Extract from an interview with Wilhelm Ornstein conducted by the Cologne public prosecution office, New York 1969
KZ-Gedenkstätte Mauthausen, M/5/14

From 1944 the Polish prisoner Wilhelm Ornstein has to work in the crematorium under the unit headed by SS man Martin Roth. In an interview he describes the sequence of events during shootings in the execution room. Ornstein refers to the *Genickschussecke* as the *Genickschussanlage*.

Bei den Tötungen von Häftlingen in der Genickschussanlage mussten wir jeweils im Leichenkühlraum warten. Die Tür zur Genickschusshalle war geschlossen. Die jeweiligen Opfer wurden einzeln in die Genickschussecke gebracht; wenn sie dort erschossen worden waren, wurde jeweils die Tür zum Leichenkühlhaus aufgerissen und wir Häftlinge mußten vorspringen, die jeweilige Leiche packen und auf möglichst schnelle Weise in den Leichenkühlraum bringen und die entstandenen Blutspuren beseitigen, damit das nachfolgende Opfer nicht sofort erkannte, was mit ihm geschehen sollte. Nach meiner Erinnerung stand dort eine zeitlang auf einem Gestell etwas mit einem schwarzen Tuch verhüllt, was wie eine Kamera aussah, so daß der jeweils zu tötende Häftling der Meinung sein konnte, fotografiert zu werden. Auch wurden von den SS-Leuten geschrien, daß diese Opfer fotografiert werden sollen. Nach Durchführung einer derartigen Tötungsaktion mußte dann von Häftlingen des Krematoriumskommandos die Genickschußanlage gesäubert werden. Hierbei wurde auch irgend ein Desinfektionsmittel verwendet. Die jeweiligen Befehle für unseren Einsatz hierbei, kamen entweder von ROTH oder über unseren Kapo KANDUTH mittelbar. Die Genickschußanlage, die ich bereits mehrfach erwähnt habe, war in ihrem oberen Teil mit einer Art Kugelfang versehen versehen, der aus Holz bestand. Der untere Teil war gekachelt und außerdem befand sich dort eine Ablaufrinne, und ein Wasserhahn damit diese Anlage jeweils gesäubert werden konnte. Für diese Erschießungen in der Genickschußanlage wurde ein Kleinkaliber-Gewehr benutzt, manchmal wurden auch Pistolen benutzt. Dieses kleine Gewehr, befand sich jeweils vor einer solchen Tötungsaktion im Dienstzimmer von ROTH. Ich kann heute allerdings nicht mehr mit Sicherheit sagen, ob dieses kleine Gewehr jeweils von einem anderen SS-Angehörigen gebracht, oder von ROTH persönlich geholt wurde. Im Allgemeinen wusste Roth von derartigen Tötungsaktionen im voraus und er befahl uns dann, alles für die Durchführung einer solchen Aktion vorzubereiten.

When prisoners were killed in the Genickschussanlage we always had to wait in the morgue. The door to the Genickschusshalle [shooting hall] was closed. The victims were brought into the Genickschussecke one at a time; when they had been shot there, the door to the morgue was thrown open and we prisoners had to leap forward, grab the corpse and get it into the morgue as quickly as possible and get rid of the traces of blood this caused, so that the next victim would not immediately know what was going to happen to him. I remember that for a while there was something on a stand covered in a black cloth that looked like a camera, so that the prisoners who were about to be killed might think that they were going to have their picture taken. The SS men also shouted that these victims were to be photographed. After this kind of killing had taken place, the Genickschussanlage then had to be cleaned by the prisoners in the crematorium detachment. Some sort of disinfectant was used for this. The orders for our assignments were given to us either by ROTH or by our Kapo KANDUTH. The Genickschussanlage, which I have already mentioned several times, had an upper section that was a sort of bullet trap made of wood. The lower part was tiled and there was also a drain there, and a tap so that the installation could be cleaned each time. For the shootings in the Genickschussanlage a small-calibre weapon was used, sometimes pistols were used too. Before this kind of killing action, this small weapon was kept in ROTH's office. Today I'm not sure any more whether this small weapon was fetched each time by a different member of the SS, or whether ROTH fetched it himself. In general Roth knew about this kind of killing action in advance and then ordered us to get everything ready for carrying it out.

Nachgestellte Erhängung, Mai 1945
Foto: U.S. Signal Corps, Fotograf unbekannt
United States National Archives and Records Administration,
RG 549, Box 345, Folder 2, p. 63

Hinrichtungen von Häftlingen, die sich der Lagerordnung widersetzt haben, werden zwecks Abschreckung meist vor den Augen aller KZ-Häftlinge auf dem Appellplatz durchgeführt.
Hinrichtungen von Personen, die nur zur Vollstreckung einer Todesstrafe im KZ inhaftiert sind, werden hingegen ohne Augenzeugen im Hinrichtungsraum vollzogen.

Reconstruction of a hanging, May 1945
Photograph: U.S. Signal Corps, unknown photographer
United States National Archives and Records Administration,
RG 549, Box 345, Folder 2, p. 63

Executions of prisoners who have violated the camp regulations are usually carried out in the roll call area in front of all the inmates in order to serve as a deterrent. By contrast, executions of people who are only imprisoned in the concentration camp because they have been given a death sentence are carried out in the execution room with no witnesses present.

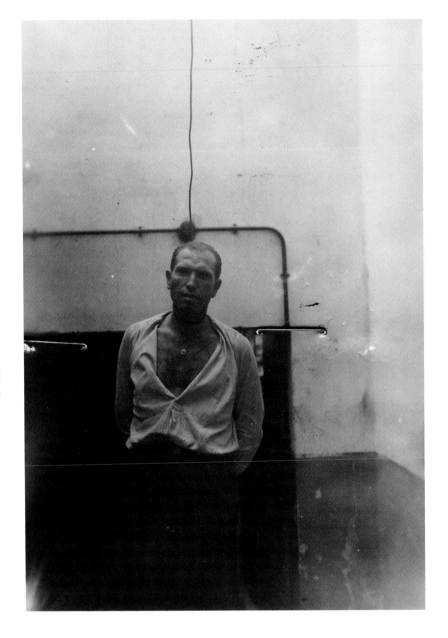

Das Verschwinden der Orte

Die SS beseitigt vor der Befreiung des Lagers beinahe alle Spuren der Hinrichtungsorte. Diese sind heute daher nicht mehr oder nur als Rekonstruktionen vorhanden. Die im Hinrichtungsraum zu sehende Eisentraverse stammt aus den Jahren 1948/1949. KZ-Überlebende wollten mit dieser Rekonstruktion die Verbrechen der SS vorstellbar machen.

The Places of Execution Disappear

Before the liberation of the camp the SS removes nearly all traces of the places of execution. Thus they no longer exist today, or only as a reconstruction. The iron cross-beam that can be seen in the execution room dates from 1948/1949. Through this reconstruction, concentration camp survivors wanted to make the crimes of the SS easier to visualise.

Ausschnitt aus einem Plan des Revierkellers mit Einträgen nach Angaben von Johann Kanduth, 1949, ergänzt 1968
Österreichisches Staatsarchiv, Wien, Archiv der Republik, Bundesministerium für Inneres, GZ. 54.309-18/68

Johann Kanduth war als Häftling im Krematoriumskommando Augenzeuge des Massenmordes. Bei einer polizeilichen Einvernahme im Jahr 1968 werden nach seinen Angaben unter anderem der Galgen (1), die Genickschussecke (2) und die Genickschussanlage (3) in den Plan eingezeichnet.

Section from a plan of the infirmary cellar with labels according to information given by Johann Kanduth, 1949, supplemented 1968
Österreichisches Staatsarchiv, Vienna, Archiv der Republik, Bundesministerium für Inneres, GZ. 54.309-18/68

As a prisoner in the crematorium detachment, Johann Kanduth was an eye-witness to mass murder. During police questioning in 1968 he adds, among others, the locations of the gallows (1), the *Genickschussecke* (2) and the *Genickschussanlage* (3) to the plan.

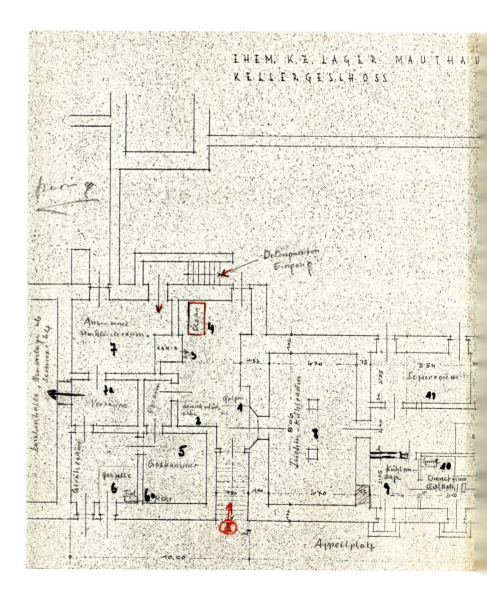

Fundamentstreifen des zweiten Krematoriums, 2008
Foto: Stephan Matyus
KZ-Gedenkstätte Mauthausen, ohne Signatur

An der Stelle, wo sich die Genickschussanlage im Hinrichtungsraum befunden hat, lässt die SS 1942 einen Krematoriumsofen errichten. Der Umbau zerstört alle Hinweise auf die Existenz der Schussanlage. Nach der Befreiung des Lagers wird der Ofen demontiert. Heute sind daher nur noch die Fundamentstreifen des Ofens, der Kaminanschluss sowie der Kamin selbst vorhanden.

Foundation strip of the second crematorium, 2008
Photograph: Stephan Matyus
KZ-Gedenkstätte Mauthausen, no archive number

In 1942 the SS has a crematorium oven built where the *Genickschussanlage* had stood in the execution room. The alterations destroy all traces of the existence of the shooting apparatus. After the liberation of the camp the oven is dismantled. Thus today only the foundation strips of the oven, the connection to the chimney, and the chimney itself are visible.

Abb. 24: MK34 (Exekutionsraum). Abdruck des Kugelfangs (Phase 5).

Abb. 25: MK34 (Exekutionsraum), Genickschussecke nach Abbau des Kugelfangs, 1945-1949 (AMM Bildarchiv. BHÖ 9 & 11).

Fazit

Der Sonderbau wurde ab Ende 1941 zwischen dem Arrest und Revier errichtet. Gaskammer, Galgen und so genannte Genickschussanlage waren von Anfang an Bestandteile, doch die Einrichtung eines zweiten Krematoriumsofens führte bald zu Umbauten, die zur Verlegung der Erschießungsanlage führten. Der Sonderbau, der spätestens ab Frühsommer 1942 „in Betrieb" ging, machte einige wenige Umbauten im Revierkeller notwendig.

Auszug aus einer bauarchäologischen Untersuchung im Hinrichtungsraum
Unveröffentlichter Projektbericht von Paul Mitchell und Günther Buchinger, Wien 2009

Die SS lässt die Genickschussecke im Zuge der Spurenbeseitigung kurz vor der Befreiung des Lagers demontieren. Die Position des Kugelfangs der Genickschussecke zeichnet sich im Boden des Hinrichtungsraumes aber noch ab.

Extract from a building archaeology report on the execution room
Unpublished project report by Paul Mitchell and Günther Buchinger, Vienna 2009

In order to cover its tracks the SS has the *Genickschussecke* dismantled shortly before the liberation of the camp. However, the position of the bullet trap at the back of the *Genickschussecke* can still be seen on the floor of the execution room.

Fig. 24: MK34 (execution room). Imprint of the bullet trap (Phase 5).
Fig. 25: MK34 (execution room). Genickschussecke *after the bullet trap has been dismantled, 1945–1949 (AMM Bildarchiv. BHÖ 9 & 11)*

Summary
The Sonderbau *[special building] was constructed at the end of 1941 between the camp prison and the infirmary. Gas chamber, gallows and the so-called* Genickschussanlage *were part of it from the beginning, but the construction of a second crematorium oven soon led to alterations which led to the relocation of the shooting area. The Sonderbau, which went 'into operation' at the latest in early summer 1942, necessitated some small alterations to the infirmary cellar.*

Zeugenberichte verorten die erste Erschießungsstätte übereinstimmend in jenem Bereich, den die SS 1944 mit dem kreisförmigen Löschteich überbauen lässt. Auf der ersten bekannten alliierten Luftaufnahme des Konzentrationslagers Mauthausen ist nur mehr der Löschteich zu sehen.

2012 beginnt eine archäologische Suche nach den Überresten der Erschießungsstätte. Die Magnetmessung zeigt Metallteile unterhalb der Erdoberfläche als schwarze Anomalien an. Die Bodenbeschaffenheit im Bereich des Löschteiches scheint zunächst auf mögliche Reste der Erschießungsstätte hinzudeuten. Grabungen zeigen aber, dass die Erschießungsstätte durch den Bau des Löschteiches restlos beseitigt worden ist.

Eyewitness reports all locate the first execution site in an area that, in 1944, the SS has built over with a circular fire water pond. The earliest known aerial photograph taken by the Allies of the concentration camp only shows the fire water pond.

In 2012 an archaeological search begins for the remains of the execution site. Pieces of metal buried in the ground show up on the magnetometer readings as black anomalies. The composition of the soil in the area around the pond at first seems to point to possible remains of the execution site. Excavations show, however, that the execution site was completely destroyed by the construction of the pond.

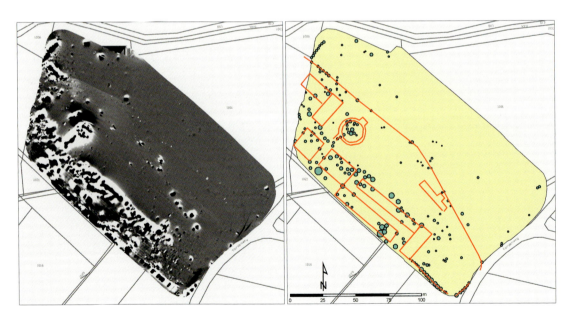

Geophysikalische Untersuchung im Bereich der ehemaligen Erschießungsstätte, Magnetmessung und Auswertung (rechts), 2010
Archeo Prospections®, Wien

Geophysical survey of the area of the former exeuction site, magnetometer reading and analysis (right), 2010
Archeo Prospections®, Vienna

Luftaufnahme des Areals der Erschießungsstätte, 2006
Amt der Oberösterreichischen Landesregierung, Linz, Digitale Orthofotos

Aerial photograph of the grounds of the execution site, 2006
Amt der Oberösterreichischen Landesregierung, Linz, Digitale Orthofotos

Alliierte Luftaufnahme des KZ Mauthausen, Ausschnitt mit dem Areal der Erschießungsstätte, September 1944
Luftbilddatenbank Dr. Carls, Esterwegen / KZ-Gedenkstätte Mauthausen, Flug Nr. 60-0744, Foto 4034

Allied aerial photograph of the Mauthausen concentration camp, detail showing the area of the execution site, September 1944
Luftbilddatenbank Dr. Carls, Esterwegen / KZ-Gedenkstätte Mauthausen, Flight no. 60-0744, Photo 4034

Todesort Lagergrenze
Death at the Camp Perimeter

Lagerzaun, 2012
Foto: Tal Adler

Camp fence, 2012
Photograph: Tal Adler

Todesort Lagergrenze

Bei vielen Todesfällen finden sich in den Akten der SS die Vermerke „Selbstmord durch Elektrizität" oder „Erschießung auf der Flucht". Diese Einträge vertuschen oft Morde. Immer wieder werden Häftlinge unter Gewaltandrohung in den mit Starkstrom geladenen Lagerzaun getrieben. Vermeintliche Fluchtversuche sind der häufigste Vorwand für gezielte Tötungen. Gefangene bestimmter Häftlingsgruppen fallen „Erschießungen auf der Flucht" besonders häufig zum Opfer. Es sind knapp hundert SS-Fotografien solcher Todesfälle an der Lagergrenze überliefert.

Death at the Camp Perimeter

Many of the deaths recorded in the files of the SS are marked 'Sucide by electrocution' or 'Shot while attempting to escape'. These entries are often a cover-up for murder. Prisoners are regularly driven by threats of violence into the camp fence, which is electrified with a high voltage current. Supposed escape attempts are the most common pretext for targeted killings. Prisoners from certain groups fall victim to being 'shot while attempting to escape' particularly often. There are nearly one hundred SS photographs still in existence showing such deaths at the camp perimeter.

Teil eines Pfostens des Mauthausener Lagerzauns
Památník Terezín, 684
Foto: Tal Adler

Section of a post from the Mauthausen camp fence
Památník Terezín, 684
Photograph: Tal Adler

An der Außenseite des Zauns ist ein Warnschild angebracht. Nicht die Häftlinge, sondern Personen, die sich von außen dem Lager nähern, werden damit vor der elektrischen Hochspannung gewarnt.
Nach der Befreiung des Lagers nehmen tschechische Überlebenden diesen Teil eines Zaunpfostens als Beweismittel und Andenken in ihre Heimat mit. Später übergeben sie ihn der Gedenkstätte Theresienstadt.

A warning sign is mounted on the outside of the fence. Not the prisoners, but rather people approaching the camp from the outside are to be warned about the high voltage. After the liberation of the camp, Czech survivors take this piece of the fence post home with them as both evidence and a reminder. Later they give it to the Terezín Memorial.

				1941	
64	Dobrowski	Thaddäus	Pole	16. Juli	Selbstmord durch Elektrizität
65	Fasching	Ignaz	BV	17. "	Auf der Flucht erschossen
66	Lopez-Munoz	Rafael	Span.	"	Selbstmord durch Ertrinken
67	Cohen	Barend	NL Jude	"	"
68	van Dam	Aaron	"	"	Auf der Flucht erschossen
69	Franzmann	Abraham	"	"	"
70	Groen	Abraham	"	"	"
71	Bauer	Maurice	"	"	"
72	Smit	Isaac	"	"	"
73	Holländer	Isaac	"	18.	"
74	Polak	Bernhard	"	"	"
75	Mamlok	Hans	"	"	"
76	Canes	David	"	"	"
77	Vischschnaper	David	"	"	"
78	Katz	Paul	"	"	"
79	von Moppis	Isaak	"	"	"
80	Kaminker	Gustav	"	"	"
81	Lierens	Manuel	"	"	"
82	Blik	Salomon	"	"	"
83	Gimenez-Ramo	Dionisio	Span.	"	Unfall
84	Pinol Mayor	Antonio	"	19. "	Selbstmord durch Elektrizität

Einträge von „Erschießungen auf der Flucht" im Verzeichnis der „unnatürlichen Todesfälle", Juli 1941
Národní archiv, Prag, OVS, inv. č. 39, karton 29

Entries listed as 'Shot while attempting to escape' in the register of 'unnatural deaths', July 1941
Národní archiv, Prague, OVS, inv. č. 39, karton 29

Ein Großteil der 1941 in Mauthausen eingelieferten Juden aus den Niederlanden wird im Lager gezielt ermordet. Im Verzeichnis der „unnatürlichen Todesfälle", in dem die SS Selbstmorde, Unfälle und Erschießungen auf der Flucht erfasst, gibt es zahlreiche Einträge, die die Erschießung ganzer Gruppen von angeblich geflohenen niederländischen Juden dokumentieren.

The majority of the Jews from the Netherlands who arrive in Mauthausen in 1941 are deliberately murdered in the camp. In the register of 'unnatural deaths', in which the SS records suicides, accidents and those shot while attempting to escape, there are numerous entries documenting the shooting of whole groups of supposedly fugitive Dutch Jews.

Kontaktabzug eines Kleinbildfilms des Mauthausener Erkennungsdienstes, Aufnahmen vermutlich 1942
Museu d'Història de Catalunya, Barcelona, fons de Amical de Mauthausen y otros campos, ohne Signatur

Neben alltäglichen Begebenheiten im KZ dokumentiert der Erkennungsdienst, die Fotoabteilung der SS, auch die sogenannten unnatürlichen Todesfälle von Häftlingen. Dazu zählen neben Unfällen Erschießungen auf der Flucht und Selbstmorde.

35mm contact sheet of the Mauthausen identification service, probably taken in 1942
Museu d'Història de Catalunya, Barcelona, fons de Amical de Mauthausen y otros campos, no archive number

As well as documenting everyday occurrences in the concentration camp, the *Erkennungsdienst* (identification service), the photographic department of the SS, also takes pictures of the so-called unnatural deaths of prisoners. Besides accidents this includes those shot while attempting to escape and suicides.

Kriegsgef.Arb.Lager Mauthausen-Gusen Mauthausen, den 18.November 1942
Kommandantur
Az.: KL 14 f 9/11.42./Mü-.

Betreff : Erschießung des SU-Kriegsgefangenen German
         P a n k r a t o w , geb.am 22.7.1915 zu Noginsk,
         Stalag Nr.128 7o2
Bezug   : Anliegender Vorgang.
Anlagen : -3-.

An das

SS - Wirtschafts - Verwaltungshauptamt
Amtsgruppe D

O r a n i e n b u r g / bei Berlin-.
Stabsgebäude.

In der Anlage überreiche ich als Gerichtsoffizier des K.L.
Mauthausen eine Sterbefallanzeige, eine Lichtbildaufnahme
sowie eine Vernehmungsniederschrift des Postens SS - Unter-
schaffführer Karl P l e s s , der am 16.November 1942 den
SU-Kriegsgefangenen German Pankratow bei einem Fluchtversuch
erschossen hat.
Meine sofort angestellten Ermittlungen haben ergeben, daß
es sich um einen Fluchtversuch des Kriegsgefangenen gehandelt hat. Nur der Wachsamkeit des Postens und seinem entschlos-
senen Waffengebrauch ist es zuzuschreiben, dass eine weitere
Flucht verhindert wurde.
Der Posten SS - Unterscharführer Karl P l e s s hat somit
in Ausübung seines Dienstes pflichtgemäß gehandelt. Eine
strafbare Handlung liegt seinerseits nicht vor.

SS-Obersturmführer u.
Gerichtsoffizier KLM.

Eingeschrieben

Schreiben des SS-Gerichtsoffiziers von Mauthausen über die Erschießung German Pankratows, 18. November 1942
Vojenský historický archiv, Prag, 164/MA/3/30

German Pankratow wird – wie laut SS-Dokumenten eine große Zahl weiterer sowjetischer Kriegsgefangener – auf der Flucht erschossen.
Der Bericht über den Vorfall endet wie üblich mit der Feststellung, der SS-Schütze habe pflichtgemäß gehandelt. Da die Dienstvorschriften ausdrücklich befohlen, auf fliehende Gefangene zu schießen, können unter dem Vorwand, einen Fluchtversuch vereitelt zu haben, gezielte Tötungen begangen werden.

Report by the Mauthausen SS legal officer regarding the shooting of German Pankratow, 18 November 1942
Vojenský historický archiv, Prague, 164/MA/3/30

German Pankratow – like a large number of other Soviet prisoners of war, according to SS documents – is shot while attempting to escape.
The report on the incident ends with the usual conclusion in such cases, namely that the SS guard who fired the shot had acted in accordance with his duty. Since official regulations expressly order the shooting of prisoners on the run, targeted murders can be committed under the pretext of thwarting an escape attempt.

POW Work Camp Mauthausen-Gusen *Mauthausen, 18th November 1942*
Camp Headquarters
File ref: KL 14 f 9 / 11.42./ Mü-.

Subject   : Shooting of the Soviet prisoner of war German
P a n k r a t o w , born 22.7.1915 at Noginsk,
Stalag No.128 702
Re   : Enclosed dossier.
Enclosures : – 3 –.

To the

SS Economic and Administrative Main Office
Branch group D

O r a n i e n b u r g / near Berlin-.
HQ building.

As legal officer of the Mauthausen concentration camp, I hereby submit a death notification, a photograph and a transcript of the questioning of the guard SS Unterscharführer Karl P l e s s , who shot the Soviet prisoner of war German Pankratow on 16 November 1942 during an escape attempt.
My investigations, launched immediately, have revealed that the case concerns an escape attempt by the prisoner of war. It is only down to the vigilance of the guard and his decisive use of arms that further escape was hindered.
The guard SS Unterscharführer Karl P l e s s thus acted in accordance with his duty. No punishable offence has been committed on his part.

[Signature]
SS Obersturmführer and
Legal Officer of
the Mauthausen Concentration Camp

Die Aufnahmen der „unnatürlichen Todesfälle": Beweismittel und Foto-Ikonen

Die spanischen Häftlinge Francisco Boix und Antonio Garcia arbeiten im Fotolabor der SS in Mauthausen. Ihnen gelingt es, mit weiteren Helfern Negative der Fotos des SS-Erkennungsdienstes aus dem Lager zu schmuggeln. Darunter sind viele Aufnahmen von „unnatürlichen Todesfällen". Die Häftlinge bewahren die Fotos so vor der Zerstörung durch die SS.

Boix stellt die Bilder unmittelbar nach der Befreiung amerikanischen Ermittlern sowie der Presse zur Verfügung. Sie werden nicht nur zu zentralen Beweismitteln in Prozessen, sondern durch ihre frühe Veröffentlichung auch zu Foto-Ikonen, die die in Mauthausen begangenen Verbrechen repräsentieren.

The 'unnatural deaths' photographs: Evidence and Iconic Images

The Spanish prisoners Francisco Boix and Antonio Garcia work in the SS photo laboratory in Mauthausen. With the help of others they manage to smuggle photograph negatives from the SS identification service out of the camp. Among them are many pictures of 'unnatural deaths'. The prisoners thus safeguard the photos from destruction by the SS.

Immediately after liberation Boix makes the pictures available to American investigators, as well as to the press. They not only become important pieces of evidence in trials, but their early publication also turns them into iconic images that represent the crimes committed at Mauthausen.

Anna Pointner (links) mit ihren beiden Töchtern und ehemaligen spanischen Häftlingen, kurz nach der Befreiung 1945
Foto: Francisco Boix
Museu d'Història de Catalunya, Barcelona, fons de Amical de Mauthausen y otros campos, ohne Signatur

Spanische Häftlinge, die als Zwangsarbeiter im Steinbruch der Mauthausener Firma Poschacher eingesetzt sind, helfen, die Fotonegative aus dem Lager herauszuschmuggeln. Die in Mauthausen lebende Anna Pointner versteckt sie bis zur Befreiung in ihrer Gartenmauer.

Anna Pointner (left) with her two daughters and former Spanish prisoners, shortly after liberation in 1945
Photograph: Francisco Boix
Museu d'Història de Catalunya, Barcelona, fons de Amical de Mauthausen y otros campos, no archive number

Spanish prisoners who are working as forced labourers in the quarry for the Mauthausen-based firm Poschacher help to smuggle the photograph negatives out of the camp. Anna Pointner, who lives in Mauthausen, hides them until liberation in her garden wall.

Francisco Boix vor dem Internationalen Militärgerichtshof in Nürnberg, Jänner 1946
Fotograf: unbekannt
United States National Archives and Records Administration, RG 111, Box 341, Serial 225801
Einige der Fotos des Mauthausener Erkennungsdienstes werden im Nürnberger Hauptkriegsverbrecherprozess als Beweismittel verwendet. Boix, befragt durch den französischen Anklagevertreter Charles Dubost, macht in seiner Aussage präzise Angaben zu den Opfern und dem Kontext der Aufnahmen.

Francisco Boix at the International Military Tribunal in Nuremberg, January 1946
Unknown Photographer
United States National Archives and Records Administration, RG 111, Box 341, Serial 225801
Some of the photos from the Mauthausen identification service are used as evidence in the Trial of the Major War Criminals in Nuremberg. Boix, questioned by the French prosecutor Charles Dubost, gives precise details about the victims and the context the pictures were taken in.

Quelle
Der Prozess gegen die Hauptkriegsverbrecher vor dem Internationalen Militärgerichtshof, Verhandlungsniederschriften, Band VI, 28. Januar 1946

Bildnachweis
1, 3: Archives Nationales, Paris, fonds de l'Amicale de Mauthausen, AJ 88; Mauthausen photos non classées 3; 88/AJ 229
2: Fédération Nationale des Déportés et Internés, Résistants et Patriotes, Paris, ohne Signatur
4: KZ-Gedenkstätte Mauthausen, Sammlung Mariano Constante, ohne Signatur

Source
Trial of the Major War Criminals before the International Military Tribunal, Proceedings, Volume VI, 28 January 1946

Photo credits
1, 3: Archives Nationales, Paris, fonds de l'Amicale de Mauthausen, AJ 88; Mauthausen photos non classées 3; 88/AJ 229
2: Fédération Nationale des Déportés et Internés, Résistants et Patriotes, Paris, no archive number
4: KZ-Gedenkstätte Mauthausen, Sammlung Mariano Constante, no archive number

Zeugenaussage von Francisco Boix

DUBOST: Sie sind am 14. August 1920 in Barcelona geboren?

BOIX: Ja.

DUBOST: Sind Sie Bildberichterstatter? Seit wann waren Sie im Lager Mauthausen interniert?

BOIX: Seit 27. Januar 1941.

DUBOST: Sie haben der Untersuchungskommission eine Anzahl von Photographien übergeben?

BOIX: Ja.

DUBOST: Sie werden jetzt auf der Leinwand gezeigt werden, und sie werden unter Eid aussagen, unter welchen Umständen und wo diese Bilder aufgenommen worden sind.

BOIX: Ja.

DUBOST: Wie sind Sie zu diesen Bildern gekommen?

BOIX: Auf Grund meines Berufes wurde ich in Mauthausen in der Abteilung „Identifizierung" [Erkennungsdienst, And. Red.] eingesetzt. In dieser befand sich ein Bilderdienst, und es konnten Photographien von allem, was im Lager passierte, aufgenommen werden. Die Photos wurden an die oberste Führung nach Berlin geschickt.

[…]

DUBOST: Wer hat diese Bilder aufgenommen?

BOIX: SS-Oberscharführer Fritz Kornatz [Kornacz, And. Red.]. Er wurde im Jahre 1944 von amerikanischen Truppen in Holland getötet.

Der russische Kriegsgefangene auf dem Bild erhielt einen Schuß in den Kopf. Man hat ihn hinaufgehoben, um den Anschein zu erwecken, als ob er versucht hätte, sich in selbstmörderischer

Testimony given by Francisco Boix

DUBOST: You were born on 14 August 1920 in Barcelona?

BOIX: Yes.

DUBOST: You are a news photographer, and you were interned in the camp of Mauthausen, since...

BOIX: Since 27 January 1941.

DUBOST: You handed over to the commission of inquiry a certain number of photographs?

BOIX: Yes.

DUBOST: They are going to be projected on the screen and you will state under oath under what circumstances and where these pictures were taken.

BOIX: Yes.

DUBOST: How did you obtain these pictures?

BOIX: Owing to my professional knowledge, I was sent to Mauthausen to work in the identification branch of the camp. There was a photographic branch, and pictures of everything happening in the camp could be taken and sent to the High Command in Berlin.

[…]

DUBOST: Who took these pictures?

BOIX: *SS Oberscharführer Fritz Kornatz* [Kornacz, editors' note]. He was killed by American troops in Holland in 1944.

This man, a Russian prisoner of war, got a bullet in the head. They hanged him to make us think he was a suicide and had

Absicht über den Stacheldraht zu werfen.

BOIX: Das nächste Bild zeigt holländische Juden in der Quarantänebaracke. Gleich am Tage ihrer Ankunft hat man die Juden dazu getrieben, sich in den Stacheldraht zu werfen, weil sie sich darüber im klaren waren, dass keine Hoffnung auf ein Entkommen bestand.

DUBOST: Von wem wurden diese Bilder aufgenommen?

BOIX: Damals von SS-Oberscharführer Paul Ricken, Professor aus Essen.

DUBOST: Das nächste Bild.

BOIX: Dies sind 2 holländische Juden. Sie können den roten [gelben, Anm. d. Red.] Stern sehen, den sie trugen.
Es handelt sich hier um einen angeblichen Fluchtversuch.

DUBOST: Was war es in Wirklichkeit?

BOIX: Die SS hatte sie in der Nähe des Stacheldrahtes zum Steineholen geschickt. Die SS-Posten an der zweiten Stacheldrahtumzäunung schossen auf sie, weil sie für jeden, den sie umbrachten, eine Prämie erhielten.

Das nächste Bild zeigt einen Juden; es war im Jahre 1941, während des Baues des sogenannten Russenlagers, das später Revier [Boix bezieht sich hier auf das „Sanitätslager", Anm. d. Red.] wurde. Er hängt an dem Strick, den er zur Befestigung seiner Hosen benutzt hatte.

DUBOST: Handelte es sich um Selbstmord?

BOIX: Angeblich. Dieser Mann hatte keine Hoffnung mehr auf ein Entkommen und ist durch Arbeit und Folterungen dazu getrieben worden.

tried to hurl himself against the barbed wire.

The other picture shows some Dutch Jews. That was taken at Barracks C, the so-called quarantine barracks.

The Jews were driven to hurl themselves against the barbed wire on the very day of their arrival because they realized that there was no hope to escape for them.

DUBOST: By whom were these pictures taken?

BOIX: At this time by SS Oberscharführer Paul Ricken, a professor from Essen.

DUBOST: Next one.

BOIX: These are 2 Dutch Jews. You can see the red yellow-star they wore. That was an alleged attempt to escape (Fluchtversuch).

DUBOST: What was it in reality?

BOIX: The SS sent them to pick up stones near the barbed wires, and the SS guards at the second barbed wire fence fired on them, because they received a reward for every man they shot down.

The other picture shows a Jew in 1941 during the construction of the so-called Russian camp, which later became the sanitary camp, hanged with the cord which he used to keep up his trousers.

DUBOST: Was it suicide?

BOIX: It was alleged to be. It was a man who no longer had any hope of escape. He was driven to desperation by forced labour and torture.

Sonderbeilage „Mauthausen. Camp de l'assassinat" (Mauthausen. Mordlager) der französischen Tageszeitung Ce Soir, 1. August 1945
Archives Nationales, Paris, fonds de l'Amicale de Mauthausen, F/9/5567

Special supplement 'Mauthausen. Camp de l'assassinat' (Mauthausen. Murder camp) published by the French daily newspaper Ce Soir, 1 August 1945
Archives Nationales, Paris, fonds de l'Amicale de Mauthausen, F/9/5567

Gedenkstättenführer in russischer Sprache, herausgegeben von der Österreichischen Lagergemeinschaft, vor 1980
KZ-Gedenkstätte Mauthausen, II.Bros.86

Guide brochure to the memorial site in Russian, published by the Österreichische Lagergemeinschaft, before 1980
KZ-Gedenkstätte Mauthausen, II.Bros.86

Vergessen in Mauthausen, Broschüre anlässlich einer Veranstaltung zur Erinnerung an das Pogrom im November 1938 („Kristallnacht"), herausgegeben von B-project, 1997
KZ-Gedenkstätte Mauthausen, II.Bros.28

Forgotten in Mauthausen, leaflet for an event commemorating the 'Kristallnacht' pogrom in November 1938, published by B-project, 1997
KZ-Gedenkstätte Mauthausen, II.Bros.28

Tod im Steinbruch
Death in the Quarry

Steinbruch Wiener Graben, 2012
Foto: Tal Adler

Wiener Graben Quarry, 2012
Photograph: Tal Adler

Tod im Steinbruch

Die SS nutzt die Zwangsarbeit im Konzentrationslager in zweifacher Hinsicht. Sie beutet die Arbeitskraft der Häftlinge zur Durchsetzung eigener wirtschaftlicher Interessen aus, sie nutzt den Arbeitseinsatz aber auch zur gezielten Ermordung ganzer Häftlingsgruppen.

Die Steinbrüche von Mauthausen und Gusen spielen dabei eine wichtige Rolle. Ihr Ausbau und ihre Bewirtschaftung setzen zeitgleich mit der Gründung des Konzentrationslagers 1938 ein. Wenig später ereignen sich die ersten Todesfälle.

Death in the Quarry

The SS uses forced labour in the concentration camp in two ways. It exploits the prisoners' labour to advance its own economic interests, and also uses the deployment of labour for the targeted killing of whole groups of prisoners.

The Mauthausen and Gusen quarries play an important role in this. Their expansion and commercialisation begin at the same time as the establishment of the concentration camp in 1938. A short time later the first deaths occur.

Lore aus dem Steinbruch, vor 1945
KZ-Gedenkstätte Mauthausen, OS1284
Foto: Tal Adler

Die Loren dienen dazu, große Mengen schwerer Steinbrocken zu transportieren. Die SS führt bei dieser Arbeit tödliche Unfälle oft gezielt herbei.
2012 wird diese Lore aus einem der Teiche des Steinbruchs geborgen.

Wagon from the quarry, before 1945
KZ-Gedenkstätte Mauthausen, OS1284
Photograph: Tal Adler

The wagons are used to transport large quantities of heavy blocks of stone. The SS often deliberately causes fatal accidents while they are in use.
In 2012 this wagon was recovered from the pond in the quarry.

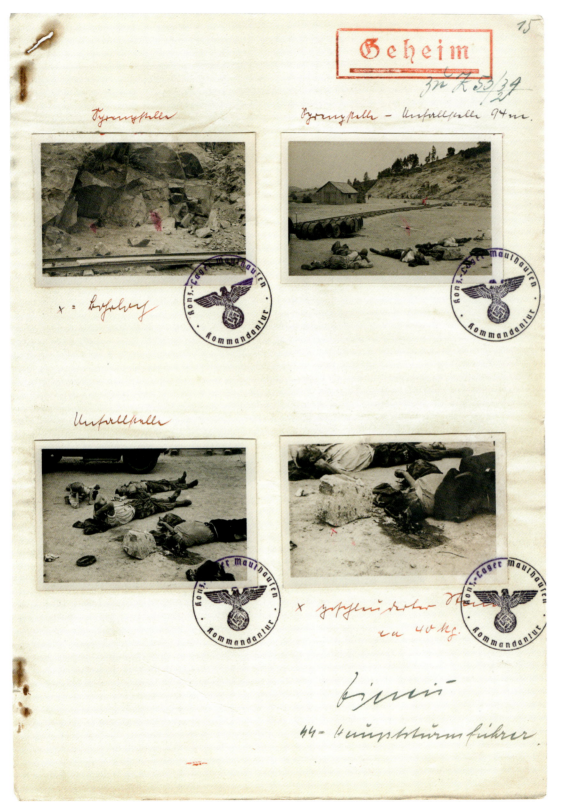

Dokumentation eines Arbeitsunfalls im Steinbruch Gusen, 1939
Oberösterreichisches Landesarchiv, Linz, BG Mauthausen, Z-Akten, Karton 70, Z53/39

Arbeitsunfälle wie dieser sind in Mauthausen und Gusen an der Tagesordnung. Grund dafür sind der schlechte körperliche Zustand der Häftlinge, die mangelhafte Schutzkleidung und das unzureichende Werkzeug. In der Anfangszeit werden diese Unfälle noch gerichtlich überprüft und deshalb dokumentiert.

Documentation of an industrial accident in the Gusen quarry, 1939
Oberösterreichisches Landesarchiv, Linz, BG Mauthausen, Z-Akten, Karton 70, Z53/39

Industrial accidents such as this are everyday occurrences in Mauthausen and Gusen. They are caused by the poor physical condition of the prisoners, a lack of protective clothing, and inadequate tools. During the initial period, these accidents are subject to a legal investigation and are therefore documented.

Protokoll einer Besprechung zwischen Reichsjustizminister Otto Georg Thierack und Reichsführer-SS Heinrich Himmler, 18. September 1942
Bundesarchiv, Berlin, R 3001/24062, Bl. 35a

Von Anfang an werden Häftlinge in den KZ durch unmenschliche Arbeitsbedingungen gezielt zu Tode gebracht. Ab September 1942 überlässt Reichsjustizminister Otto Georg Thierack dem Polizei- und SS-Apparat ganze Gruppen von Justizgefangenen. Diese werden zur „Vernichtung durch Arbeit" in die Konzentrationslager deportiert.
Von etwa 10.000 Justizgefangenen in Mauthausen, hier „Sicherheitsverwahrte" genannt, sterben zwischen 1942 und 1943 innerhalb von 15 Monaten fast 7.000.

Minutes of a meeting between Reich Minister of Justice Otto Georg Thierack and Reich Chief of the SS Heinrich Himmler, 18 September 1942
Bundesarchiv, Berlin, R 3001/24062, Bl. 35a

From the start inhuman working conditions are deliberately used to kill prisoners in the concentration camps. From September 1942 onwards Reich Minister of Justice Otto Georg Thierack hands over whole groups of prisoners in the justice system to the police and SS apparatus. They are deported to the concentration camps for 'annihilation through work'.
Out of around 10,000 prisoners from the justice system in Mauthausen, here termed 'Sicherheitsverwahrte' ('preventative detention prisoners'), nearly 7,000 die within 15 months between 1942 and 1943.

[...] Transfer of antisocial elements from the prison system to the Reich Chief of the SS for annihilation through work. Without exception, preventative detention prisoners, Jews, Gypsies, Russians and Ukrainians, Poles with sentences over 3 years, Czechs or Germans with sentences over 8 years are to be handed over in accordance with the decision by the Reich Minister of Justice. First to be handed over are the worst antisocial elements from the last group in this list. [...]

Steinträger im Steinbruch Wienergraben, nach 1940
SS-Foto, Fotograf unbekannt
NIOD, Amsterdam, 67338

Angehörige der Strafkompanie, viele von ihnen sogenannte Sicherheitsverwahrte, werden bei den gefährlichsten Arbeiten eingesetzt. Sie geraten unter die Räder der Loren oder stürzen bei der Arbeit als Steinträger über die Treppe, die sie oft im Laufschritt und unter Schlägen überwinden müssen. Stürzende Häftlinge reißen andere mit in den Tod.

Carrying stones in the Wiener Graben quarry, after 1940
SS photograph, unknown photographer
NIOD, Amsterdam, 67338

Members of the *Strafkompanie* (penal company), many of them so-called preventative detention prisoners, are assigned the most dangerous work. They fall under the wheels of the wagons or trip while carrying stones on the stairs, which they are often forced to climb at a run or amid blows from the guards. Prisoners who fall take others with them to their deaths.

Toter Häftling an der Kante des Steinbruchs, 1941
SS-Foto, Fotograf unbekannt
L'Humanité, Paris, 4 HU 22

Dead prisoner at the edge of the quarry, 1941
SS photograph, unknown photographer
L'Humanité, Paris, 4 HU 22

Eine weitere Gruppe, die zur gezielten und oft auch sofortigen Tötung ins KZ Mauthausen gebracht wird, sind Juden aus den Niederlanden. Die meisten dieser Häftlinge überleben nur wenige Wochen. Sie werden während des Arbeitseinsatzes erschossen oder über die steilen Felswände gestoßen. Die SS nennt diese Opfer zynisch „Fallschirmspringer".
Der spanische Überlebende Francisco Boix kann nach dem Krieg das hier abgebildete Opfer als holländischen Juden identifizieren.

Another group brought to the Mauthausen concentration camp for targeted and often immediate execution are Jews from the Netherlands. Most of these prisoners only survive a few weeks. They are shot during labour deployment or pushed over the steep sides of the quarry. The SS cynically terms these victims 'parachutists'.
After the war the Spanish survivor Francisco Boix is able to identify the victim pictured here as a Dutch Jew.

Die Todesstiege

Heute sind im Steinbruch kaum Spuren der hier begangenen Verbrechen zu erkennen. Nur die Stiege gibt es noch. Sie ist zu einem Symbol für die Grausamkeit im KZ geworden.

The Stairs of Death

Today hardly any traces of the crimes committed in the quarry are visible. Only the stairs remain. They have become a symbol for the cruelty of the concentration camp.

Hinweisschild der Gedenkstätte Mauthausen, vor 1949
KZ-Gedenkstätte Mauthausen, OS1285
Foto: Tal Adler

Bereits kurz nach der Befreiung taucht die Bezeichnung „Todesstiege" auf. Der Begriff zeigt die Bedeutung, die diese Treppenanlage in der Erinnerung der überlebenden Häftlinge einnimmt.

Sign from the Mauthausen memorial site, before 1949
KZ-Gedenkstätte Mauthausen, OS1285
Photograph: Tal Adler

Only a short time after liberation the name 'Todesstiege' ('Stairs of Death') appears. The term shows the importance given to this stairway in survivors' memories.

Tschechische Überlebende auf der Todesstiege,
Mauthausen, um 1950
Fotograf/Fotografin unbekannt
Národní archiv, Prag, SPB, karton 21/124

Schon bald nach der Befreiung nutzen Überlebende bei ihren Besuchen der Gedenkstätte die Treppe als Erinnerungsort. Auch die ersten Befreiungsfeiern finden am Fuß der Treppe statt. Im Jahr 1948 wird sie in das Gelände der Gedenkstätte integriert.

Czech survivors on the Stairs of Death, Mauthausen, around 1950
Unknown photographer
Národní archiv, Prague, SPB, karton 21/124

Survivors already start using the stairs as a place of remembrance on their visits to the memorial site in the first years after the liberation. Early commemoration ceremonies also take place at the bottom of the stairs. In 1948 they become part of the memorial site.

Ersttag mit Sonderpostmarke der Österreichischen Post, 2005
KZ-Gedenkstätte Mauthausen, AMM 1.8.3.0001

Die Treppe erhält als Symbol im Lauf der Jahre universelle Bedeutung für das Gedenken an die Opfer des KZ Mauthausen. Ihr Abbild findet sich auf einer österreichischen Briefmarke ebenso wie auf dem Titelblatt einer antifaschistischen Broschüre.

First day cover with a special edition postage stamp issued by the Austrian Post, 2005
KZ-Gedenkstätte Mauthausen, AMM 1.8.3.0001

Over time the stairs become a universal symbol for the remembrance of the victims of the Mauthausen concentration camp. Their image is to be found on the cover of antifascist leaflets as well as on an Austrian postage stamp.

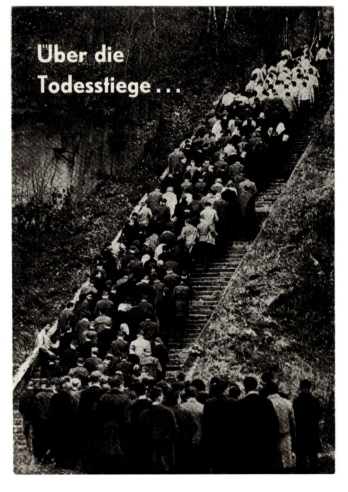

Über die Todesstiege …,
Broschüre der Gewerkschaft der Gemeindebediensteten,
Wien, undatiert [ca. 1960]
KZ-Gedenkstätte Mauthausen,
II.Bros.143

On the Stairs of Death …,
brochure produced by the Union of Local Authority Employees,
Vienna, undated [circa 1960]
KZ-Gedenkstätte Mauthausen,
II.Bros.143

Mauthausen-Mahnmal am Pariser Friedhof Père-Lachaise, 1958
Foto: Pierre Freteaud, 2004
Amicale française de Mauthausen, Paris, ohne Signatur

Der Gedenkstein für die Opfer des KZ Mauthausen am Pariser Friedhof Père-Lachaise ist das Werk des Bildhauers Gérard Choain aus dem Jahr 1958. Die symbolisierte Darstellung der Todesstiege ist aus Mauthausener Granit geschlagen.

Mauthausen memorial in the Père-Lachaise cemetery in Paris, 1958
Photograph: Pierre Freteaud, 2004
Amicale française de Mauthausen, Paris, no archive number

The memorial for victims of the Mauthausen concentration camp in the Père-Lachaise cemetery in Paris is a work by the sculptor Gérard Choain from 1958. The symbolic representation of the Stairs of Death is carved from Mauthausen granite.

Tödliche Medizin
Deadly Medicine

Ehemaliges Sanitätslagergelände, 2012
Foto: Tal Adler

Site of the former infirmary camp, 2012
Photograph: Tal Adler

Tödliche Medizin

SS-Ärzte und SS-Sanitätsdienstgrade, die in Gusen, Mauthausen oder den Außenlagern eingesetzt sind, ordnen die Ermordung tausender kranker Gefangener an. Viele töten sie auch eigenhändig. Einige SS-Ärzte missbrauchen Häftlinge für Experimente und nehmen dabei auch ihren Tod in Kauf. Die Körper von Gestorbenen dienen ihnen zur Herstellung zahlreicher medizinischer Präparate; manchmal töten sie Häftlinge nur zu diesem Zweck. Um ihre Morde zu verschleiern, lassen die SS-Ärzte Dokumente fälschen.

Deadly Medicine

SS doctors and SS *Sanitätsdienstgrade* (medical orderlies) assigned to Gusen, Mauthausen and the sub-camps order the deaths of thousands of sick inmates. They also kill many themselves. Some SS doctors misuse prisoners for experiments, not caring whether they die. They use the bodies of the dead to make numerous anatomical specimens; sometimes they kill prisoners for this reason alone. In order to conceal the murders, the SS doctors have documents falsified.

Spritze aus Mauthausen
KZ-Gedenkstätte Mauthausen, OS451
Foto: Tal Adler

Syringe from Mauthausen
KZ-Gedenkstätte Mauthausen, OS451
Photograph: Tal Adler

Die defekte Spritze, die zur Injektion tödlicher Substanzen verwendet worden ist, schmuggelt der in der Apotheke des Krankenreviers eingesetzte Häftling Alois Stockinger 1943 aus dem Lager. Er übergibt sie 1946 den Ermittlern im Vorfeld der Mauthausen-Prozesse als Beweisstück und sagt selbst als Zeuge zu den Giftinjektionen aus. Später überlässt Stockinger die Spritze der Sammlung der KZ-Gedenkstätte Mauthausen.

The damaged syringe, which was used to inject lethal substances, is smuggled out of the camp in 1943 by the prisoner Alois Stockinger, who is assigned to work in the infirmary pharmacy. In 1946, in the run-up to the Mauthausen trials, he turns it over to the investigators as a piece of evidence and he himself testifies as a witness to the lethal injections. Later Stockinger presents the syringe to the collection of the Mauthausen Memorial.

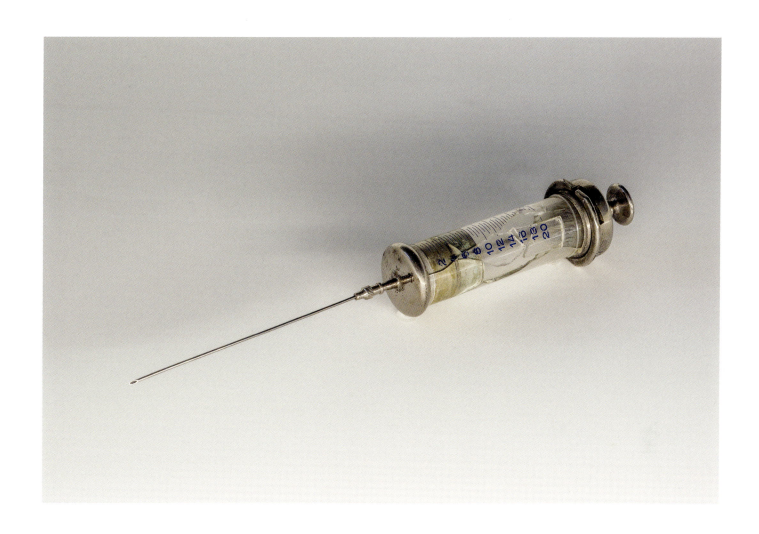

```
K.L.Mauthausen/Unterkunft Gusen.                    Gusen, den 4.Dezember 1941.
Liste der am 4.12.41 nach dem K.L.Dachau/Hftl-Sanat.überstellten Häftlinge:
```

Lfdr.Nr.	Name	Vorname	Geb.Dat.	Hftl-Nr.	Nation.	Transp.Liste N
1	Alonso-Millan	Timoteo	19.12.00	11644	Spanier	12
2	Benna	Romann	8.4.02	-8004	Pole	9
3	Bibula	Siegmund	15.7.15	11036	Pol-Jude	22
4	Ciesielski	Andreas	1.11.22	1286	Pole	17
5	Drazek	Josef	1.1.04	6113	Pole	18
6	Dura	Hieronim	17.9.98	8364	Pole	10
7	Epstein	Michael	14.9.98	8371	Pole	18
8	Fernandez-Sanz	Juan	17.2.00	10892	Spanier	11
9	Guzenda	Czeslaus	7.7.08	3682	Pole	20
10	Gryska	Ladislaus	1.6.84	12570	Pole	17
11	Gonzales-Sanchez	Joaquin	29.9.02	9909	Spanier	22
12	Gawronski	Felix	27.7.20	6185	Pole	7
13	Maslinski	Stanislaus	16.11.07	2363	Pole	9
14	Hajdasz	Felix	16.5.23	3686	Pole	19
15	Hantzko	Siegmund	2.12.97	5148	Pole	10
16	Herschmann	Rudolf	14.1.99	7550	Pol.Jude/AZR	15
17	Jarzembowski	Bruno	31.3.15	7578	Pole	20
18	Jendykiewicz	Edmund	28.3.17	8461	Pole	18
19	Kaczmarek	Czeslaus	16.5.20	8466	Pole	22
20	Kobylinski	Heinrich	2.1.07	3883	Pole	18
21	Kolenda	Ladislaus	17.2.08	3895	Pole	17
22	Kornacki	Mieczyslaus	1.1.22	1773	Pole	17
23	Korotki	Wladimir	27.6.98	12605	Pole	17
24	Kucharski	Georg	27.7.14	12610	Pole	17
25	Kus	Stanislaus	15.5.17	4028	Pole	18
26	Lanoszka	Thaddäus	24.12.12	4044	Pole	20
27	Lea-Arranda	Evaristo	26.2.19	10961	Spanier	17
28	Lis	Johann	22.6.05	6637	Pole	17
29	Lopez-Barberan	Esteban	27.12.10	9378	Spanier	8
30	Mazur	Paul	26.6.00	12283	Pole	22
31	Mauro-Giovani	Giovani	25.1.00	8612	Spanier	21
32	Navarro-Munera	Francisco	19.8.19	11525	Spanier	17
33	Oliva-Olivera	Josef	7.12.06	11545	Spanier	8
34	Ososik	Sylvester	18.12.20	4290	Pole	18
35	Paguina-Mula	Baldomero	25.1.06	10185	Spanier	22
36	Pankowiak	Adam	21.12.08	5552	Pole	21
37	Paszek	Kasimir	12.4.23	6846	Pole	10
38	Petzold	Josef	8.11.07	4329	Pole	21
39	Perez-Valero	Jose	15.10.22	9569	Spanier	17
40	Pikora	Stanislaus	30.12.02	730	Pole	9
41	Polakowski	Ladislaus	1.6.10	6906	Pole	21
42	Przymusinski	Josef	11.3.16	6943	Pole	10
43	Ptaszkiewicz	Ladislaus	17.6.02	8759	Pole	15
44	Puig-Cerve	Marcel	12.2.00	9592	Spanier	10
45	Ranke	Friedrich	28.12.89	12712	AZR-Deutsch	17
46	Rudzinski	Kasimir	6.1.06	8792	Pole	21
47	Schulz	Josef	7.4.02	8808	AZR-Deutsch	20
48	Semrad	Josef	30.9.22	7797	Tschech/Schutz	17
49	Sewina	Johann	13.12.10	8193	Pole	20
50	Smigielski	Anton	2.3.93	4545	Pole	16
51	Surmacewicz	Eduard	18.10.99	7103	Pole	10
52	Schmidt	Peter	16.4.04	886	Pole	16
53	Sznajder	Czeslaus	21.3.99	4653	Pole	10
54	Szyszkowski	Josef	28.7.22	8881	Pole	17
55	Toll	Johann	22.12.03	8229	Pole	20
56	Umiastowski	Marian	25.3.05	12757	Pole	17
57	Vogtschmied	Fritz	15.1.83	12760	AZR/Deutsch	17
58	Witkowski	Isidor	15.3.09	3148	Pole	21
59	Zapedowski	Eduard	12.2.09	4840	Pole	20
60	Zgid	Thaddäus	22.5.22	7906	Pole	17

Liste eines Transports von Gusen nach Hartheim,
4. Dezember 1941

Amicale française de Mauthausen, Paris, ohne Signatur

Im Frühjahr 1941 beginnt die erste reichsweit organisierte Massenmordaktion an KZ-Häftlingen. Sie trifft vor allem kranke und arbeitsunfähige Häftlinge. Sie werden in Tötungsanstalten vergast, die ursprünglich für die „Euthanasie-Aktion" zur Ermordung behinderter Menschen eingerichtet worden sind. Die SS tarnt diese Morde. So wird als Zielort dieses Gefangenentransports aus Gusen ein „Häftlingssanatorium" im KZ Dachau angegeben. Tatsächlich ist das Ziel die Gaskammer der Tötungsanstalt Hartheim bei Linz.

List of a transport from Gusen to Hartheim,
4 December 1941

Amicale française de Mauthausen, Paris, no archive number

In spring 1941 the first organised mass murder programme of concentration camp inmates throughout Reich territory begins. In particular, it targets prisoners who are sick and unable to work. They are gassed in killing centres that were originally set up for murdering disabled people as part of the 'euthanasia programme'. The SS disguises these murders. Thus the destination given on this list of a prisoner transport from Gusen is a 'Prisoner Sanatorium' in Dachau concentration camp. In reality the destination is the gas chamber of the Hartheim killing centre near Linz.

Nummernmarken, Grabungsfunde 2002
Dokumentationsstelle Hartheim des Oberösterreichischen
Landesarchivs, Alkoven, Bestand Fundgegenstände
Foto: Tal Adler

Archäologische Grabungen bei der ehemaligen
Tötungsanstalt Hartheim fördern knapp 60 Marken mit
Nummern von KZ-Häftlingen zutage. Über 40 dieser
Nummern finden sich auf Listen, in denen die SS Transporte
aus Gusen in das „Häftlingssanatorium Dachau"
verzeichnet hat.

Number tags, archaeological find in 2002
Dokumentationsstelle Hartheim des Oberösterreichischen
Landesarchivs, Alkoven, Bestand Fundgegenstände
Photograph: Tal Adler

Archaeological digs at the former Hartheim killing centre
in 2002 unearth nearly 60 tags bearing the numbers of
concentration camp prisoners. Over 40 of these numbers
can be found on SS lists of transports from Gusen to the
Dachau 'Prisoner Sanatorium'.

Sammlung medizinischer Präparate in Gusen, 1945
KZ-Gedenkstätte Mauthausen, H/17/1/1

Collection of anatomical specimens in Gusen, 1945
KZ-Gedenkstätte Mauthausen, H/17/1/1 and H/17/1/2

Schreiben des SS-Standortarztes Krebsbach an die
SS-Ärztliche Akademie in Graz, 21. Juli 1943
Vojenský historický archiv, Prag, SS-Ärztliche Akademie Graz,
Mappe 5, Aktenzeichen 278

Der im Schreiben genannte jüdische Häftling ist
kleinwüchsig. Er wird in Mauthausen getötet, um sein
Skelett für Studienzwecke nutzen zu können.

Letter from SS chief camp physician Krebsbach to the
SS medical academy in Graz, 21 July 1943
Vojenský historický archiv, Prague, SS-Ärztliche Akademie Graz,
Mappe 5, Aktenzeichen 278

The Jewish prisoner named in the letter is of unusually
short stature. He is killed in Mauthausen so that his
skeleton can be used for study.

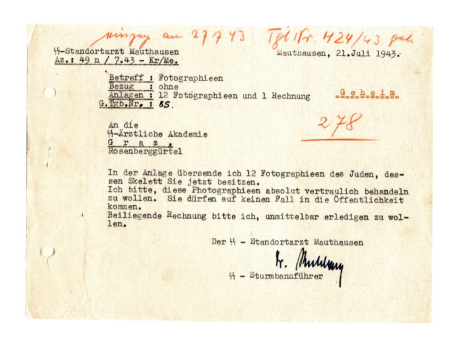

Darstellung einer Hautreaktion aus Unterlagen zu
Impfversuchen an Häftlingen in Mauthausen, 1943
Bundesarchiv, Berlin, NS 4 Ma/30, Bl. 5

Neben Testreihen mit Impfstoffen führen SS-Ärzte
in Gusen und Mauthausen auch Arzneimittel- und
Ernährungsversuche mit Häftlingen durch. Weit über 500
Todesfälle sind als Folge solcher Experimente bekannt.

Illustration of a skin reaction from files relating to
vaccination experiments on prisoners in Mauthausen, 1943
Bundesarchiv, Berlin, NS 4 Ma/30, Bl. 5

As well as conducting series of tests for vaccinations,
SS doctors in Mauthausen and Gusen also carry out
pharmaceutical and nutritional experiments on prisoners.
Well over 500 deaths are known to have resulted from
these kinds of experiments.

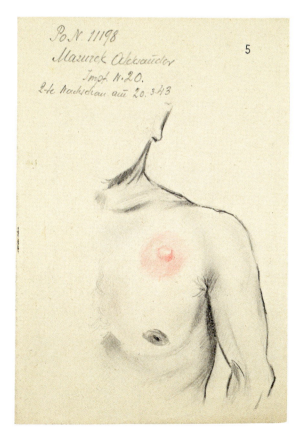

Totenbuch des SS-Standortarztes von Mauthausen, 1942
United States National Archives and Records Administration,
RG 238, Entry 2A, Location: 190/10/35/06, Vol. 3

Death register of the SS chief camp physician of
Mauthausen, 1942
United States National Archives and Records Administration,
RG 238, Entry 2A, Location: 190/10/35/06, Vol. 3

Die SS lässt falsche Todesursachen registrieren. Der als Schreiber eingesetzte Häftling Ernst Martin markiert im Totenbuch heimlich jene Fälle, bei denen er erfährt, dass es sich um gezielte Tötungen handelt. Durch einen Punkt hinter dem Geburtsort kennzeichnet er Opfer von Giftinjektionen.

The SS has false causes of death registered. The prisoner Ernst Martin, assigned as a clerk, puts secret marks in the death register against cases where he learns that the prisoners were killed deliberately. By putting a dot after the place of birth, he identifies the victims of lethal injections.

Medizinisches SS-Personal vor Gericht

Zwischen 1946 und 1947 führt ein amerikanisches Militärgericht in Dachau gegen mehr als 300 Männer Prozesse wegen in Mauthausen und seinen Außenlagern begangenen Verbrechen. Unter den Angeklagten sind neun SS-Ärzte und sechs Sanitätsdienstgrade. In späteren Verfahren vor Militärtribunalen oder nationalen Gerichtshöfen werden ebenfalls Medizinverbrechen verhandelt. Viele der in Mauthausen, Gusen und den Außenlagern tätigen SS-Ärzte und Sanitätsdienstgrade entgehen alledings einer Bestrafung.

SS Medical Personnel in Court

Between 1946 and 1947 an American military court in Dachau tries over 300 men for crimes committed in Mauthausen and its subcamps. Among the defendants are nine SS doctors and six medical orderlies. Medical crimes are also dealt with in later military tribunals and national courts of law. However, many of the SS doctors and medical orderlies active in Mauthausen, Gusen and the subcamps escape punishment.

Gruppenfoto aller Angeklagten des Mauthausen-Hauptprozesses in Dachau, 1946
Fotograf unbekannt
United States National Archives and Records Administration, RG 549, Box 346, Folder 5

Group photograph of all the defendants at the Mauthausen trial in Dachau, 1946
Unknown photographer
United States National Archives and Records Administration, RG 549, Box 346, Folder 5

Dr. Eduard Krebsbach (1894–1947)
Standortarzt in Mauthausen von 1941 bis 1943
Als Standortarzt ist Eduard Krebsbach Vorgesetzter des gesamten medizinischen Personals im Hauptlager und in allen Außenlagern. Eigenhändig ermordet er zahlreiche Häftlinge mit Giftinjektionen. Sein Spitzname im Lager ist „Dr. Spritzbach". Er ist bei Vergasungen anwesend und selektiert Häftlinge für die Ermordung in Hartheim.
1944 verlässt Krebsbach die Waffen-SS und wird Betriebsarzt in Kassel.
Das amerikanische Militärgericht in Dachau verurteilt Krebsbach wegen seiner Beteiligung an den im KZ Mauthausen begangenen Verbrechen zum Tode. Im Mai 1947 wird er gehängt.

Dr. Eduard Krebsbach (1894–1947)
Chief Camp Physician in Mauthausen from 1941 to 1943
As chief camp physician, Eduard Krebsbach is in charge of the entire medical staff in the main camp and all the subcamps. He himself murders numerous prisoners by lethal injection. His nickname in the camp is 'Dr. Spritzbach' (a *Spritze* is an injection in German). He is present at gassings and selects prisoners to be murdered in Hartheim.
In 1944 Krebsbach leaves the Waffen SS and becomes a company doctor in Kassel.
The American military court in Dachau sentences Krebsbach to death for his part in the crimes committed at the Mauthausen concentration camp. He is hanged in May 1947.

Eduard Krebsbach (links) vor dem Dachauer Militärgericht, 1946
Fotograf unbekannt
United States National Archives and Records Administration, RG 549, Box 346, Folder 5

Eduard Krebsbach (left) in front of the Dachau military court, 1946
Unknown photographer
United States National Archives and Records Administration, RG 549, Box 346, Folder 5

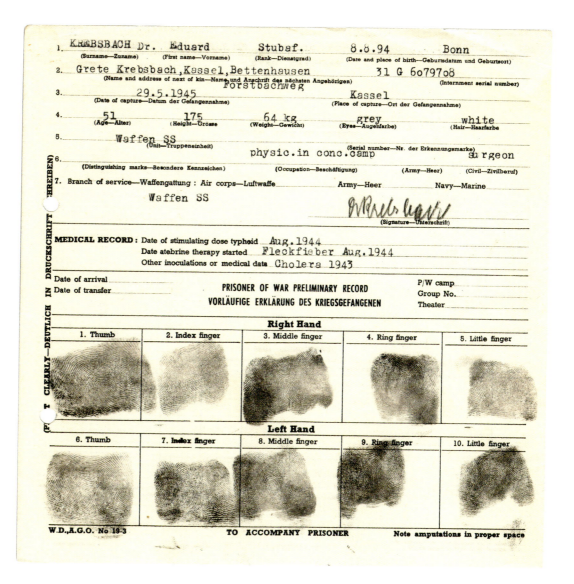

Datenblatt von Eduard Krebsbach, angelegt nach seiner Verhaftung im Mai 1945
United States National Archives and Records Administration, RG 549, Executee Files, Box 12, Folder Krebsbach, E.

Personal information sheet for Eduard Krebsbach, created after his arrest in May 1945
United States National Archives and Records Administration, RG 549, Executee Files, Box 12, Folder Krebsbach, E.

Otto Kleingünther (1896–1962)
SS-Sanitätsdienstgrad in Mauthausen von 1940 bis 1943
Otto Kleingünther arbeitet als Pfleger im Krankenrevier des Lagers. Wie die meisten SS-Sanitätsdienstgrade verfügt er nur über spärliche medizinische Kenntnisse und hat lediglich eine Erste-Hilfe-Ausbildung absolviert. Er ermordet zahlreiche Häftlinge durch tödliche Injektionen. Im Juni 1943 wird er ins Außenlager Loiblpaß versetzt.
Das nach Kriegsende über Kleingünther in Dachau verhängte Todesurteil wird bald in lebenslange Haft umgewandelt. 1955 kommt er auf Bewährung frei. Zwei Jahre später wird ihm der Rest der Haftstrafe erlassen.

Otto Kleingünther (1896–1962)
Medical orderly in Mauthausen from 1940 to 1943
Otto Kleingünther works as an orderly in the camp infirmary. Like most SS *Sanitätsdienstgrade* (medical orderlies) he has very little medical knowledge and has merely completed a first-aid course. He murders numerous prisoners by lethal injection. In June 1943 he is transferred to the Loiblpaß subcamp.
The death sentence Kleingünther receives in Dachau after the war is soon commuted to life imprisonment. In 1955 he is released on parole. Two years later the remaining sentence is dropped.

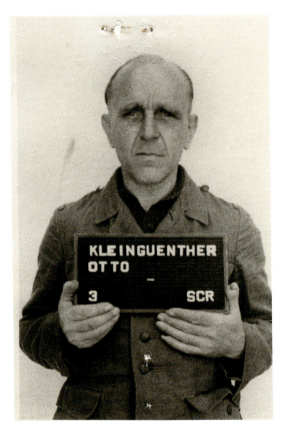

Otto Kleingünther in amerikanischer Gefangenschaft, 1945
Fotograf unbekannt
United States National Archives and Records
Administration, RG 549, Box 392, Folder 4

Otto Kleingünther in American custody, 1945
Unknown photographer
United States National Archives and Records
Administration, RG 549, Box 392, Folder 4

Erlass der Reststrafe von Otto Kleingünther, Juli 1957
United States National Archives and Records Administration, RG 549, Box 393, Folder 1

Order to remit the remaining sentence of Otto Kleingünther, July 1957
United States National Archives and Records Administration, RG 549, Box 393, Folder 1

HEADQUARTERS
U. S. ARMY, EUROPE
Office of the Commander in Chief
16 JUL 1957

UNITED STATES vs Josef Kettner, et al., Case No. 000-50-5-21
VEREINIGTE STAATEN gegen Josef Kettner, et al., Fall Nr. 000-50-5-21

ORDER FOR REMISSION OF UNEXECUTED PORTION OF SENTENCE
VERFUEGUNG ZUM ERLASS DES UNVERBUESSTEN TEILS DER STRAFE

BE IT KNOWN TO ALL MEN BY THESE PRESENTS THAT by virtue of the authority
Es wird hiermit bekanntgegeben, dass kraft der mir verliehenen Befugnisse,

vested in me, and as Commander in Chief, United States Army, Europe, and
in meiner Eigenschaft als Oberbefehlshaber der US-Armee in Europa und ent-

pursuant to a unanimous and therefore mandatory recommendation of the Mixed
sprechend einer einstimmigen und darum bindenden Empfehlung des Gemischten Aus-

Board created by Article 6, Chapter One, Settlement Convention, Bonn Con-
schusses, der durch Artikel 6, Absatz 1, des Regelungsvertrages der Bonner Ver-

ventions, the unexecuted portion of the sentence of:
traege errichtet wurde, der unverbuesste Teil der Strafe des:

Otto Kleinguenther, born 19 August 1896,
Otto Kleinguenther, geboren am 19 August 1896,

convicted by a General Military Government Court in the case styled and
der in dem oben bezeichneten Fall und unter der oben bezeichneten Nummer von

numbered above, shall be and the same is hereby remitted effective upon
einem Oberen Militaergericht verurteilt worden ist, hiermit erlassen werde, und

service of this order on him and execution by him of the written Acknowl-
zwar mit Wirkung von der Zustellung dieser Verfuegung, und nachdem er die nach-

edgment of Service & Receipt below, at which time he shall become finally
stehende Zustellungs- und Empfangsbestaetigung unterschrieben hat, worauf seine

released and discharged.
entgueltige Entlassung erfolgen wird.

Certified True Copy

GLEN WALKER
GLEN WALKER
Major JAGC

/s/ H. I. Hodes
H. I. HODES
General, United States Army
Commander in Chief

ACKNOWLEDGMENT OF SERVICE & RECEIPT
ZUSTELLUNGS- UND EMPFANGSBESTAETIGUNG

I acknowledge that on this date, August 17, 1957, a signed copy of
Ich bestaetige, dass mir heute, am 17 August 1957, eine unterschriebene

the within and foregoing Order was served on and delivered to me.
Ausfertigung der obigen Verfuegung zugestellt und ausgehaendigt wurde.

WITNESS:
Zeuge:

Anton ASANGER
Parole Supervisor

Name (signed): Otto Kleingünther
Name (Unterschrift)

Name (typed): Otto KLEINGEUNTHER
Name (Unterschrift in Maschinenschrift)

Bericht des ehemaligen Häftlings Ernst Martin über die Giftinjektionen, verfasst für das in Mauthausen tätige War Crimes Investigation Team, Mai 1945
United States National Archives and Records Administration, RG 238, USA Prosecution Exhibit 249

Die beliebteste Todesart, insbesondere für Lungenkranke, Kranke die an Infektionskrankheiten, schweren Phlegmonen usw. litten, war ihnen eine Spritze zu geben. Dies ging so meist vor sich, daß der Häftling auf den Operationstisch gelegt wurde zwecks Vornahme einer Operation. Er wurde kurz mit Chloraethyl narkotisiert und sodann wurde mit einer Injektionsspritze und langer Nadel in das Herz eine Lösung von Magnesiumchlorat, von Cyan-Rhodan-Verbindungen und andere, von Benzin usw. injiziert. Der Tod trat schockartig ein, meist nach Sekunden, oft aber, wenn diese Injektionen nicht von Ärzten gemacht wurden, quälte sich der Häftling noch stundenlang ab.

Report by former prisoner Ernst Martin on lethal injections, compiled for the War Crimes Investigation Team working in Mauthausen, May 1945
United States National Archives and Records Administration, RG 238, USA Prosecution Exhibit 249

The most common way to get rid of prisoners who suffered from a disease of the lungs or another contagious disease was to give an injection. This was usually done in the following manner:
The patient was put on the operating table. He was then given ether, and given an injection with a long needle into his heart.
This solution consisted of Magnesium chloride and Cyan Rhodan and others, among them gasoline. Death occurred in the way of shocks and cramps most of the time after a few seconds. If the solution was not prepared by a doctor the patient would suffer for hours afterwards.

Ernst Martin als Zeuge im Mauthausen-Hauptprozesses in Dachau, 1946
Fotograf unbekannt
KZ-Gedenkstätte Mauthausen, P/19/10/12

Ernst Martin as a witness at the Mauthausen trial in Dachau, 1946
Unknown photographer
KZ-Gedenkstätte Mauthausen, P/19/10/12

Aussage des ehemaligen Häftlings Alois Stockinger im Prozess gegen Otto Kleingünther in Dachau, August 1947 United States National Archives and Records Administration, RG 549, Box 392, Folder 3	Testimony given by former prisoner Alois Stockinger in the trial against Otto Kleingünther in Dachau, August 1947 United States National Archives and Records Administration, RG 549, Box 392, Folder 3
F: Wo sind sie dem Angeklagten Kleingünther begegnet? A: In der Apotheke in den Krankenbaracken. F: Welche Arbeit war Ihnen zugewiesen, als Sie in Mauthausen waren? A: Ich habe in verschiedenen Kommandos gearbeitet. Zum Schluss war ich in der Apotheke. […] F: In der Zeit, als die in der Apotheke eingesetzt waren, kamen sie da überhaupt in Kontakt mit dem Angeklagten Kleingünther? A: Sehr häufig. […] F: Wissen Sie, ob im KZ Mauthausen Häftlinge getötet wurden, in dem ihnen körperfremde Substanzen ins Herz gespritzt wurden? […] A: Ja. F: Wissen Sie, wer an diesen Injektionen beteiligt war? A: Kleingünther, und ich glaube, da war August Becker und der Lagerarzt Krebsbach. […] F: Waren Sie Zeuge davon, dass der Angeklagte zu dieser Zeit Häftlingen Injektionen gab? A: Ja. […] F: Wie viele Häftlinge waren in diesem Fall betroffen. A: Das war unterschiedlich, später war die Zahl der Männer, die eine Injektion erhielten, sehr hoch. Zu dieser Zeit hat er an einem halben Tag 30 Männer tot gespritzt, an anderen Tagen 40. […] F: Haben Sie all diese Injektionen gesehen? A: Einen Teil. Aber es ist sehr leicht auszurechen: Für eine Injektion brauchte man 20 Kubikzentimeter, und Kleingünther hat normalerweise 3 bis 4 Liter dieser Flüssigkeit bestellt. Und ein Liter war normalerweise ausreichend für 50 Mann. So können Sie selbst ausrechnen, wie viele er getötet hat. […] F: Wurde ein Betäubungsmittel oder Narkotikum gegeben, bevor gespritzt wurde? A: Sie wurden auf den Tisch gelegt und es gab ein Stück in Chloräthyl getauchte Baumwolle auf ihre Nase, und dann hat Kleingünther schon die Spritze gesetzt. Dass die Leute den Schmerz spürten, konnte man daran sehen, dass sie an Händen und Füßen festgehalten werden mussten.	Q: Where did you meet the defendant Kleingünther? A: In the dispensary, in the sick barracks. Q: What work were you assigned to while you were at Mauthausen? A: I worked on several details. During the last time I was there I worked in the pharmacy. […] Q: During the time that you were assigned to the Pharmacy did you come in contact with the defendant Kleingünther at all? A: Very frequently. […] Q: Do you know if prisoners were killed at Camp Mauthausen by injections of a foreign substance into the heart? […] A: Yes Q: Do you know who took part in these injections? A: Kleingünther, and then I believe there was August Becker and the camp physician Krebsbach. Q: Did you witness the defendant injecting any inmates at that time? A: Yes. […] Q: How many inmates were involved in this incident? A: That varied form time to time, later on the amount of men who received injections was very high. At that time there were half days when he injected 30 men, on other days he injected 40 men. […] Q: You saw all these injections? A: Part of them I have seen, but this is very easy to figure out: For one injection you needed 20 cubic centimetres and Kleingünther usually requested 3 to 4 litres of that liquid, and one litre was usually sufficient for 50 men, this is how you can figure out for yourself how many he killed. […] Q: Was any anaesthetic or narcotic given before the injection was administered? A: They were put on the table and then there was a piece of cotton soaked in chloro-ethyl on their nose, and when this was done Kleingünther already administered the injection. That the people felt the pain could be seen by the fact that one had to hold them back by their hands and feet.

Mord durch Giftgas
Murder by Poison Gas

Ehemalige Gaskammer, 2012
Foto: Tal Adler

Former gas chamber, 2012
Photograph: Tal Adler

Mord durch Giftgas

Im Herbst 1941 wird in Mauthausen eine Gaskammer errichtet, in der Häftlinge mit dem Schädlingsbekämpfungsmittel Zyklon B getötet werden. In den Jahren 1942 und 1943 kommt zusätzlich ein mobiler Gaswagen zum Einsatz, der auch in Gusen verwendet wird.

Zunächst richten sich die Mordaktionen vor allem gegen politische Gegner, später vermehrt gegen Kranke und unliebsame Zeugen. Die Vergasungen geschehen im Verborgenen. Die SS ist um größte Geheimhaltung bemüht und versucht später alle Spuren zu verwischen.

Murder by Poison Gas

In autumn 1941 a gas chamber is constructed at Mauthausen in which prisoners are killed using the pesticide Zyklon B. In addition, a mobile gas van is in operation in 1942 and 1943 that is also used in Gusen.

At first the killing actions are primarily directed against political opponents; later on they increasingly target the sick and unwanted witnesses. The gassings take place in secret. The SS takes great trouble to conceal them and later tries to destroy all traces of them.

Abluftventilator der Gaskammer
Památník Terezín, 213
Foto: Tal Adler

Nach der Vergasung der Häftlinge wird die Gaskammer mit diesem Ventilator entlüftet.
Kurz vor der Befreiung des Lagers lässt die SS alle technischen Einrichtungen der Gaskammer abbauen. Tschechische Häftlinge sichern den Ventilator und nehmen ihn mit nach Prag. In den 1950er Jahren wird er der Gedenkstätte Theresienstadt übergeben.

Extractor fan from the gas chamber
Památník Terezín, 213
Photograph: Tal Adler

After the prisoners have been gassed the gas chamber is ventilated using this extractor fan.
Shortly before the liberation of the camp the SS has all technical equipment removed from the gas chamber. Czech prisoners save the extractor fan and take it with them to Prague. In the 1950s it is donated to the Terezín Memorial.

Eingang zur ehemaligen Gaskammer und zerstörte
„Gaszelle", 1948
Fotograf/Fotografin unbekannt
Burghauptmannschaft Österreich, Wien

Die sogenannte Gaszelle ist ein kleiner, an die Gaskammer angrenzender Raum. Mit Hilfe einer speziellen Vorrichtung wird hier die im Zyklon B gebundene Blausäure gasförmig gemacht und in die Gaskammer eingeleitet.
Der Vergasungsvorgang dauert bis zu 20 Minuten, die Opfer sterben qualvoll.
Um die Spuren der Verbrechen zu verwischen, lässt die SS vor der Befreiung des Lagers die Mauer der Gaszelle niederreißen. Auch die Gaskammertüren werden entfernt.

Entrance to the former gas chamber and demolished
'gas cell', 1948
Unknown photographer
Burghauptmannschaft Österreich, Vienna

The so-called *Gaszelle* (gas cell) is a small room adjoining the gas chamber. With the help of a special device, the prussic acid in Zyklon B is turned into gas and fed into the gas chamber.
The gassing lasts up to 20 minutes, the victims die in agony.
In order to cover up the traces of its crimes, the SS has the wall of the gas cell torn down before the camp is liberated. The doors to the gas chamber are also removed.

Abluftrohr der Gaskammer, Mai 1945
Fotograf unbekannt
KZ-Gedenkstätte Mauthausen, Sammlung Mariano Constante Campo, ohne Signatur

Durch dieses Rohr rechts des Krematoriumskamins wird das Giftgas nach dem Tötungsvorgang aus der Gaskammer ins Freie geleitet.
Bei archäologischen Untersuchungen im Jahr 2011 werden Reste des Rohres in der Decke über der Gaskammer freigelegt.

Ventilation pipe of the gas chamber, May 1945
Unknown photographer
KZ-Gedenkstätte Mauthausen, Mariano Constante Campo Collection, no archive number

Through this pipe to the right of the crematorium chimney, poison gas from the gas chamber is released into the air after the killing procedure.
During archaeological investigations in 2011, remains of the pipe are uncovered in the ceiling above the gas chamber.

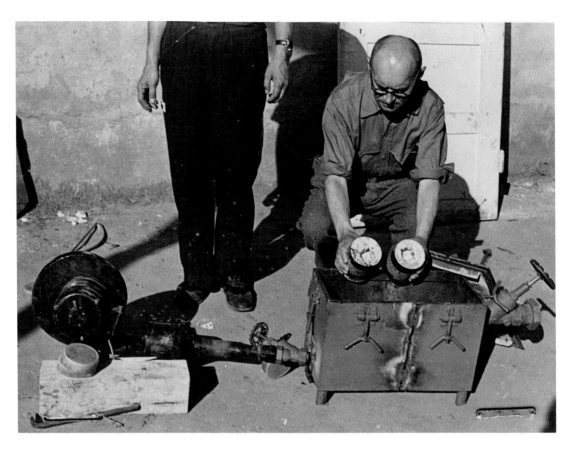

Jack H. Taylor mit dem Gaseinfüllapparat, Mai 1945
Fotograf unbekannt
United States National Archives and Records Administration,
RG 226, Entry 110

Jack H. Taylor with the gas filling apparatus, May 1945
Unknown photographer
United States National Archives and Records Administration,
RG 226, Entry 110

Obwohl die SS die Beseitigung sämtlicher Hinweise auf die Existenz der Gaskammer anordnet, stellen Häftlinge unter Lebensgefahr Beweise sicher. Ein von dem befreiten KZ-Häftling und US-Geheimdienstoffizier Jack H. Taylor verfasster Bericht dokumentiert die sichergestellten Gegenstände. Heute ist nur noch der Abluftventilator erhalten. Der Gaseinfüllapparat und die Gaskammertüren sind verschollen.

Although the SS orders the removal of any sign of the existence of the gas chamber, prisoners risk their lives to secure evidence of it. A report by US intelligence officer Jack H. Taylor, himself a liberated prisoner, documents the objects that were saved. Today only the extractor fan remains. The *Gaseinfüllapparat* (gas filling apparatus) and the doors to the gas chamber have vanished.

Auszug aus dem Totenbuch des SS-Standortarztes,
24. April 1945
United States National Archives and Records Administration,
RG 238, Entry 2A, Location: 190/10/35/06

Ende April 1945 tötet die SS wiederholt kranke Gefangene
in der Gaskammer. Um keine Beweise zu hinterlassen,
werden im Totenbuch natürliche Todesursachen vermerkt.
Der tschechische Häftling und Schreiber Josef Ulbrecht fügt
nach der Befreiung des Lagers den Vermerk „Gaz" hinzu.
Das ist der einzige Hinweis auf die wahren Todesumstände
dieser Gefangenen.

Extract from the death register of the SS chief camp
physician, 24 April 1945
United States National Archives and Records Administration,
RG 238, Entry 2A, Location: 190/10/35/06

At the end of April 1945 the SS kills groups of sick prisoners
in the gas chamber. So that no evidence is left, natural
causes of death are recorded in the death register. After
liberation the Czech prisoner and clerk Josef Ulbrecht adds
the note 'Gaz' to their entries. This is the only indication of
the true circumstances of these prisoners' deaths.

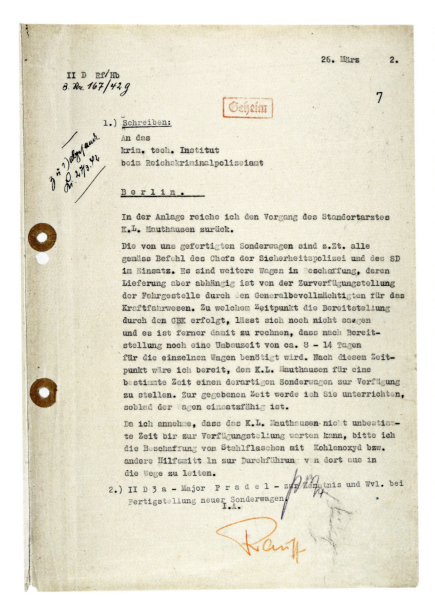

Schreiben von Walter Rauff an das Kriminaltechnische Institut des Reichskriminalpolizeiamts, 26. März 1942
Bundesarchiv, Berlin, R 58/871

Walter Rauff ist Leiter der Abteilung Technischer Dienst bei der Sicherheitspolizei und für die Bereitstellung von Gaswagen zuständig. Bei ihm beantragt die Leitung des KZ Mauthausen zunächst vergeblich einen als „Sonderwagen" bezeichneten Gaswagen.
In den Jahren 1942 und 1943 setzt die SS in Mauthausen und Gusen schließlich doch Gaswagen ein. Insgesamt werden in diesen Wagen mindestens 900 kranke Häftlinge getötet.

Letter from Walter Rauff to the Criminal Technical Institute of the Reich Criminal Police Department, 26 March 1942
Bundesarchiv, Berlin, R 58/871

Walter Rauff is the head of the technical services department of the Security Police and is responsible for the allocation of gas vans. The head of the Mauthausen concentration camp at first unsuccessfully requests a gas van, known as a 'Sonderwagen' ('special van'), from him. In 1942 and 1943 the SS finally does operate gas vans in Mauthausen and Gusen. In total at least 900 sick prisoners are killed using these vans.

[...] The Sonderwagen *manufactured by us are all currently in use in accordance with orders from the Head of the Security Police and the SD [Security Service]. Further vans have been procured but their delivery is subject to chassis being made available by the commissioner general for motor vehicles [GBK]. A date for allocation by the GBK cannot be determined at present and, furthermore, a necessary refit period of c. 8 – 14 days for the individual vans following allocation must be reckoned with. At that point I would be willing to supply the Mauthausen concentration camp with this kind of* Sonderwagen *for a certain period of time. I will inform you at the given time as soon as the van is ready for use.*

Assuming that the Mauthausen concentration camp cannot wait for it to be ready for an indefinite period, I ask that the procurement of steel bottles of carbon monoxide and other necessary equipment be arranged from there [...].

Leugnung und Beweis

Die gezielte Vernichtung von Beweisen durch die SS ermöglicht es sogenannten Revisionisten nach 1945, den Gasmord zu leugnen. Immer wieder bestreiten sie die Existenz der Gaskammer. Wissenschaftler, Juristen und Überlebende tragen aber eine Unzahl von Indizien zusammen. Dank mehrerer Gerichtsverfahren sowie zahlreicher wissenschaftlicher Arbeiten ist der Gasmord heute zweifelsfrei bewiesen.

Denial and Proof

After 1945 the deliberate destruction of evidence by the SS enables so-called revisionists to deny that murder by poison gas took place. Time and again they contest the existence of the gas chambers. However, researchers, jurists and survivors compile a mass of evidence. Thanks to several court cases as well as numerous academic studies, murder by gas has long been proven beyond doubt.

Eingang zur ehemaligen Gaskammer und wiedererrichtete „Gaszelle", 2012
Foto: Tal Adler

In den Jahrzehnten nach dem Krieg rückt die ehemalige Gaskammer des KZ Mauthausen ins Zentrum jedes Gedenkstättenbesuchs. Daher wird sie auf Betreiben von KZ-Überlebenden in Teilen wiederhergestellt: Die Mauern der „Gaszelle" werden wieder aufgebaut, die ebenfalls entfernten, ursprünglich luftdichten Türen werden durch einfache Luftschutztüren ersetzt. Diese Rekonstruktionen bilden die Basis für die Leugnung des Gasmords in Mauthausen durch Revisionisten.

Entrance to the gas chamber and reconstructed 'gas cell', 2012
Photograph: Tal Adler

In the decades after the war, the former gas chamber of the Mauthausen concentration camp becomes a focal point for visits to the memorial site. It is therefore partly reconstructed on the initiative of concentration camp survivors: the walls of the 'gas cell' are rebuilt and the original airtight doors, which had also been removed, are replaced with simple air-raid shelter doors. These reconstructions constitute the basis for the denial of gassings in Mauthausen by revisionists.

Auszug aus dem Bericht von Jack H. Taylor an die US-Armee, Mai 1945
United States National Archives and Records Administration, RG 226, Entry 110

Jack H. Taylor wird als Angehöriger des US-amerikanischen Geheimdienstes Ende November 1944 östlich von Wien verhaftet. Am 1. April 1945 überstellt man ihn nach Mauthausen. Dort muss er beim Bau des dritten Krematoriumsofens mitarbeiten und wird so zum Zeugen des Massenmords. Nach der Befreiung verfasst er einen Bericht, der die erste systematische Dokumentation des Gasmords in Mauthausen enthält. In seinem Bericht geht er allerdings fälschlicherweise davon aus, dass das Gas über die Duschanlage eingeleitet worden ist.

[…] Das Gas, das man verwendete, war Zyklon B Zyanid (siehe Muster), ein Granulatpulver, das in etwa einen halben Liter fassenden Dosen aufbewahrt und auch für die Desinfektion von Kleidern verwendet wurde. In einem kleinen, an die Gaskammer angrenzenden Raum befand sich ein direkt an ein Gebläse angeschlossener Stahlbehälter, der wiederum mit der Duschanlage verbunden war. Eine Gasmaske tragend schlug der Zuständige die Enden zweier Dosen des Pulvers (eine davon tötet 100 Personen) mit einem Hammer ein. Nachdem er diese in den Behälter legte, verschloss er den Deckel hermetisch und schaltete das Gebläse ein. […]

Extract from the report by Jack H. Taylor to the US army, May 1945
United States National Archives and Records Administration, RG 226, Entry 110

Jack H. Taylor is arrested as a member of the US intelligence service at the end of November 1944 to the east of Vienna. On 1 April 1945 he is transferred to Mauthausen. There is made to work on the construction of the third crematorium oven and thus becomes a witness to mass murder. After liberation he writes a report which contains the first systematic documentation of murder by gas in Mauthausen. However, in his report he wrongly believes that the gas is delivered via the showers.

Pierre Serge Choumoff, Les chambres à gaz de Mauthausen (Titelseite)
Paris: Amicale des Déportés de Mauthausen 1972
KZ-Gedenkstätte Mauthausen, I.F.90

Die Leugnung des Gasmords vor allem ab den 1960er Jahren veranlasst den ehemaligen Häftling Pierre-Serge Choumoff, Beweise für die Existenz der Gaskammer in Mauthausen zusammenzutragen. Das Gerichtsverfahren gegen den ehemaligen SS-Krematoriumskommandanten Martin Roth im Jahr 1970 liefert ihm dafür wichtige Informationen.
1972 veröffentlich er seine Forschungsergebnisse erstmals auf Französisch. Choumoff weist nach, dass mindestens 5.200 Häftlinge in Mauthausen und Gusen durch Giftgas getötet wurden.

Pierre-Serge Choumoff, Les chambres à gaz de Mauthausen (front cover)
Paris: Amicale des Déportés de Mauthausen 1972
KZ-Gedenkstätte Mauthausen, I.F.90

The denial of murder by gas, in particular from the 1960s onwards, prompts the former prisoner Pierre-Serge Choumoff to gather evidence proving the existence of the gas chamber in Mauthausen. The trial against Martin Roth, the former head of the SS crematorium unit, in 1970 supplies him with important information.
In 1972 he publishes the results of his research in French. Choumoff proves that at least 5,200 prisoners were killed in Mauthausen and Gusen using poison gas.

Titelseite einer neonazistischen Zeitschrift, November 1987
Dokumentationsarchiv des österreichischen Widerstandes, Wien, ohne Signatur

1987 veröffentlicht die in Österreich erscheinende Zeitschrift *Halt* ein vermeintlich historisches Dokument, das den Mord durch Giftgas in NS-Konzentrationslagern widerlegen soll. Das vom österreichischen Beamten Emil Lachout in Umlauf gebrachte Schriftstück behauptet unter Berufung auf „alliierte Untersuchungskommissionen", in Mauthausen und anderen Lagern seien „keine Menschen durch Giftgas getötet worden".
Das so genannte Lachout-Dokument stellt sich schnell als Fälschung heraus. So haben etwa die in dem Schriftstück genannten Behörden nie existiert.

Front cover of a neo-Nazi magazine, November 1987
Dokumentationsarchiv des österreichischen Widerstandes, Vienna, no archive number

In 1987 the Austrian magazine *Halt* publishes a supposedly historical document that will disprove murder by poison gas in National Socialist concentration camps. The file, circulated by the Austrian civil servant Emil Lachout, cites the findings of 'Allied investigation commissions' to claim that, in Mauthausen and other camps, 'no people were killed using poison gas'.
The so-called Lachout-Document soon turns out to be a fake. For example the authorities cited in the file never existed.

Alles Gesehene, Berechnete, und Kalkulierte wird genauestens aufnotiert.

Die Röhren, Heizkörper, Leitungen, alles wird gründlich untersucht.

Fred Leuchter in der ehemaligen Gaskammer von Mauthausen, Auszug aus dem „Zweiten Leuchter-Report", 15. Juni 1989
Dokumentationsarchiv des österreichischen Widerstandes, Wien, 41962

Im Auftrag des Holocaust-Leugners Ernst Zündel untersucht der selbsternannte US-amerikanische „Hinrichtungsexperte" Fred Leuchter Ende der 1980er Jahre die Gaskammer von Mauthausen. In seinem Bericht bestreitet er, dass in Mauthausen Vergasungen durchgeführt worden seien. Innerhalb kürzester Zeit widerlegen zahlreiche Expertisen Leuchters pseudowissenschaftliche Behauptungen.

Fred Leuchter in the former gas chamber at Mauthausen, extract from the 'Second Leuchter Report', 15 June 1989
Dokumentationsarchiv des österreichischen Widerstandes, Vienna, 41962

Commissioned by the Holocaust denier Ernst Zündel, the self-proclaimed US 'execution expert' Fred Leuchter investigates the Mauthausen gas chamber at the end of the 1980s. In his report he denies that gassings were carried out at Mauthausen. Within a very short space of time, numerous expert reports disprove Leuchter's pseudoscientific claims.

Die Beseitigung der Leichen
The Disposal of the Corpses

Ehemaliger Krematoriumsofen 3, 2014
Fotograf: Tal Adler

Former crematorium oven 3, 2014
Photograph: Tal Adler

Die Beseitigung der Leichen

Lagereigene Verbrennungsöfen ermöglichen es der SS, die zahlreichen KZ-Toten zu entsorgen. Durch das Verbrennen der Leichen im KZ kann sie – verborgen vor der Öffentlichkeit – die Spuren ihrer Gewalttaten verwischen.

Die erhaltenen Ofenanlagen sind heute zentrale Orte des Totengedenkens. Sie sind Ersatz für die fehlenden Gräber der in den KZ-Krematorien verbrannten Opfer.

The Disposal of the Corpses

Having its own incinerators in the camp enables the SS to dispose of the large number of dead prisoners. By burning the corpses in the concentration camp – away from public view – it can conceal the traces left by its acts of violence.

Today the remaining oven installations are central sites for the remembrance of the dead. They stand in for the missing graves of victims who were burned in the concentration camp crematoria.

Verzeichnis der Einäscherungen im Krematorium des KZ Gusen, November 1941 bis Februar 1942
Gosudarstvennyj Archiv Rossijskoj Federacii, Moskau, F.7021, op.112, d.14
Foto: Tal Adler

Register of cremations in the Gusen concentration camp crematorium, November 1941 to February 1942
Gosudarstvennyj Archiv Rossijskoj Federacii, Moscow, F.7021, op.112, d.14
Photograph: Tal Adler

Die SS führt genau Buch über die Verbrennungen, die von einem Häftlingskommando durchgeführt werden. In diesem Buch ist auch vermerkt, welchen Leichen vor der Einäscherung Goldzähne aus dem Kiefer gebrochen worden sind.

The SS keeps exact records of the cremations, which are carried out by a prisoner work detachment. Records are also kept in this book of which corpses had the gold teeth broken out of their jaws before cremation.

...chopik Stanislaus	16	40472	22.1.21 Lesma	-"-	/.	k	
...chow Aleksiej	16	40442	16.5.19 Hodicha	-"-	/.	k	
... Andrej	16	41608	-.10.09 Jalowka	-"-	/.	k	
...yn Pawel	16	40907	27.10.18 Sosnowka	-"-	/.	k	am 0...
...tchkin	16	38727	20.12.21 Gosdycha	✓	/.	k	
...go Martin Cecilio	R4	12354	17.2.17 Jetabucha	✓	/.	k	
... Bastida Antonio	R12	11383	21.4.93 Quintana de Serrano	-"-	/.	k	
... Quintana Juan	R12	10299	9.2.21 Lorca	✓	/.	k	
...ez Suarez Enrique	R10	13957	15.2.15 Veler	-"-	/.	k	am 5.3.42 verraicht
...o Zamora Celestino	R17	13663	24.7.11 La Fulgera	✓	/.	k	
...lorente Sandalio	R12	10495	3.9.10 Mazarron	✓	/.	k	
...o Hernandez Lorenzo	R20	12235	12.4.11 Camarma	✓	/.	k	
...z Marquiz Martin	R11	13734	29.3.18 Almonacid	✓	/.	k	
...cher Moreno Victoriano	R18	13885	17.11.09 Madrid	✓	/.	k	
...a Molina Jose	R9	9488	2.3.17 Movera	✓	/.	k	3.42...
...ly August	R18	12497	5.10.87 Santa Barbara	-"-	/.	k	
...dinger Karl	R4	14981	8.9.05 Herne	✓	/.	k	
... Piotr	16	×3258	Alberweiler	✓	/.	k	
...nurkowski Bronislaus	16	41328	23.8.14 Schykiejewo	✓	/.	k	
...chew Aleksandr	16	40399	21.2.18 Stare Kupiski	✓	/.	k	am 7.3.72
... Adolf	16	40265	-.-.1914 Czernyje	-"-	/.	k	
... Michail	16	40243	-.-.1920 Hnatowka	-"-	/.	k	
	16						

Bei der Errichtung des KZ wird zunächst kein eigenes Krematorium geschaffen. Die SS lässt daher bis 1940 die Leichen aller KZ-Häftlinge in den städtischen Krematorien von Steyr und Linz verbrennen. Später werden die Verstorbenen mancher Mauthausener Außenlager auch in den Feuerhallen in Wien und Graz eingeäschert.

When the concentration camp is first built it does not have its own crematorium. Therefore until 1940, the SS has the corpses of all concentration camp prisoners burned in the Steyr and Linz municipal crematoria. Later on the dead from some of the Mauthausen subcamps are cremated in Vienna and Graz.

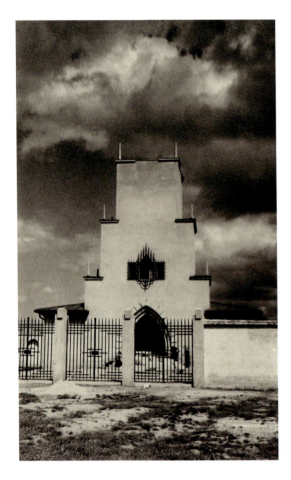

Feuerhalle der Stadt Steyr, um 1927
Fotograf/Fotografin unbekannt
Museum der Stadt Steyr, ohne Signatur

Municipal crematorium in the town of Steyr, around 1927
Unknown photographer
Museum der Stadt Steyr, no archive number

Feuerhalle in Linz, zwischen 1929 und 1933
Fotograf/Fotografin unbekannt
Aus: Hans Arndt/Paul Theer, Julius Schulte und seine Schüler,
Linz: Wagner in Innsbruck 1933

Crematorium in Linz, between 1929 and 1933
Unknown photographer
From: Hans Arndt/Paul Theer, Julius Schulte und seine Schüler,
Linz: Wagner in Innsbruck 1933

Die KZ-Krematorien

Im Mai 1940 nimmt die Mauthausener SS im Keller des Lagergefängnisses einen ersten Verbrennungsofen in Betrieb. Im selben Jahr wird auch im KZ Gusen eine Verbrennungsanlage gebaut. Später lässt die SS im Keller des Reviergebäudes noch zwei weitere Ofenanlagen aufstellen. Diese werden von den Firmen Heinrich Kori und Topf & Söhne geliefert, die Öfen für die Tierkadaver- und Abfallentsorgung herstellen.

Die Leichen werden in den KZ-Krematorien fabrikmäßig und ohne jede Bestattungszeremonie verbrannt.

The Concentration Camp Crematoria

In May 1940 the Mauthausen SS starts operating its first incinerator in the cellar of the camp prison. In the same year incineration facilities are also built at the Gusen concentration camp. Later the SS has two further oven installations constructed in the cellar of the infirmary. These are supplied by the firms Heinrich Kori and Topf & Söhne, who produce incinerators for the disposal of waste and animal carcasses.

The concentration camp crematoria operate like a factory and the corpses are burned without any form of burial rite.

Der erste Krematoriumsofen in Mauthausen, Mai 1945
Fotograf/Fotografin unbekannt
KZ-Gedenkstätte Mauthausen,
N/7/1/4

The first crematorium oven in Mauthausen, May 1945
Unknown photographer
KZ-Gedenkstätte Mauthausen,
N/7/1/4

Der Krematoriumsofen im KZ Gusen, Mai 1945
Foto: Francisco Boix
L'Humanité, Paris

The crematorium oven in Gusen concentration camp, May 1945
Photograph: Francisco Boix
L'Humanité, Paris

Erste Seite eines Kostenvoranschlags der Firma Topf & Söhne für einen Krematoriumsofen, 6. Jänner 1941
Bundesarchiv, Berlin, NS 4-Ma/54, Bl. 48

Bereits wenige Monate nach der Errichtung des ersten KZ-Krematoriums plant die SS den Bau zusätzlicher Öfen. Im Mai 1942 wird im Hinrichtungsraum schließlich ein weiterer Ofen in Betrieb genommen. Da dieser mit Öl befeuert wird, ist er wegen des kriegsbedingten Treibstoffmangels nur kurz in Betrieb. Der Ofen wird nach der Befreiung des Lagers demontiert.

First page of a quote from the firm Topf & Söhne for a crematorium oven, 6 January 1941
Bundesarchiv, Berlin, NS 4-Ma/54, Bl. 48

Just a few months after the construction of the first concentration camp crematorium the SS makes plans to install additional incinerators. Finally, in May 1942, a second oven becomes operational in the execution room. Because it is oil-fired, it is only in use for a short period due to war-time fuel shortages. The oven is dismantled after the liberation of the camp.

Der dritte Krematoriumsofen im KZ Mauthausen,
Mai 1945
Foto: Francisco Boix
Museu d'Història de Catalunya, Barcelona, fons de Amical de Mauthausen y otros campos, ohne Signatur

Im April 1945 wird in Mauthausen ein dritter Verbrennungsofen in Betrieb genommen. Selbst dieser zusätzliche Ofen reicht nicht, um die ständig steigende Zahl von Toten zu beseitigen.

The third crematorium oven in Mauthausen concentration camp, May 1945
Photograph: Francisco Boix
Museu d'Història de Catalunya, Barcelona, fons de Amical de Mauthausen y otros campos, no archive number

In April 1945 a third incinerator is put into operation in Mauthausen. Even the addition of this oven is not enough for the disposal of the ever increasing number of dead.

> Konzentrationslager Mauthausen Mauthausen, den 16. 7. 1943.
> Kommandantur
>
> Frau
> Helene Sänftl
> Mittenbach 42½
> Bez. Landshut/Nbb.
>
> Ihr Ehemann Josef Sänftl geb. 1.4.05
> ist am 12.7.43 an den Folgen Kreislaufschwäche
> .... im hiesigen Krankenhaus verstorben.-
> Die Leiche wurde am 15.7.43 im staatlichen Krematorium
> eingeäschert.-
> Gegen die Ausfolgung der Urne bestehen, wenn eine Bescheinigung
> der örtlichen Friedhofsverwaltung beigebracht wird, daß für ord-
> nungsgemäße Beisetzung Sorge getragen ist, keine Bedenken.-
> Eine Sterbeurkunde können Sie bei Einsendung der Gebühr von
> RM -.72 beim Standesamt Mauthausen II anfordern.-
>
> i.A. [Unterschrift]
> SS-Untersturmführer.-

Verständigung über den Tod von Josef Sänftl, 16. Juli 1943
Privatbesitz Karl Sänftl, Niederaichbach

Werden Angehörige vom Tod eines Häftlings informiert, so enthält die Benachrichtigung auch die Mitteilung, dass der Verstorbene bereits eingeäschert worden ist. Eine Überprüfung der Todesursache ist somit ausgeschlossen. Urnen werden nur selten an die Angehörigen versendet.

Notification of the death of Josef Sänftl, 16 July 1943
Owned by Karl Sänftl, Niederaichbach

If relatives are informed of the death of a prisoner, the notification also contains the message that the body has already been cremated. An investigation into the cause of death is thereby ruled out. Urns are only rarely sent to relatives.

Krematorien in den Außenlagern

Leichen aus den KZ-Außenlagern lässt die SS zunächst zur Verbrennung nach Mauthausen und Gusen transportieren. Weil so viele Häftlinge in den Außenlagern Melk und Ebensee sterben, werden 1944 auch dort eigene Krematoriumsöfen errichtet.

Crematoria in the Subcamps

At first the SS has corpses from the subcamps transported to Mauthausen or Gusen for incineration. Because so many prisoners die in the Melk and Ebensee subcamps, crematorium ovens are constructed there too in 1944.

Krematoriumsbaracke im KZ-Außenlager Ebensee, 22./23. Mai 1945
Foto: Bohuslav Bárta
KZ-Gedenkstätte Mauthausen, B/5/17/12

Crematorium barracks in the Ebensee subcamp, 22/23 May 1945
Photograph: Bohuslav Bárta
KZ-Gedenkstätte Mauthausen, B/5/17/12

Tafel aus dem Krematorium in Ebensee
United States Holocaust Memorial Museum, Washington, DC, 1993.24.1

Diese Tafel mit dem Gedicht des Schriftstellers Peter Rosegger ist über dem Krematoriumsofen in Ebensee angebracht. Mit diesen Versen hat Rosegger Ende des 19. Jahrhunderts die Feuerbestattung als Errungenschaft angepriesen.

Nicht ekle Würmer
soll'n einst von meinem Leichnam nähr'n!
Die reine Flamme soll mich einst verzehr'n.
Ich liebte stets die Wärme und das Licht
Drum verbrennt mich und begrabt mich nicht.

Plaque from the crematorium in Ebensee
United States Holocaust Memorial Museum, Washington, DC, 1993.24.1

This plaque with a poem by the writer Peter Rosegger is mounted over the crematorium oven in Ebensee. With these verses, Rosegger praised cremation as an achievement at the end of the 19th century.

No slimy worm
Shall some day feed upon my corpse!
The purest flames mine shall consume.
Constant was my love for the warmth and the light
So burn me and do not bury me.

Das KZ-Außenlager in Melk, links das
Krematoriumsgebäude, vermutlich Herbst 1945
Foto: Hilda Lepetit
KZ-Gedenkstätte Ebensee, Sammlung Hilda Lepetit, KLE P4

The Melk subcamp with the crematorium building on the
left, probably autumn 1945
Photograph: Hilda Lepetit
KZ-Gedenkstätte Ebensee, Hilda Lepetit Collection, KLE P4

Skizze von František Kord mit der Verortung des Bauplatzes für die Krematorien aus Auschwitz-Birkenau, Prag 1996
Institut für Zeitgeschichte, Wien, Sammlung Bertrand Perz, ohne Signatur

In den Monaten vor der Befreiung können tausende Leichen in den bestehenden Krematoriumsöfen nicht mehr verbrannt werden. Die SS plant die Errichtung weiterer Einäscherungsöfen. Nahe dem KZ Mauthausen sollen zehn im KZ Auschwitz-Birkenau demontierte Verbrennungsanlagen wieder aufgestellt werden. Der KZ-Häftling František Kord muss bei der Planung mitarbeiten. Das Vorhaben wird aber nicht mehr verwirklicht.

Sketch by František Kord showing the location of the site intended for the crematoria from Auschwitz-Birkenau, Prague 1996
Institut für Zeitgeschichte, Vienna, Bertrand Perz Collection, no archive number

In the months before liberation thousands of corpses can no longer be burned in the existing crematorium ovens. The SS plans to construct further cremation facilities. Ten incinerators dismantled and brought from the Auschwitz-Birkenau concentration camp are to be erected near to Mauthausen. The prisoner František Kord is made to work on the planning process. The proposal, however, is not realised.

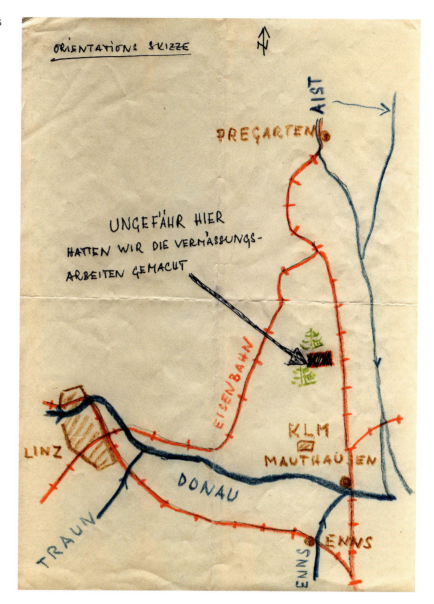

Gräber

Die SS verstreut die Asche der verbrannten Leichen meist auf Baustellen des Konzentrationslagers, in Wäldern der Umgebung, auf einer Mülhalde neben dem Lager oder kippt sie in die Donau.

Im Frühjahr 1945 lässt die SS zusätzlich Massengräber anlegen. Bei der Marbacher Linde nahe dem Lager Mauthausen verscharrt sie etwa 10.000 Leichen, die nicht mehr verbrannt werden können.

Das US-Militär bestattet die in den Lagern vorgefundenen Leichen sowie die nach der Befreiung Verstorbenen in neu geschaffenen Friedhöfen. Die Anlage von Gräbern und die Abhaltung würdevoller Bestattungszeremonien bilden einen bewussten Bruch mit der Art der Leichenentsorgung in den Konzentrationslagern.

Graves

The SS usually spreads the ashes of the incinerated corpses on concentration camp construction sites, in nearby woods, on a rubbish dump next to the camp, or it tips them into the Danube.

In early 1945 the SS also has mass graves dug. At the *Marbacher Linde* (lit. Marbach lime tree) near to the Mauthausen camp it buries around 10,000 corpses that can no longer be burned.

The US military buries the corpses it finds in the camps, as well as those who die after liberation, in newly-created cemeteries. Laying out graves and holding dignified burial ceremonies mark a deliberate break with the way in which corpses were disposed of in the concentration camps.

Massengrab bei der Marbacher Linde, Mai 1948
Fotograf/Fotografin unbekannt
Burghauptmannschaft Österreich, Wien

Nach der Befreiung wird das von der SS angelegte Massengrab zu einem Friedhof umgestaltet. Nach dessen Auflösung in den 1960er Jahren werden die Gebeine der KZ-Toten in ein Gräberfeld auf dem Gedenkstättengelände umgebettet.

Mass grave at the Marbacher Linde, May 1948
Unknown photographer
Burghauptmannschaft Österreich, Vienna

After liberation the mass grave created by the SS is turned into a cemetery. After its dissolution in the 1960s, the remains of the concentration camp dead are reinterred in a burial ground within the memorial site.

„Camp Cemetery Mauthausen" (Lagerfriedhof Mauthausen), 22. Juni 1945
Foto: Gabriel Bonnet
Archives Nationales, Paris, fonds de l'Amicale de Mauthausen, ohne Signatur

Das US-Militär legt nahe dem Areal des KZ Gusen sowie auf dem ehemaligen SS-Sportplatz in Mauthausen Friedhöfe an, wo tausende Opfer bestattet werden. Nach der Auflösung dieser Camp Cemeteries in den 1950er Jahren werden die sterblichen Überreste der Häftlinge in deren Herkunftsländer überführt oder im ehemaligen Häftlingslager beerdigt.

'Camp Cemetery Mauthausen', 22 June 1945
Photograph: Gabriel Bonnet
Archives Nationales, Paris, fonds de l'Amicale de Mauthausen, no archive number

The US military lays out cemeteries on the site of the Gusen concentration camp as well as on the former SS sports field in Mauthausen. Thousands of victims are buried here. After the dissolution of these camp cemeteries in the 1950s, the mortal remains of the prisoners are either transferred to their native countries or buried within the former prisoners' camp.

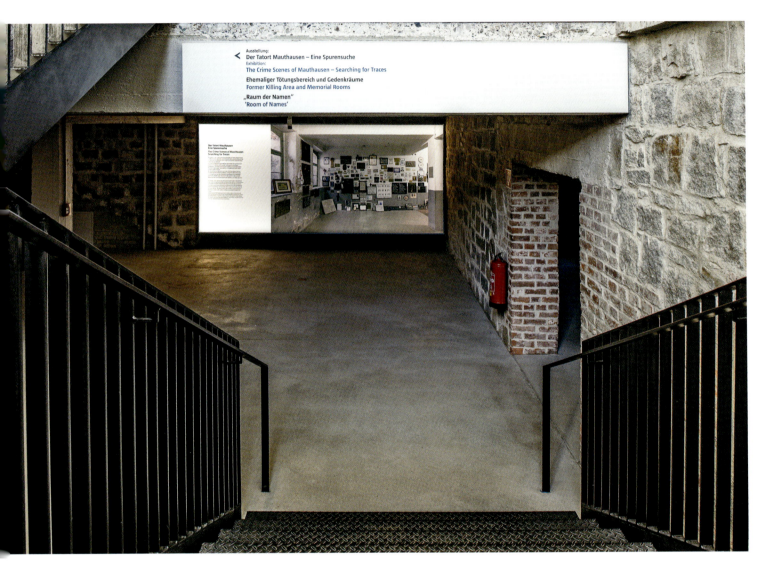

Eingangsbereich zur Ausstellung *Der Tatort Mauthausen – Eine Spurensuche* im Untergeschoss des ehemaligen Reviergebäudes in der KZ-Gedenkstätte Mauthausen.
Foto: Tal Adler

Entrance area to the exhibition *The Crime Scenes of Mauthausen – Searching for Traces* in the basement of the former infirmary building at the Mauthausen Memorial.
Photograph: Tal Adler

Bertrand Perz/Jörg Skriebeleit

Exhibiting Death

Should a guillotine be exhibited?

This was the question preoccupying historians, museum experts, politicians and Germany's arts pages at the beginning of 2014.[1] These debates, intense rather than controversial, had been sparked by the (re-)discovery of a guillotine in the Bavarian National Museum in Munich. An ethnologist working there had stumbled across it in the museum depot in the department for 'Antiquities relating to Punishment and Justice', where executioners' swords, thumb screws and the like are stored. Highlighting the prominence of those it had been used to execute, this member of museum staff thought it would be a good idea to offer the object to various exhibition projects as an audience attraction, for example the future Munich Documentation Centre for the History of National Socialism or the new Centre of Bavarian History. For this wasn't just any old guillotine – in the depths of its collections, the Bavarian National Museum has several of these killing machines at its disposal. Rather, what was being offered as a worthy showpiece was a guillotine allegedly used to behead the members of the 'White Rose' resistance group on 22 February 1943, namely Sophie and Hans Scholl and their fellow student Hans Probst.[2]

Public reaction was swift and deservedly unambiguous. There was talk of 'disrespect', displaying the object was simply pandering to 'base instincts'. Others spoke of 'intellectual poverty'[3] or, like the founding director of the Munich Documentation Centre for the History of National Socialism Winfried Nerdinger, they questioned the display of this type of object in any form in the context of an exhibition on National Socialism: 'I am doubtful whether such a killing apparatus, with which over 1,000 people were executed, can be shown in public in any kind of museum context at

einem musealen Kontext öffentlich gezeigt werden kann, ohne dass er eine fragwürdige Faszination oder nur einen Schauereffekt auslöst."[4]

Lediglich die Vorsitzende der „Stiftung Weiße Rose", Hildegard Kronawitter, wollte eine museale Zurschaustellung nicht gänzlich ausschließen. Mit dem Verweis auf eigene Erfahrungen hob sie in einem emotionalen Statement die „Beeindruckungsqualität" authentischer Objekte und Orte hervor. Als Jugendliche habe sie der Besuch der Gedenkstätte Berlin-Plötzensee und die dort (bis heute) zu besichtigenden Fleischerhaken, an der Widerstandskämpfer aufgehängt wurden, sehr beeindruckt und bewegt. Die nun diskutierte Guillotine zeige doch den „Vernichtungswillen des NS-Staates"[5], so die Stiftungsvorsitzende.

Darf man den Tod ausstellen?

Darf man nun Tötungsinstrumente ausstellen? Oder ganz grundsätzlich formuliert: Darf man den Tod ausstellen? Guillotinen und anderes Folter-, Tötungs- und Mordwerkzeug gehören für ganze Gattungen von Museen zur Grundausstattung. Kein Mittelaltermuseum ohne Streckbank, kein Kriminalmuseum ohne Tatwaffen. Ein weithin unbekanntes Haus, das sich dieser Präsentationsformen offensiv bedient, ist beispielsweise das Wiener Kriminalmuseum. In einem Parcours durch lokalhistorisch bedeutsame Kriminalfälle mit Todesfolge, die dem Besucher mittels expliziter Tatortdarstellungen und exzessiver Mordbeschreibungen präsentiert werden, trifft man dort en passant auch auf drei Guillotinen, von denen mindestens eine auch zwischen 1938 und 1945 in Gebrauch war. Ähnlich ungezwungen geht das Kriminalmuseum im württembergischen Ludwigsburg mit zwei Guillotinen zur Veranschaulichung historischen Strafvollzugs um, darunter ebenfalls ein Exemplar, das während der NS-Zeit in einem Gefängnis betrieben wurde. „Natürlich kann man die nicht einfach so hinstellen", argumentiert der Leiter des Museums, aber eingebettet in eine Ausstellung sei das durchaus möglich, „wir schmieren ja kein Blut oder Ketchup dran."[6]

Die Frage nach der Zulässigkeit, Tatwerkzeuge, Tötungsinstrumente oder gar „den Tod" per se aus-

all without arousing a questionable fascination or simply a chilling effect.'[4]

Only Hildegard Kronawitter, director of the *Stiftung Weiße Rose* (White Rose Foundation), did not want to rule out displaying it entirely. With reference to her own experiences, she gave an emotional statement highlighting the 'striking quality' of authentic objects and places. As a young person she had visited the Berlin-Plötzensee Memorial Centre and the meat hooks visible there (to this day) on which the resistance fighters were hanged made a deep and moving impression on her. The guillotine now under discussion surely showed the 'exterminatory will of the National Socialist state'[5], said the foundation's director.

Should death be exhibited?

Should the instruments used to kill be exhibited? Or, to put it simply, should death be exhibited? For whole genres of museum, guillotines and the other implements of torture, killing and murder are their tools of the trade: no medieval museum without a rack, no crime museum without the murder weapon. An example of a largely unheard-of museum that draws heavily on this type of presentation is the Vienna Crime Museum. Visitors are led past displays on the history of prominent, local murder cases, which are illustrated with explicit depictions of the crime scenes and excessive descriptions of the killings and, en passant, take in three guillotines, at least one of which was in use between 1938 and 1945. The Württemberg criminal museum in Ludwigsburg treats its two guillotines in a similarly casual manner, using them to illustrate historical forms of punishment. One of them was likewise in operation in a prison during the National Socialist era. 'Of course you can't display them just like that', argues the museum's director, but it's entirely possible when embedded in an exhibition, 'it's not as if we smear them with blood or ketchup.'[6]

For a concentration camp memorial museum, the question of the permissibility of exhibiting murder weapons, the instruments used to kill, or even death per se is of a very different order. In

zustellen, hat für eine KZ-Gedenkstätte eine ganz andere Dimension. In den nationalsozialistischen Konzentrationslagern wurde täglich gestorben, getötet, gemordet und hingerichtet. Ein Konzentrationslager ist per se ein Ort des Todes, ein Sterbensort, ein Tatort.

Bei der sorgsamen Neu-Konzeption einer KZ-Gedenkstätte, definiert als früherer Tatort tausendfachen Tötens, Mordens, intentional herbeigeführten oder billigend in Kauf genommenen Sterbens, stellt sich die Frage „darf man den Tod ausstellen?" anders. Es kann hier gar nicht um das „ob" gehen. Die Frage nach dem „wie" muss für konzeptionelles und kuratorisches Entwickeln handlungsleitend sein.

Wie stellt man den Tod in einem Konzentrationslager aus?

Den nach 1945 zu Gedenkstätten gewordenen Tatorten sieht man die Spuren des Todes nicht immer und nicht überall eindeutig an – nicht auf den ersten Blick und oft auch nicht auf den zweiten. Während einige Relikte des Lagers unmittelbar mit Tod und Massensterben identifiziert werden können, wie etwa die ehemaligen Krematorien, sind andere Mord- und Sterbeplätze völlig undecodierbar, so die früheren Kranken-, Sanitäts- und Quarantänelager oder Erschießungsstätten. Während die unmittelbar sichtbaren Relikte des Todes rasch zu Symbolen und Ikonen wurden, fielen andere Mordstätten und Todesorte – und damit oft auch ihre Opfer – dem völligen Vergessen anheim. Pointiert formuliert: Die Krematorien von Mauthausen will jeder Besucher sehen, das tägliche dem Tode Entgegen-Vegetieren der Gefangenen entzieht sich jedoch eindeutiger Visualisierung und damit auch oft kognitiver oder emotionaler Wahrnehmung.

Der Tod in einem Konzentrationslager hat viele konkrete Orte. Das Sterben in einem Konzentrationslager hat viele schreckliche Formen. Und es hat viele Namen und Gesichter, womit eine der zentralen Kategorien des „wie" benannt ist. Es geht bei aller Notwendigkeit historisch korrekter und differenzierter museologischer Darstellung von Verbrechen stets um den pietätvollen und würdigen Umgang mit den Opfern. Dennoch: eine Ausstellung in einem ehemaligen Konzentrationslager muss sich gegenüber der

the National Socialist concentration camps people died, were killed, murdered and executed on a daily basis. A concentration camp is per se a place of death, the scene of dying, a crime scene.

The question 'can death be exhibited?' has to be asked differently within the context of a careful redesign of a concentration camp memorial site, a site defined as the scene of past crimes, of killings and murders in their tens of thousands, of deaths caused intentionally or simply allowed to take place. There is no question here of 'whether'. It is the question of 'how' that must guide curators' actions when it comes to developing concepts for the site.

How do you exhibit death in a concentration camp?

At the crime scenes, which became memorial sites after 1945, the traces of death are not always clearly visible – not at first glance and often not at second. While some of the relics of the camp are instantly identifiable with death and mass killing – the former crematoria, for example – other sites such as the former sick, sanitary and quarantine camps or the execution site are impossible to decode. While the relics of death that were in plain sight quickly became symbols or icons, other murder sites and places of death faded into oblivion, and often their victims with them. To put it bluntly: Every visitor to Mauthausen wants to see the crematoria, yet the prisoners' daily decline towards death often goes unnoticed – cognitively and emotionally – because it eludes clear visualisation.

Death in a concentration camp had many concrete locations. Dying in a concentration camp had many terrible forms. It also had many names and faces, which brings us to one of the central categories of the 'how'. For all the necessity of a historically correct and differentiated museological presentation of the crimes, what matters is dealing with the victims in a respectful and dignified way. Nevertheless, an exhibition at a former concentration camp must also be able to take a step back from this deferential, commemorative

Funktion des ehrenden Gedenkens ebenso bewusst abheben. Eine Ausstellung an einem ehemaligen Tatort hat die Aufgabe der Aufklärung, Verifizierung und Einordnung des dort Geschehenen, allerdings unter der Prämisse, die Opfer pietätvoll zu behandeln, nicht mit ihnen und ihrem Leid publikumswirksam hausieren zu gehen.

Daher hat die für die Ausstellung verantwortliche Konzeptgruppe frühzeitig einen völlig anderen museologischen Ansatz gewählt als jenen, der unlängst mit der Münchener Guillotine und der Prominenz ihrer Opfer versucht wurde. Sie hat sich für einen forensischen Ansatz der Spurensuche, Spurensicherung und Spurendokumentation entschieden – in einem konkret (bau)historischen Forschungskontext, in einer historiografisch-analytischen Thesenbildung sowie in der museologischen Umsetzung. Es ging zunächst darum, die konkreten Orte des Tötens, Mordens, Sterbens und der Leichenentsorgung zu definieren. Um den Tod im KZ-Komplex Mauthausen historiografisch präzise zu beschreiben, bedarf es vieler Begriffe. Um Leugnun-

role. The task of an exhibition at a former crime scene is to explain, verify and contextualise the events that took place there, albeit on the condition that the victims are treated with respect and that they and their suffering are not peddled as an audience attraction.

The group responsible for developing the exhibition therefore decided early on to take a totally different museological approach to that attempted recently for the Munich guillotine and its prominent victims. They settled on a forensic approach of searching for, securing and documenting traces – whether in the (building) historical research context on the ground, in the formulation of analytical, historiographical theses or in the creation of the exhibition. The first step was to define the concrete locations of killing, murder, death and corpse disposal. Many terms are required in order to describe death in the Mauthausen concentration camp complex with historiographical precision. Both the visible and the invisible need

BesucherInnen bei der Eröffnung der Ausstellung am 5. Mai 2013.
Foto: Tal Adler

Visitors at the exhibition opening on 5 May 2013.
Photograph: Tal Adler

gen, Relativierungen und falschen Analogisierungen entschieden entgegenzutreten, braucht es eine Dekonstruktion von Sichtbarem wie Unsichtbarem. Um den Opfern möglichst nahe zu kommen, bedarf es Empathie und Pietät.

Zur historischen Einordnung: Das Konzentrationslager Mauthausen als Ort des Massenmordes

Detlev Garbe, der Leiter der KZ-Gedenkstätte Neuengamme, hat zur Frage der Tötungen in Konzentrationslagern im Unterschied zu den Vernichtungsstätten, die fast ausschließlich dem Mord an den europäischen Juden und Jüdinnen dienten, darauf hingewiesen, dass nur eine Minderheit unter den KZ-Opfern durch direkte Gewaltakte getötet wurde – klammert man Auschwitz-Birkenau und auch Majdanek in ihrer Doppelfunktion als Konzentrations- wie Vernichtungslager für den Judenmord einmal aus. Eklatante Unterversorgung, lebensbedrohende Arbeitsbedingungen, Hunger sowie permanente Schikanen und Demütigungen waren die Faktoren, die mehrheitlich den Tod von KZ-Häftlingen verursachten. Dennoch, so Garbe „gehörten Massenmorde von Anfang an zur Geschichte der Konzentrationslager. Wie die vielfältigen Praktiken der Entwürdigung und der tagtägliche Terror waren Morde dem KZ-System wesensimmanent."[7] Richteten sich gezielte Morde durch die SS in der Vorkriegszeit noch gegen einzelne Häftlinge, kam es nach Kriegsbeginn zu einer Entgrenzung der Gewalt. Immer öfter wurden ganze Gruppen gezielt getötet.

Das Konzentrationslager Mauthausen und sein Zweiglager Gusen waren in besonderer Weise Schauplätze gezielter Tötungen und Massenmorde. Als Doppellager war dieser Lagerkomplex in den ersten Kriegsjahren nicht nur der größte unter allen Konzentrationslagern, sondern auch jener mit der weitaus höchsten Todesrate, verursacht durch extrem lebensfeindliche Haftbedingungen, aber auch gezielte Tötungen. Die Einstufung von Mauthausen und Gusen in die schwerste Lagerstufe III durch Heinrich Himmler schrieb diesen schon zuvor bestehenden Zustand im Sommer 1940 fest.[8] Mauthausen und Gusen waren auch nach dem generellen Funktionswandel der Konzentrationslager zu Ar-

to be deconstructed in order to counter denials, relativisations and false analogies decisively. Empathy and respect are called for in order to get as close to the victims as possible.

The historical context: The Mauthausen concentration camp as a site of mass murder

On the question of killings in concentration camps as opposed to extermination camps, whose purpose was almost solely the murder of the European Jews, the director of the Neuengamme Concentration Camp Memorial, Detlev Garbe, has pointed out that only a minority of concentration camp victims were killed through direct acts of violence – leaving aside for now Auschwitz-Birkenau and Majdanek with their double function as both concentration and extermination camps. Blatant deprivation, life-threatening working conditions and hunger as well as permanent harassment and humiliation – these were the factors behind the majority of deaths among concentration camp prisoners. Nevertheless, according to Garbe, 'mass murder was part of the concentration camp's history from the start. Just like the various practices of degradation and the everyday terror, killings were integral to the system.'[7] While in the pre-war period the SS was still targeting individual prisoners, violence lost all restraint following the outbreak of war. With increasing frequency, whole groups were singled out and murdered.

The Mauthausen concentration camp and its branch camp at Gusen provided a very particular setting for targeted killings and mass murder. As a double camp, this camp complex was not only the largest of all the concentration camps in the first years of the war but also the camp with the highest death rate. This was due to the extremely hostile living and imprisonment conditions but also to targeted killings. Heinrich Himmler's classification of Mauthausen and Gusen in summer 1940 as a grade III camp, the harshest grade, simply confirmed the conditions already in existence.[8] Even after the general role of the concentration camps changed to that of labour reserves for the arms industry, Mauthausen and Gusen remained

beitskräftereservoirs der Rüstungsindustrie Stätten, an denen bestimmte Häftlingsgruppen in großem Umfang gezielt getötet wurden.

Eine genaue Abschätzung, wie viele der insgesamt über 90.000 Toten im Lagerkomplex Mauthausen an den Folgen der Haft- und Zwangsarbeitsbedingungen starben und wie viele Opfer gezielter direkter Tötungen waren, ist fast unmöglich, da sich gezielte Tötungen oft nur schwer vom massenhaften Sterben als Folge struktureller Gewalt abgrenzen lassen. Ein genauerer Blick auf die unterschiedlichen Formen, wie Menschen im KZ ums Leben kamen, ist dennoch nicht nur für das historische Verständnis der Gewaltdynamik des KZ-Systems, die Häftlinge in höchst unterschiedlicher Weise betraf, von großer Bedeutung. Schon für die US-amerikanischen *War Crimes Investigating-Teams* war die genaue Rekonstruktion von Tathergängen und die Beweisaufnahme am Tatort über Zeugenaussagen, Dokumente und Tatgegenstände Voraussetzung für die nachfolgenden juristische Verfahren gegen das Lagerpersonal und andere Täter.

Analysiert man die in großer Zahl vorgenommenen direkten Tötungshandlungen, so muss zwischen drei Formen unterschieden werden:

1. Angeordnete Tötungen

Eine erste Art von direkten Tötungshandlungen waren diejenigen, die zentral für die Konzentrationslager oder auch spezifisch für den Lagerkomplex Mauthausen angeordnet wurden. So dienten die Konzentrationslager ab Kriegsbeginn offiziell als polizeiliche Hinrichtungsstätten, in denen vom Reichssicherheits-Hauptamt, vom Chef der Sicherheitspolizei und des SD und von SS- und Polizeigerichten angeordnete Todesurteile unauffällig vollstreckt werden konnten. Im Rahmen einer der Justiz entzogenen Polizeigewalt wurden im Lager Personen mit Häftlingsstatus ermordet, denn von Beginn an ahndet die SS schwerwiegende Verstöße gegen die Lagerordnung mit der Todesstrafe. Darüber hinaus wurden auch auf Befehl des Reichsführers SS Personen bzw. Personengruppen ausschließlich zur Exekution eingewiesen.[9]

places where certain groups of prisoners continued to be targeted and killed in large numbers.

In total, there were over 90,000 deaths in the Mauthausen camp complex. A precise estimate of how many people died as a result of the imprisonment and forced labour conditions and how many were the victims of direct, targeted killings is almost impossible since it is often difficult to distinguish between targeted killings and mass death as a result of structural violence. Nonetheless, a closer look at the different ways in which people died in the concentration camps is hugely important not only in terms of gaining historical understanding of the dynamic of violence in the concentration camp system and the very different ways in which the prisoners were affected by it. Even for the American *War Crimes Investigating Teams*, the exact reconstruction of the circumstances of the crimes was a prerequisite for the subsequent judicial trials against camp personnel and other perpetrators and evidence was collected at the crime scene in the form of witness statements, documents and the implements used.

Any analysis of the large number of targeted killing actions carried out needs to distinguish between three forms:

1. Ordered killings

The first type of targeted killing actions were those ordered centrally either for all concentration camps or specifically for the Mauthausen camp complex. From the start of the war onwards, the concentration camps served as official police execution sites at which death sentences handed down by the Reich Main Security Office, the head of the Security Police or the SD (Security Service), and by SS and police courts could be carried out away from the public eye. In the context of state violence divorced from the judicial system, people with prisoner status were killed in the camps; from the outset, the SS punished serious violations of the camp rules with the death penalty. Furthermore, people or groups were sent to the camps on the orders of the Reich Chief of the SS solely for the purpose of execution.[9]

Unter den zentral angeordneten Tötungen, die einen geplanten systematischen Massenmord darstellen, sind weiters vier Aktionen zu nennen, in die das Konzentrationslager Mauthausen und das Zweiglager Gusen bezüglich Umfang und Intensität in unterschiedlicher Weise eingebunden waren. Die erste systematische Massenmordaktion an KZ-Häftlingen erfolgte im Rahmen der „Aktion 14f13", der Selektion nicht oder nicht mehr arbeitsfähiger KZ-Häftlinge durch die Ärzte der zentral gesteuerten NS-Euthanasie (sogenannte „Aktion T4") und ihre Verbringung in die Euthanasie-Tötungsanstalten, im Falle von Mauthausen-Gusen ab Sommer 1941 nach Hartheim.[10] Erfasst wurden bei dieser Mordaktion aber auch eine erhebliche Anzahl niederländischer Juden, die kurze Zeit davor nach Mauthausen eingewiesen worden waren. Diese Tötungen fanden 1944 ihre Fortsetzung, in dem nochmals über 3.200 körperlich zugrunde gearbeitete und kranke Häftlinge nach Hartheim transportiert und mittels Giftgas getötet wurden.

Das zweite große Massentötungsprogramm in den Konzentrationslagern betraf die ab Herbst 1941 in die Konzentrationslager eingelieferten sowjetischen Kriegsgefangenen. Das Doppellager Mauthausen/Gusen war darin weniger intensiv eingebunden als andere Lager, die genauen Gründe dafür sind nicht bekannt. Zwar wurden im Oktober 1941 etwa 4.000 sowjetische Kriegsgefangene nach Mauthausen und Gusen eingewiesen, diese waren aber als „Arbeitsrussen" zur Zwangsarbeit und nicht zur Exekution bestimmt.[11] Das hinderte die Lager-SS allerdings nicht daran, die Mehrzahl dieser Kriegsgefangenen innerhalb weniger Monate durch brutale Behandlung und Unterversorgung zu Tode zu bringen. Ob dies allein in der Verantwortung der Lagerführung lag oder von der übergeordneten Inspektion der Konzentrationslager (IKL) befürwortet oder gewünscht wurde, ist nicht geklärt; ähnliche Entwicklungen in anderen Lagern – etwa Sachsenhausen[12] – lassen jedoch darauf schließen, dass diese mörderische Vorgangsweise nicht alleine auf die Initiative der Lagerkommandantur zurückzuführen ist.[13] Über die Gruppe der „Arbeitsrussen" hinaus wurden Hunderte sowjetische Kriegsgefangene, die in Kriegsgefangenenlagern auf österreichischem Ge-

Among these centrally-ordered killings, which constitute planned, systematic mass murder, further mention should be made of four actions that involved the Mauthausen concentration camp and Gusen branch camp to varying degrees. The first systematic mass murder of concentration camp prisoners took place as part of 'Action 14f13', under which doctors attached to the centrally-organised National Socialist 'euthanasia' programme (known as 'Action T4') selected concentration camp prisoners who were unable or no longer able to work for transfer to the programme's killing centres, which for Mauthausen-Gusen was Hartheim from summer 1941.[10] Large numbers of Dutch Jews who had been deported to Mauthausen shortly beforehand were caught up in this killing programme. It was continued in 1944 when over 3,200 prisoners, sick or worked to physical exhaustion, were again transported to Hartheim and murdered with poison gas.

The second of the larger mass killing programmes in the concentration camps concerned Soviet prisoners of war, who were imprisoned in the camps from autumn 1941 onwards. The double camp at Mauthausen/Gusen was less intensively involved in this than other camps and the precise reasons for this are unknown. In October 1941, around 4,000 Soviet prisoners of war were in fact admitted to Mauthausen and Gusen but as 'Arbeitsrussen' ('labour Russians') designated for forced labour and not for execution.[11] However, this did not prevent the camp SS from bringing about the deaths of the majority of these prisoners of war within a few months through brutality and deprivation. Whether the camp administration alone was responsible for this or whether it was sanctioned or desired by the higher-ranking *Inspektion der Konzentrationslager* (or *IKL* - Inspectorate of the Concentration Camps) is not clear. However, similar developments in other camps – Sachsenhausen, for example[12] – suggest that these murderous strategies cannot be attributed solely to the initiative of the camp administration.[13] In addition to the group of 'labour Russians', hundreds of Soviet prisoners of war in camps on Austrian territory were selected as being

biet als „untragbar" ausgesondert worden waren, zur Exekution nach Mauthausen deportiert.[14]

In die dritte zentral geplante Massenmordaktion, der Überstellung von tausenden Justizgefangenen an die Konzentrationslager ab Ende 1942, war Mauthausen massiv involviert. Wie es in der entsprechenden Vereinbarung zwischen Heinrich Himmler und Reichsjustizminister Otto Georg Thierack im September 1942 formuliert wurde, sollte es zur „Auslieferung asozialer Elemente aus dem Strafvollzug an den Reichsführer SS zur Vernichtung durch Arbeit"[15] kommen. Von den etwa 7.500 Ende 1942 nach Mauthausen und Gusen eingewiesenen Justizgefangenen (als Sicherheitsverwahrungs-Häftlinge oder kurz SV-Häftlinge bezeichnet) wurden innerhalb von wenigen Wochen 3.800 erschlagen, zu Tode geschunden und erschossen.[16]

Eine vierte zentral geplante Massenmordaktion, die „Aktion Kugel", die fast ausschließlich das KZ Mauthausen betraf, war die Einweisung von ca. 5.000 vorwiegend sowjetischen sogenannten K-Häftlingen – wiederergriffene Zwangsarbeiter und Kriegsgefangenen – zur Exekution ab dem Frühjahr 1944.[17]

Die Methoden, die die SS bei diesen zentral angeordneten Tötungshandlungen benutzte, waren sehr unterschiedlich. Wurden zunächst bei Exekutionen tausende Menschen erschossen oder gehenkt, so ist ab Herbst 1941 eine Technisierung der Tötungsverfahren festzustellen. Die Einrichtung einer sogenannten „Genickschuss"-Vorrichtung zielte ebenso wie der Bau einer Zyklon-B-Gaskammer vor allem auf eine Erhöhung der Tötungskapazitäten für Exekutionen ab.[18]

Der Mord an nicht mehr arbeitsfähigen kranken Häftlingen in der Tötungsanstalt Hartheim durch Kohlenmonoxyd verweist darauf, dass hier quasi in einer Art „Amtshilfe" durch die T4-Organisation auf ein bereits erprobtes Tötungsverfahren inklusive der aus Sicht der SS notwendigen Verschleierung der Todesursachen zugegriffen werden konnte.[19]

'untragbar' (lit. 'unbearable') and were deported to Mauthausen for execution.[14]

The third centrally-planned programme of mass murder – the transfer of thousands of judicial prisoners to the concentration camps starting in late 1942 – involved Mauthausen on a vast scale. In the corresponding agreement between Heinrich Himmler and Reich Minister of Justice Otto Georg Thierack in September 1942, this was formulated as a '[t]ransfer of antisocial elements from the prison system to the Reich Chief of the SS for annihilation through work.'[15] Of the 7,500 or so prisoners (termed 'Sicherheitsverwahrungs-Häftlinge' / 'preventative detention prisoners', or SV-prisoners for short) transferred from the justice system to Mauthausen and Gusen at the end of 1942, 3,800 had been beaten or worked to death or shot within a few weeks.[16]

'Aktion Kugel' ('Action Bullet'), a fourth centrally-planned programme of mass murder, was almost exclusive to the Mauthausen concentration camp. Starting in early 1944, it involved the deportation to Mauthausen for execution of around 5,000 predominantly Soviet recaptured forced labourers or prisoners of war known as 'K'-prisoners.[17]

The SS used a variety of different methods to carry out these centrally-ordered killing actions. While at first thousands were executed by shooting or hanging, the technologisation of killing procedures becomes clear from autumn 1941 onwards. The aim of installing a so-called *'Genickschuss'*-device (an apparatus for shooting people in the back of the neck), along with building a Zyklon-B gas chamber was above all to increase capacity for executions.[18]

The use of carbon monoxide at the Harthim killing centre for the murder of prisoners who were sick and unable to work indicates that here, through a sort of 'official cooperation' on the part of the T4 organisation, the SS was able to draw on a tried and tested killing procedure that had, from its point of view, the necessary benefit of concealing the cause of death.[19]

Im Gegensatz dazu blieb die Tötungsart bei den SV-Häftlingen weitgehend unbestimmt. Die vereinbarte „Vernichtung durch Arbeit" war in den Steinbrüchen von Mauthausen und Gusen von Anbeginn eine übliche Form der Tötung, man kann aber davon ausgehen, dass im Falle der SV-Häftlinge von der Lagerleitung erwartete wurde, den Tod mittels brutaler Behandlung bei der Zwangsarbeit schnell und konsequent herbeizuführen. Eine klare Abgrenzung zu der im Lager ohnedies vorhandenen strukturellen Gewalt, die die Realität der Lager prägte, ist hier aber nicht möglich, die Differenz zu Todesraten für Häftlinge anderer Nationalitäten und Kategorien machen aber den Grad an Intentionalität bei der Vernichtung der SV-Häftlinge deutlich. Dass hier überhaupt Zwangsarbeit und Vernichtung kombiniert wurden, liegt vermutlich am Zeitpunkt des Abkommens zwischen Himmler und Thierack. Denn im Herbst 1942 war der Bedarf an KZ-Zwangsarbeitern für die Rüstungsindustrie bereits erheblich, die SS stand gerade auch im Bereich des KZ Mauthausen mit der Industrie in Verhandlungen über diverse Kooperationen und die Errichtung entsprechender Außenlager.[20]

2. Tötungen ohne zentrale Anordnung – „Auf der Flucht erschossen"

Eine zweite Art von Tötungshandlungen stellten Morde dar, die zwar nicht zentral angeordnet worden waren, aber durch zentrale Befehle bzw. Dienstvorschriften für die Konzentrationslager legitimiert und gedeckt wurden. Die häufigste Tötungsart war dabei die Erschießung von Häftlingen durch Wachposten, die Fluchtversuche unternahmen. „Fliehende Schutzhäftlinge werden nach Anruf scharf beschossen"[21], so legte es die Dienstvorschrift für die Wachposten 1941 fest. Der unbedingte Schusswaffengebrauch bei Fluchtversuchen eröffnete für das Lagerpersonal die Möglichkeit, gezielte Tötungen – spontan oder von langer Hand geplant – missliebiger Häftlinge vorzunehmen, in dem diese Morde als Akt der Fluchtvereitelung getarnt werden konnten, die in der Regel auch noch zu Belobigung des Todesschützen – etwa Sonderurlaub – führten. Dass als Vereitelung von Fluchtversuchen getarnte Morde an der Tagesordnung waren, ist durch Aussagen in Nachkriegsprozessen wie auch in Erinnerungen ehemaliger Häftlinge vielfach thematisiert worden.[22]

In contrast, no particular method was designated for killing SV-prisoners. The 'annihilation through work' of the agreement was, from the outset, the usual form of killing in the Mauthausen and Gusen quarries but in the case of the SV-prisoners, the camp administration would have expected their deaths to be brought about quickly and relentlessly through brutal treatment during forced labour. However, no clear distinction is possible between this and the structural violence that existed in the camp regardless, which shaped the very reality of the camp, although the level of intentionality behind the extermination of these inmates becomes clear from looking at the death rates for prisoners of other nationalities and categories. That forced labour and annihilation could be combined at all lies, in all likelihood, in the timing of the agreement between Himmler and Thierack. By autumn 1942, the need for forced labourers from the concentration camps for the arms industry was already great and, in particular with regard to the Mauthausen concentration camp, the SS was in negotiations with industry about various cooperations and the establishment of the requisite subcamps.[20]

2. Killings without central orders – 'Shot while attempting to escape'

Representing a second type of killing action were those murders that, while not having been ordered from the centre, were legitimised and sanctioned by the orders or regulations issued centrally for the concentration camps. The most common form these killings took was the shooting by guards of prisoners as they tried to escape. 'Prisoners attempting to escape are to be hailed then shot at'[21], as stated in the official regulations for guards in 1941. The compulsory use of firearms during escape attempts opened up the possibility for camp personnel to carry out – either spontaneously or planned in advance – the targeted killing of undesirable prisoners, since this act of murder could be covered up as having tried to prevent an escape, something that usually also led to a commendation for the shooter in the form of special leave, for example. That murder disguised as escape prevention was the order of the day was

Häftlinge nach Belieben zu töten erlaubte aber auch noch eine zweite Regelung der Dienstvorschrift, da der Grund für die Tötung im Einzelfall, auch wenn es gewollt worden wäre, kaum überprüfbar war: „Greift ein Häftling einen SS-Posten, SS-Aufsichtsführenden oder SS-Vorgesetzten an, bedroht er sie mit einem Gegenstand oder gibt deutlich zu erkennen, daß er tätlich werden will, so wird sofort von der Schußwaffe Gebrauch gemacht."[23]

Tötungshandlungen im Ermessen des SS-Angehörigen, die auf Grundlage der Dienstvorschriften für Konzentrationslager basierten, erfolgten meist durch Einsatz von Schusswaffen, bei tatsächlichen Fluchtversuchen kamen im Falle der Wiederergreifung aber unterschiedlichste Tötungsarten zur Anwendung, die oft mit demonstrativen Bestrafungsritualen und Folterungen einhergingen, nicht zuletzt zur Abschreckung der anderen Lagerinsassen.

3. Intentionales und „in Kauf-genommenes" Töten

Eine dritte Form der Tötungen sind jene, die zwar nicht auf Befehl, aber mit Einverständnis der Inspektion der Konzentrationslager oder zumindest im Einverständnis mit der Lagerführung begangen wurden und die sich gegen Einzelpersonen, aber auch ganze Gruppen richten konnten. Dazu zählen die vom medizinischen Personal der Lager durchgeführten individuellen Tötungen von Kranken (die Analogie zum dezentralen Krankenmord in den Heil- und Pflegeanstalten im Rahmen der NS-Euthanasie nach dem offiziellen Abbruch der T4-Aktion), aber auch Massenrepressalien wie etwa die berüchtigten Totbadeaktionen, bei denen 1941/42 mehrere tausend Häftling ermordet wurden. Dazu zählen auch Einzelaktionen wie die brutale Tötung von etwa 600 kranken Häftlingen des KZ Gusen in der Endphase des Lagers.

In Bezug auf die Zwangsarbeit von Häftlingen ist bei dieser Form der Tötungen ein fließender Übergang zwischen intendiertem Tod (etwa in Bezug auf Spanier und Polen in der ersten Kriegshälfte bei der Steinbrucharbeit) und in Kauf genommenem Tod in Folge katastrophaler Arbeitsbedingungen (etwa bei dem Bau unterirdischer Anlagen) festzustellen, eine genaue analytische Unterscheidung ist hier oft kaum möglich.

something thematised repeatedly in testimonies at the post-war trials, as well as in the memories of former prisoners.[22]

Murdering prisoners at will was also made possible by a second official regulation, since the grounds for killing would hardly have been verifiable in individual cases, assuming such verification would even have been sought: 'Should a prisoner attack an SS guard, SS officer or SS superior, if he threatens him with an object or makes it clear that he will become violent, immediate use will be made of a firearm.'[23]

Killings at the discretion of members of the SS on the basis of the regulations for the concentration camps were generally carried out using firearms. For genuine escape attempts where there was a recapture, various killing methods were employed and these often went hand in hand with demonstrative rituals of punishment or torture, not least to deter the other prisoners.

3. Intentional and 'accepted' killings

A third type of killings are those that, while not the result of a direct order, were carried out with the consent of the *Inspektion der Konzentrationslager*, or at least with the consent of the camp authorities. These killings might be aimed at individuals or whole groups and included the murder of individual, sick patients by the camp's medical personnel (corresponding to the decentralised murder of the ill in sanatoria as part of the National Socialist 'euthanasia' programme after the official end of 'Action T4') as well as mass repressions such as the infamous 'Totbadeaktionen' ('death baths'), during which several thousand prisoners were killed in 1941/42. They also include individual instances such as the brutal killing of some 600 prisoners in the Gusen concentration camp during the final phase of the camp's existence.

Where forced labour and this form of killing are concerned, a dividing line can been seen that fluctuates between intentional killings (as was the case for Spaniards and Poles working in the quarry in the first half of the war, for example) and

Die Dimension gezielter Tötungen

Der Umfang direkter Tötungen, die auf Basis der Aufzeichnungen der SS oder über Gerichtsverfahren in ihrer Dimension erfasst werden können, wie Erschießungen „auf der Flucht", Exekutionen, Tötung der K-Häftlinge, Tötungen durch Giftgas in Mauthausen und Gusen, mittels Gaswagen und in der T4-Anstalt Hartheim war im Lagerkomplex Mauthausen beträchtlich. Bei einer vorsichtigen Schätzung kann von mindestens 16.000 Todesfällen ausgegangen werden.

Berücksichtigt man weitere Tötungsaktionen wie jene gegen die SV-Häftlinge, Massenrepressalien wie die „Totbadeaktionen", Krankenmorde durch das medizinische Personal sowie als Selbstmorde getarnte Tötungen, so kann von einer doppelt so hohen Zahl ausgegangen werden. Demnach ist im Lagerkomplex Mauthausen etwa ein Drittel aller Todesfälle auf direkte Tötungshandlungen zurückzuführen.

Die Spuren der Verbrechen

Begibt man sich auf die Spurensuche[24] nach Belegen der Massentötungen, die vom SS-Lagerpersonal des KZ Mauthausen begangen wurden, so ist zunächst festzuhalten, dass wir es hier mit einer Institution zu tun haben, die systematisch versuchte, ihre verbrecherischen Handlungen schon im Prozess des Handelns selbst zu verschleiern und möglichst keine Spuren zu hinterlassen. Dies gilt sowohl für die schriftlichen Zeugnisse, die ab Anfang 1945 verbrannt wurden, als auch für dingliche Quellen, die zerstört wurden. Dies gilt aber auch für zentrale Zeugen der Massenverbrechen unter den Häftlingen, etwa die Angehörigen der Krematoriums-Kommandos, die man unmittelbar vor der Befreiung des Lagers zu töten beabsichtigte.

Die Verschleierung der Tötungen erfolgte vor allem auf zwei Ebenen. Einerseits wurde dies durch Verwendung von Tarnbegriffen in der Korrespondenz der verschiedenen SS-Dienststellen sowie durch die Fälschung von Todesmeldungen versucht, in dem natürliche anstelle der tatsächlichen Todesursachen eingetragen wurden.[25] Andererseits wollte die SS

death accepted as a by-product of the catastrophic working conditions (during construction of underground installations, for example). Precise analytical differentiation is often impossible here.

The dimensions of the targeted killings

The extent of direct killings in the Mauthausen camp complex was considerable. From figures ascertained on the basis of records kept by the SS or via court trials for shootings 'while attempting to escape', executions, the killing of K-prisoners, and killings using poison gas in Mauthausen and Gusen, in mobile gas vans and in the Hartheim T4 killing centre, a cautious estimate puts it at at least 16,000 deaths.

If further killing actions such as those aimed at SV-prisoners, mass repressions such as the 'death baths', the murder of the sick by medical personnel and killings disguised as suicide are taken into account, then the figure is twice as high. Therefore, around a third of all deaths in the Mauthausen camp complex can be traced back to direct killing actions.

The traces of the crime

When setting out to search for the traces,[24] for the evidence of the mass killings carried out by the SS personnel of the Mauthausen concentration camp, the first thing to note is that we are dealing with an institution which systematically sought to cover up its criminal activities while in the process of carrying them out and which endeavoured to leave behind as few traces as possible. This applies to the written forms of evidence that were burned from early 1945 onwards and to the material objects that were destroyed. This also applies to the central witnesses to the large-scale crimes from among the prisoners: members of the crematorium work detachment, for example, whom the SS intended to kill immediately before the liberation of the camp.

Efforts to conceal the killings mostly took one of two forms. Firstly, the various SS departments used code words in their correspondence and falsified death reports, registering natural causes of death in place of the actual causes.[25] Secondly, the SS pursued their aim of concealment by trying to get rid of the physical evidence, by dismantling the

dieses Ziel durch die Beseitigung von Beweismitteln erreichen, etwa durch die Demontage von baulichen und technischen Objekten, die auf Tötungen hinweisen, wie die Einrichtungen der Gaskammer.

Die SS kam dabei allerdings in der Endphase an die Grenzen ihrer Vertuschungsmöglichkeiten, da die Verschleierung mit der Weiterführung der Massentötungen in praktische Konkurrenz geriet. So musste einerseits ein Häftlingskommando aus Mauthausen Ende 1944 in Hartheim die Spuren der Massentötungen beseitigen, in dem die Gaskammer rückgebaut und der Krematoriumsofen samt Kamin abgetragen wurden, während andererseits der SS in Mauthausen angesichts der enorm hohen Todesraten Verbrennungskapazitäten fehlten, sodass etwa zehntausend Tote in Massengräbern unweit des Lagers verscharrt wurden und noch im April 1945 ein Krematoriumsofen in Mauthausen in Betrieb genommen wurde, um Abhilfe zu schaffen.

Auch die Gaskammer in Mauthausen wurde bis wenige Tage vor dem Abzug der SS zur Tötung verwendet, um dann hastig und scheinbar ohne größere Planung durch die Entfernung von Gaseinfüllapparat, Abluftventilator und Türen Spuren zu verwischen, die dann wenig später auf dem Lagergelände von den US-amerikanischen Befreiern sichergestellt werden konnten und damit zu wichtigen Beweismitteln wurden.[26]

Selbst schriftliche Quellen waren nicht einfach zu beseitigen. Zwar wurden in Mauthausen ab Anfang 1945 systematisch Akten verbrannt, auf der anderen Seite wurden aber, um die Kontrolle und Herrschaft über das Lager nicht zu verlieren, weiterhin bis weit in den April 1945 hinein fein säuberlich Transportlisten, Exekutions- und Totenbücher geführt und auch noch für die zentrale maschinelle Informationsverarbeitung der KZ-Verwaltung diese Häftlingsdaten in für Hollerithmaschinen lesbare Codes umgeschrieben.

Überdies stand gerade die hohe Arbeitsteilung bei der Durchführung der Verbrechen einer völligen Beseitigung von Dokumenten im Wege. Fast alle im KZ Mauthausen produzierten schriftlichen Quellen wurden in Abschriften, Durchschlägen und Kopien

buildings and technical objects that pointed to the killings, such as the installations in the gas chamber.

However, during the final phase of the war, the SS reached the limits of its cover-up capabilities because, on a practical level, concealment conflicted with the continuation of the mass killings. At the end of 1944, for example, while a prisoner work detachment from Mauthausen was having to erase the traces of mass killing in Hartheim by dismantling the gas chamber and removing the crematorium oven including the chimney, in Mauthausen the SS was so short of incineration capacity due to the extremely high death rate that some ten thousand dead had to be hastily buried in mass graves not far from the camp and, as late as April 1945, another crematorium oven went into operation in Mauthausen in order to provide relief.

The gas chamber in Mauthausen was also still being used for killings until a few days before the withdrawal of the SS, who, hastily and seemingly without any overall plan, then removed the gas filling apparatus, the extractor fan and the doors. These were recovered a short time later within the camp grounds by the American liberators and thus became important pieces of evidence.[26]

Even written sources were not so easy to dispose of. Files were indeed burned systematically at Mauthausen from early 1945 onwards but, at the same time, nice, neat transport lists and execution and death registers continued to be kept until well into April 1945 in order to maintain control and authority over the camp. This prisoner information was even still being converted into codes to be read by the Hollerith machines used by the concentration camp administration for centralised, machine data processing.

Moreover, it was precisely this high division of labour that hindered the destruction of all documentation. Almost all of the written sources produced in the Mauthausen concentration camp were sent as duplicates, carbon copies

an andere Konzentrationslager, an übergeordnete Ämter, an andere Verfolgungsbehörden, an Wehrmachtseinrichtungen und Wirtschaftsunternehmen verschickt – dasselbe gilt für Dokumente, bei denen das Lager Mauthausen der Empfänger war.

Das heutige Wissen über Tatorte, Tatkomplexe und Opferzahlen im KZ Mauthausen verdanken wir an erster Stelle denjenigen Häftlingen, die unter Todesgefahr versuchten, Dokumente, Fotografien und Beweisobjekte vor der Zerstörung durch die SS zu bewahren und diese den Alliierten für Gerichtsverfahren nach der Befreiung übergeben konnten.[27] Die Beweissicherung durch die alliierten Befreier sowie die darauf folgenden juristischen Verfahren, die wesentlich auf Aussagen von Überlebenden, aber auch auf Aussagen von SS-Angehörigen beruhten, waren weitere zentrale Bausteine für die Rekonstruktion der Verbrechen im Lagerkomplex Mauthausen. Der jahrelangen Sammlung von Dokumenten durch Überlebende – insbesondere durch Hans Maršálek für die 1970 eröffnete Dauerausstellung in der KZ-Gedenkstätte Mauthausen – war ein wichtiger Schritt in der Sicherung von Quellen, von der auch die seit den 1980er-Jahren intensivierte historische Forschung profitierte. Mittels weiterer aufwändiger Recherchen der zunehmend international vernetzten Forschung über Konzentrationslager, nicht zuletzt in den seit den 1990er-Jahren neu zugänglichen osteuropäischen Archiven, konnten seitdem viele zusätzliche Erkenntnisse gewonnen werden.

Die meisten Tatorte auf dem heutigen Gedenkstättengelände sind stark verändert und verraten ihre Geschichte nicht, denkt man an den Exekutionsplatz nordöstlich des Lagers, der heute eine grüne Wiese ist. Auch vorhandene bauliche Überreste der Tötungseinrichtungen wie die Gaskammer und der Hinrichtungsraum, vor allem aber die für die Leichenbeseitigung errichteten Krematoriumsöfen sind verändert worden, nicht zuletzt durch ihre frühe Inanspruchnahme als zentrale Gedenkbereiche. Aus Sicht der Überlebenden waren bauliche Veränderungen im Zuge der Errichtung der Gedenkstätte wie der Wiedereinbau der von der SS entfernten Türen in der Gaskammer offensichtlich kein Problem, ging es doch um eine erklärende wie würdige Präsentation

or transcripts to other concentration camps, to departments further up the hierarchy, to other authorities involved in persecution, to *Wehrmacht* organisations and to commercial companies – the same applies to documents for which the Mauthausen camp was the receiving party.

Today's knowledge about the crime scenes, 'crime complexes' and the number of victims at the Mauthausen concentration camp is thanks, first and foremost, to those prisoners who risked their own lives to try and save documents, photographs and other pieces of evidence from destruction by the SS and who, after liberation, were able to hand these over to the Allies for use in the trials.[27] Another significant building block in reconstructing the crimes committed at the Mauthausen camp complex was evidence secured by the Allied liberators together with the subsequent legal proceedings, which drew heavily on the testimonies of both survivors and members of the SS. Collecting work over many years by survivors – in particular by Hans Maršálek for the permanent exhibition that opened at the Mauthausen Memorial in 1970 – was an important step in securing source documents, from which historical research has also profited as it has intensified since the 1980s. A great deal of additional knowledge has since been gained through further painstaking and increasingly internationally networked research on the concentration camps, not least from the eastern European archives that became accessible in the 1990s.

Most of the crime scenes within the grounds of today's memorial site have undergone significant alteration and give no clues as to their history – take, for example, the execution site to the northeast of the camp that is now a green field. Even the surviving structural remains of the killing installations such as the gas chamber and execution room and, above all, the crematorium ovens installed for corpse disposal have been changed, not least through their early adoption as central places of remembrance. Making structural changes in the course of establishing the memorial museum – reinstalling the doors to the gas chamber that had been removed by the SS, for

der Orte und nicht um die präzise Erhaltung eines Tatortes mit den heutigen Ansprüchen einer *Crime Scene Investigation*. Dass Leugnungsstrategien Jahre oder Jahrzehnte später an solchen Veränderungen ansetzten, war für Überlebende des Lagers wohl kaum vorstellbar. Die Geschichte der Transformation der Tatorte und Tatobjekte in Gedenkorte und -objekte ist damit selbst Teil der Spurensuche und Spurensicherung, wenn es um den Tatort Mauthausen geht.

Nicht zuletzt haben in den letzten Jahren bauarchäologische Untersuchungen wesentlich zur Sicherung auch minimaler Spuren der Verbrechen beigetragen – gerade in den Bereichen von Hinrichtungsraum und Gaskammer, wo etwa die Reste des Abluftrohres zur Entlüftung der Gaskammer freigelegt wurden. Auch durch die Untersuchung der seit 1949 als Gedenkbereich gestalteten „Aschenhalde" oder der kürzlich erfolgten Renovierung des Krematoriumsofens in Gusen wurde eine langfristige Sicherung dieser Spuren gewährleistet.[28]

„Der Tatort Mauthausen" – Die Ausstellung

Um auf die eingangs erwähnte Debatte über die Möglichkeit der Ausstellung einer Guillotine zurückzukommen: Ein derartiges zentrales Beweisstück für die Tötungsverbrechen im KZ Mauthausen kann es nicht geben, auch wenn mit dem Klappgalgen und dem Abluftventilator der Gaskammer wichtige Objekte von Tötungsverbrechen vorhanden sind.

Ein „arbeitsteiliges" Verbrechen in dieser Dimension kann nicht durch ein Objekt alleine repräsentiert werden. Bei aller notwendigen Differenzierung der Tatorte und der Tötungsverbrechen im KZ-Komplex Mauthausen muss immer wieder daran erinnert werden, dass das Lager als ganzes als Tatort zu sehen ist, der dadurch definiert ist, dass an diesem Ort entweder das Verbrechen stattgefunden hat oder Beweise für das Verbrechen gefunden werden können.

In diesem Sinne geht es in einer quellenorientierten Ausstellung über den Tatort Mauthausen um die Präsentation der vielfältigen Spuren, die auch 70 Jahre nach den Geschehnissen erhalten geblieben sind.

example – obviously posed no problem from the survivors' point of view. What mattered was that the sites were presented in an informative yet respectful manner, not preserved as if aspiring to a contemporary *Crime Scene Investigation*. For the survivors of the camp it was unthinkable that years or decades later, these kinds of changes would form the basis for strategies of denial. Therefore, in dealing with Mauthausen as the scene of a crime, the history of the transformation of the crime scenes and murder weapons into places and objects of remembrance is itself part of the search for and securing of traces.

Last but not least, building-archaeological investigations have made a significant contribution to securing even the smallest traces of the crimes in recent years – particularly in the area of the execution room and gas chamber where the remains of the pipe for ventilating the gas chamber were uncovered. Investigations carried out at the 'Aschenhalde' ('ash dump'), landscaped as a memorial area in 1949, and recent renovations to the crematorium oven in Gusen have also ensured that these traces will remain safeguarded in the long term.[28]

'The Crime Scenes of Mauthausen' – the exhibition

To return to the opening debate on the possibilities for exhibiting a guillotine, there can be no central piece of evidence for the murderous crimes committed at the Mauthausen concentration camp, even if the collapsing gallows and the extractor fan for the gas chamber mean that important objects relating to them are available.

A crime of these dimensions which was based on a 'division of labour' cannot be represented by one object alone. For all the necessary differentiation of the various crime scenes and killing actions within the Mauthausen concentration camp complex, there needs to be a constant reminder that the camp as a whole should be viewed as a crime scene and that, as such, it is defined by a crime having been committed there or evidence for it found there.

Die Ausstellung *Der Tatort-Mauthausen – Eine Spurensuche* ist der bisher erste Versuch, die vielen Funktionen, die eine KZ-Gedenkstätte heute in sich vereint, miteinander zu verknüpfen. Die Bewahrung des Baudenkmals hat die Funktion der Tatortsicherung. Die behutsame ästhetische Aufwertung der ehemaligen Krematorien und die Ergänzung durch einen *Raum der Namen* dienen der pietätvollen Erinnerung an alle im KZ-Komplex Mauthausen Umgekommen. Die Ausstellung selbst hilft der Vorbereitung und Einordnung der historischen Sachverhalte und Sachzeugnisse. Sie versucht exakt jenen Kontext herzustellen, in dem Mordwerkzeuge nicht effektheischend und publikumswirksam präsentiert, sondern forensisch und damit kognitiv eingeordnet werden.

Forensisch bedeutet hier konkret, dass der hier ausgestellte Klappgalgen sowohl als Tatwerkzeug als auch als Beweismittel gezeigt wird. Ein zweites weniger eindeutiges, aber in seinem Kontext umso eindrücklicheres Beispiel ist eine Injektionsspritze. Beide Objekte sind eingebettet in den thematischen Gesamtkontext von konkreten Tötungsarten im Konzentrationslager, nämlich den beiden Stationen „Hinrichtungen" und „Tödliche Medizin". Gleichzeitig werden beide Objekte mit ihrer eigenen Überlieferungsgeschichte präsentiert und somit der Funktionswandel vom Tatwerkzeug zum Beweisstück sowie zum symbolisch-museologischen Objekt beschrieben. Die Opfer der hier erwähnten Tötungsarten und Mordaktionen sind in jeder der Vitrinen präsent. Nicht als Schaustücke, sondern als Individuen, die in den Quellen der Täter oftmals nur als namenlose Nummern vermerkt sind. Die Re-Individualisierung der Opfer geschieht im *Raum der Namen*, der als integraler Bestandteil der Neugestaltung geplant wurde.

Mit ihrer Gesamtkonzeption will die neue Ausstellung und die an sie anschließenden historischen Räume weniger Stätte voyeuristischer Sensationslust und emotionaler Erschütterung sein, als vielmehr Ort erkenntnisgeleiteter Aufklärung und moralischer Wertebildung.

In this sense, the purpose of a source-based exhibition on the crime scenes of Mauthausen is a presentation of the many and varied traces that can still be found even 70 years after the events.

The exhibition *The Crime Scenes of Mauthausen – Searcing for Traces* is the first attempt to date to link together the many functions that come together in a contemporary concentration camp memorial museum. The preservation of the historic building structures means the crime scene is secured. The sensitive redesign of the former crematoria and the addition of a *Room of Names* promotes the respectful remembrance of all those who died in the Mauthausen concentration camp complex. The exhibition itself facilitates the absorption and contextualisation of the historical facts and evidence. It attempts to create just that context in which murder weapons are not presented as attention-grabbers or crowd-pleasers but are given a forensic and therefore cognitive context.

Forensic here means that the collapsing gallows are displayed as both murder weapon and evidence. A second less obvious but, in its context, no less impressive example is a syringe. Both objects are embedded in overarching thematic concepts that relate to a concrete method of killing in the concentration camp, namely the two stations 'Executions' and 'Deadly Medicine'. At the same time, both objects are presented with the history of their own survival, meaning that their changing function from murder weapon to evidence to symbolic-museological object is described. The victims of the killing methods and murders described here are present in every display case. Not as show pieces but as individuals who, in sources created by the perpetrators, often appear only as nameless numbers. The victims' re-individualisation takes place in the *Room of Names,* which was planned as an integral element of the redesign.

In its conceptual entirety, the new exhibition and the historical rooms leading from it seek to be less the site of voyeuristic sensationalism and emotional shock than a place of knowledge-based education and moral development.

1 Vgl. exemplarisch „Darf man eine Guillotine ausstellen?", die tageszeitung (taz) vom 24. Jänner 2014.
2 „Was tun?", Süddeutsche Zeitung (SZ) vom 17. Jänner 2014.
3 „Darf man eine Guillotine ausstellen?", taz vom 24. Jänner 2014.
4 „Wohin mit dem Fallbeil?", SZ vom 13. Jänner 2014.
5 „Darf man eine Guillotine ausstellen?", taz vom 24. Jänner 2014.
6 Ebenda.
7 Detlev Garbe: Die Konzentrationslager als Stätten des Massenmordes. Zur Geschichte anderer Tötungsverfahren und der notwendigen Einordnung des Gasmordes, in: Günter Morsch/Bertrand Perz unter Mitarbeit von Astrid Ley (Hg.): Neue Studien zu nationalsozialistischen Massentötungen durch Giftgas. Historische Bedeutung, technische Entwicklung, revisionistische Leugnung (Berlin 2011), S. 316–334, hier S. 316.
8 In Konzentrationslager mit der Stufe III sollten „schwerbelastete, insbesondere auch gleichzeitig kriminell vorbestrafte, ausgesprochen asoziale und daher kaum noch erziehbare Schutzhäftlinge" deportiert werden. Vgl. Johannes Tuchel: Die Inspektion der Konzentrationslager 1938–1945. Das System des Terrors (Berlin 1994), S. 67; Verein für Gedenken und Geschichtsforschung in österreichischen KZ-Gedenkstätten (Hg.): Das Konzentrationslager Mauthausen 1938–1945. Katalog zur Ausstellung in der KZ-Gedenkstätte Mauthausen (Wien 2013), S. 136.
9 Vgl. Garbe: Die Konzentrationslager als Stätten des Massenmordes, S. 322.
10 Vgl. Astrid Ley: Die „Aktion 14f13" in den nationalsozialistischen Konzentrationslagern, in: Morsch/Perz (Hg.): Massentötungen durch Giftgas (Berlin 2011), S. 231–243.
11 Vgl. Bertrand Perz/Florian Freund: Tötungen durch Giftgas im Konzentrationslager Mauthausen, in: Morsch/Perz (Hg.): Massentötungen durch Giftgas (Berlin 2011), S. 244–259.
12 Vgl. Dirk Riedel: Ordnungshüter und Massenmörder im Dienst der „Volksgemeinschaft": Der KZ-Kommandant Hans Loritz (Berlin 2010), S. 271f.
13 Vgl. zur Frage der Todesursache Andreas Kranebitter: Zahlen als Zeugen. Quantitative Analysen zur „Häftlingsgesellschaft" des KZ Mauthausen-Gusen, Dipl.Arb. Univ. (Wien 2012, erscheint Ende 2014 als Band 9 der Mauthausen-Studien), S. 154–165.
14 Vgl. dazu allgemein Reinhard Otto: Wehrmacht, Gestapo und sowjetische Kriegsgefangene im deutschen Reichsgebiet 1941/42. Schriftenreihe der Vierteljahreshefte des Instituts für Zeitgeschichte (München 1998).
15 Garbe: Die Konzentrationslager als Stätten des Massenmordes, S. 330.
16 Vgl. Florian Freund/Bertrand Perz: Mauthausen – Stammlager, in: Wolfgang Benz/Barbara Distel (Hg.): Der Ort des Terrors. Geschichte der nationalsozialistischen Konzentrationslager. Band 4. Flossenbürg – Mauthausen – Ravensbrück (München 2006), S. 331.
17 Vgl. allgemein dazu: Matthias Kaltenbrunner: Flucht aus dem Todesblock. Der Massenausbruch sowjetischer Offiziere aus dem Block 20 des KZ Mauthausen und die „Mühlviertler Hasenjagd" – Hintergründe, Folgen, Aufarbeitung (Innsbruck 2012).
18 Vgl. Pierre Serge Choumoff: Nationalsozialistische Massentötungen durch Giftgas auf österreichischem Gebiet 1940 – 1945, Wien 2000 (Mauthausen-Studien Band 1a); Perz/Freund: Tötungen durch Giftgas im Konzentrationslager Mauthausen, S. 250.

1 Cf. as an example 'Darf man eine Guillotine ausstellen?' ['Should a guillotine be exhibited?'], die tageszeitung (taz) dated 24 January 2014.
2 'Was tun?' ['What to do?'], Süddeutsche Zeitung (SZ) dated 17 January 2014.
3 'Darf man eine Guillotine ausstellen'?, taz dated 24 January 2014.
4 'Wohin mit dem Fallbeil?' ['Where to put the guillotine?'], SZ dated 13 January 2014.
5 'Darf man eine Guillotine ausstellen?', taz dated 24 January 2014.
6 Ibid.
7 Detlev Garbe: Die Konzentrationslager als Stätten des Massenmordes. Zur Geschichte anderer Tötungsverfahren und der notwendigen Einordnung des Gasmordes, in: Günter Morsch/Bertrand Perz assisted by Astrid Ley (ed.): Neue Studien zu nationalsozialistischen Massentötungen durch Giftgas. Historische Bedeutung, technische Entwicklung, revisionistische Leugnung (Berlin 2011), p. 316–334, here p. 316.
8 Those 'with major offences, particularly those with criminal records and marked antisocial element who therefore cannot be re-educated' were to be deported to Grade III concentration camps. Cf. Johannes Tuchel: Die Inspektion der Konzentrationslager 1938–1945. Das System des Terrors (Berlin 1994), p. 67; Association for Remembrance and Research in Austrian Concentration Camp Memorials (ed.): The Concentration Camp Mauthausen 1938–1945. Catalogue to the Exhibition at the Mauthausen Memorial (Vienna 2013), p. 136.
9 Cf. Garbe: Die Konzentrationslager als Stätten des Massenmordes, p. 322.
10 Cf. Astrid Ley: Die "Aktion 14f13" in den nationalsozialistischen Konzentrationslagern, in: Morsch/Perz (ed.): Massentötungen durch Giftgas (Berlin 2011), p. 231–243.
11 Cf. Bertrand Perz/Florian Freund: Tötungen durch Giftgas im Konzentrationslager Mauthausen, in: Morsch/Perz (ed.): Massentötungen durch Giftgas (Berlin 2011), p. 244–259.
12 Cf. Dirk Riedel: Ordnungshüter und Massenmörder im Dienst der "Volksgemeinschaft": Der KZ-Kommandant Hans Loritz (Berlin 2010), p. 271f.
13 On the question of the causes of death cf. Andreas Kranebitter: Zahlen als Zeugen. Quantitative Analysen zur "Häftlingsgesellschaft" des KZ Mauthausen-Gusen, Masters Thesis (University of Vienna 2012, to be published in late 2014 as volume 9 of the Mauthausen-Studien), p. 154–165.
14 On this topic in general, cf. Reinhard Otto: Wehrmacht, Gestapo und sowjetische Kriegsgefangene im deutschen Reichsgebiet 1941/42. Schriftenreihe der Vierteljahreshefte des Instituts für Zeitgeschichte (Munich 1998).
15 Garbe: Die Konzentrationslager als Stätten des Massenmordes, p. 330.
16 Cf. Florian Freund/Bertrand Perz: Mauthausen – Stammlager, in: Wolfgang Benz/Barbara Distel (ed.): Der Ort des Terrors. Geschichte der nationalsozialistischen Konzentrationslager. Vol. 4. Flossenbürg – Mauthausen – Ravensbrück (Munich 2006), p. 331.
17 On this topic in general, cf. Matthias Kaltenbrunner: Flucht aus dem Todesblock. Der Massenausbruch sowjetischer Offiziere aus dem Block 20 des KZ Mauthausen und die "Mühlviertler Hasenjagd" – Hintergründe, Folgen, Aufarbeitung (Innsbruck 2012).
18 Cf. Pierre Serge Choumoff: Nationalsozialistische Massentötungen durch Giftgas auf österreichischem Gebiet 1940 – 1945, Vienna 2000 (Mauthausen-Studien vol. 1a);

19 Vgl. Astrid Ley, Die „Aktion 14f13", S. 231–243.

20 Vgl. Bertrand Perz: Zwangsarbeit von KZ-Häftlingen der Reichswerke „Hermann Göring" in Österreich, Deutschland und Polen. Vergleichende Perspektiven, in: Gabriella Hauch unter Mitarbeit von Peter Gutschner und Birgit Kirchmayr (Hg.): Industrie und Zwangsarbeit im Nationalsozialismus. Mercedes Benz – VW – Reichswerke Hermann Göring in Linz und Salzgitter (Innsbruck/Wien/München/Bozen 2003), S. 85–99.

21 Dienstvorschrift für Konzentrationslager (Lagerordnung). Gedruckt im RSHA, Berlin 1941, S. 48.

22 Vgl. Gregor Holzinger: „…da mordqualifizierende Umstände nicht hinreichend sicher nachgewiesen werden können…" Die juristische Verfolgung von Angehörigen der SS-Wachmannschaft des Konzentrationslagers Mauthausen wegen „Erschießungen auf der Flucht", in: Dokumentationsarchiv des österreichischen Widerstandes (Hg.): Täter. Österreichische Akteure im Nationalsozialismus. Jahrbuch 2014 (Wien 2014), S. 135–163; Jutta Fuchshuber: „Auf der Flucht erschossen"? Tötungen im KZ-Komplex Mauthausen, in: InnenAnsichten, Jahrgang 1 (2012), Nr. 1, S. 9–26.

23 Dienstvorschrift für Konzentrationslager (Lagerordnung). Gedruckt im RSHA, Berlin 1941, S. 48.

24 Generell zur Frage der Quellen der NS-Verbrechen, allerdings spezifisch zum Judenmord vgl. Raul Hilberg: Die Quellen des Holocaust. Entschlüsseln und Interpretieren (Frankfurt a.M. 2002).

25 In der Mehrzahl der Todesfälle wurden diese in den Konzentrationslagern, analog zur „Aktion T4" nicht grundsätzlich bestritten, sondern die Ursachen verfälscht. Das unterscheidet die Morde in den KZs grundsätzlich vom Mord an den europäischen Juden, der von den Nationalsozialisten zur Gänze geleugnet wurde. Hier wäre die Verfälschung der Todesursachen schon wegen der enormen Zahl an Toten – zeitweise bis zu 20.000 pro Tag – völlig unmöglich gewesen. Vgl. Bertrand Perz: Tod ohne Ritual. Der nationalsozialistische Massenmord, in: Wolfgang Hameter/Meta Niederkorn/Martin Scheutz (Hg.): Freund Hain? Tod und Ritual in der Geschichte (Innsbruck/Wien/Bozen 2007), S. 157–176 (Querschnitte Bd. 22, Einführungstexte zur Sozial-, Wirtschafts- und Kulturgeschichte).

26 Vgl. Florian Freund/Bertrand Perz/Karl Stuhlpfarrer: Einleitung zur Dokumentation: Der Bericht des US-Geheimagenten Jack H. Taylor über das Konzentrationslager Mauthausen, in: Zeitgeschichte 22 (1995) 9/10, S. 318–341.

27 Vgl. etwa zur Rettung von Fotografien Benito Bermejo: Francisco Boix, der Fotograf von Mauthausen. Mauthausen-Studien, Sonderband (Wien 2007) bzw. Bundesministerium für Inneres (Hg.): Das sichtbare Unfassbare: Fotografien vom Konzentrationslager Mauthausen. Katalog zur gleichnamigen Ausstellung (Wien 2005).

28 Zur Bau-Archäologie siehe den Beitrag von Paul Mitchell in diesem Band sowie Claudia Theune: Zeitschichten. Archäologische Untersuchungen in der Gedenkstätte Mauthausen, in: Bundesministerium für Inneres (Hg.): KZ-Gedenkstätte Mauthausen | Mauthausen Memorial 2009. Forschung – Dokumentation – Information, Jahrbuch der KZ-Gedenkstätte Mauthausen (Wien 2010), S. 25–30; Paul Mitchell/Günter Buchinger: Die Baugeschichte des neuen Reviergebäudes, KL Mauthausen, unveröffentlichtes Manuskript (Wien 2010); dieselben, Die Baugeschichte des Tötungs- und Einäscherungskomplexes am Appellplatz, KL Mauthausen (mit einem Anhang von Karl Scherzer), unveröffentlichtes Manuskript (Wien 2009).

Perz/Freund: Tötungen durch Giftgas im Konzentrationslager Mauthausen, p. 250.

19 Cf. Astrid Ley, Die "Aktion 14f13", p. 231–243.

20 Cf. Bertrand Perz: Zwangsarbeit von KZ-Häftlingen der Reichswerke "Hermann Göring" in Österreich, Deutschland und Polen. Vergleichende Perspektiven, in: Gabriella Hauch assisted by Peter Gutschner and Birgit Kirchmayr (ed.): Industrie und Zwangsarbeit im Nationalsozialismus. Mercedes Benz – VW – Reichswerke Hermann Göring in Linz und Salzgitter (Innsbruck/Vienna/Munich/Bolzano 2003), p. 85–99.

21 Dienstvorschrift für Konzentrationslager (Lagerordnung). Gedruckt im RSHA, Berlin 1941 [Official Regulations for Concentration Camps (camp regulations). Printed by the Reich Main Security Office, Berlin 1941], p. 48.

22 Cf. Gregor Holzinger: "…da mordqualifizierende Umstände nicht hinreichend sicher nachgewiesen werden können…" Die juristische Verfolgung von Angehörigen der SS-Wachmannschaft des Konzentrationslagers Mauthausen wegen "Erschießungen auf der Flucht", in: Dokumentationsarchiv des österreichischen Widerstandes (ed.): Täter. Österreichische Akteure im Nationalsozialismus. Jahrbuch 2014 (Vienna 2014), p. 135–163; Jutta Fuchshuber: "Auf der Flucht erschossen"? Tötungen im KZ-Komplex Mauthausen, in: InnenAnsichten, Jahrgang 1 (2012), Nr. 1, S. 9–26.

23 Dienstvorschrift für Konzentrationslager (Lagerordnung). Gedruckt im RSHA, Berlin 1941, p. 48.

24 On the more general question of source material for National Socialist crimes, albeit specifically on the destruction of the Jews, cf. Raul Hilberg: Sources of Holocaust Research. An Analysis (Chicago 2001).

25 For the majority of these cases, the deaths were not essentially disputed in the concentration camps but, like those of 'Action T4', the cause of death was falsified. This marks a fundamental difference between murders in the concentration camps and the murder of the European Jews, which was denied in its entirety. Given the vast number of deaths – at times up to 20,000 per day – falsification of the cause of death would have been completely out of the question. Cf. Bertrand Perz: Tod ohne Ritual. Der nationalsozialistische Massenmord, in: Wolfgang Hameter/Meta Niederkorn/Martin Scheutz (ed.): Freund Hain? Tod und Ritual in der Geschichte (Innsbruck/Vienna/Bolzano 2007), p. 157–176 (Querschnitte vol. 22, introductory texts on social, economic and cultural history).

26 Cf. Florian Freund/Bertrand Perz/Karl Stuhlpfarrer: Einleitung zur Dokumentation: Der Bericht des US-Geheimagenten Jack H. Taylor über das Konzentrationslager Mauthausen, in: Zeitgeschichte 22 (1995) 9/10, p. 318–341.

27 On saving photographs, for example, cf. Benito Bermejo: Francisco Boix, der Fotograf von Mauthausen. Mauthausen-Studien, Sonderband (Vienna 2007) and Federal Ministry of the Interior (ed.): The Visible Part. Photographs of Mauthausen Concentration Camp. Catalogue to accompany the exhibition of the same name (Vienna 2005).

28 On building-archaeology see the article by Paul Mitchell in this volume, also Claudia Theune: Zeitschichten. Archäologische Untersuchungen in der Gedenkstätte Mauthausen, in: Bundesministerium für Inneres (ed.): KZ-Gedenkstätte Mauthausen | Mauthausen Memorial 2009. Forschung – Dokumentation – Information, Jahrbuch der KZ-Gedenkstätte Mauthausen (Vienna 2010), p. 25-30; Paul Mitchell/Günter Buchinger: Die Baugeschichte des neuen Reviergebäudes, KL Mauthausen, unpublished manuscript (Vienna 2010); Paul Mitchell/Günter Buchinger, Die Baugeschichte des Tötungs- und Einäscherungskomplexes am Appellplatz, KL Mauthausen (with an appendix by Karl Scherzer), unpublished manuscript (Vienna 2009).

Christian Dürr/Ralf Lechner/Niko Wahl/Johanna Wensch

„Der Tatort Mauthausen – Eine Spurensuche". Zum Konzept der Ausstellung

Die Vertiefungs-Ausstellung *Der Tatort Mauthausen – Eine Spurensuche* wurde im Mai 2013 zeitgleich mit der Überblicks-Ausstellung *Das Konzentrationslager Mauthausen 1938–1945* eröffnet. Damit war die erste Phase der Umsetzung des Rahmenkonzepts zur Neugestaltung der KZ-Gedenkstätte Mauthausen abgeschlossen. Dieses Konzept wurde 2009 von einer international besetzten Arbeitsgruppe vorgelegt.[1] Wichtigstes Ziel der Neugestaltung ist es, den historischen Ort des ehemaligen Konzentrationslagers durch verschiedene Gestaltungsmaßnahmen so zu erschließen, dass Topographie und bauliche Überreste zu Anknüpfungspunkten für die Vermittlung der Lagergeschichte werden. Entlang eines neuen, durch ein einheitliches Informations- und Leitsystem ausgeschilderten Rundgangs durch die Gedenk-

Christian Dürr/Ralf Lechner/Niko Wahl/Johanna Wensch

'The Crime Scenes of Mauthausen – Searching for Traces'. On the concept behind the exhibition

The thematic exhibition *The Crime Scenes of Mauthausen – Searching for Traces* opened in May 2013 at the same time as the overview exhibition *The Mauthausen Concentration Camp 1938-1945*. This marked the completion of the first implementation phase of the framework concept for the redesign of the Mauthausen Memorial. This concept was presented in 2009 by an international working group.[1] The most important aim of the redesign is to open up the historical site of the former concentration camp in such a way that, through the use of a variety of planning and design measures, the topography and structural remains become the starting point for learning about the history of the camp. A new tour route around the memorial site, signposted with a single, unified

Die Themenstationen der Ausstellung werden inhaltlich durch großflächige Fotografien eingeleitet, die die jeweiligen Tatorte in ihrem heutigen Zustand zeigen.
Foto: Tal Adler

The topic of each thematic station in the exhibition is introduced by a large-format photograph showing the crime scene in its current state.
Photograph: Tal Adler

stätte sollen insgesamt sechs neue Ausstellungen installiert werden. Diese dezentral angeordneten Ausstellungen ermöglichen den BesucherInnen eine Annäherung an die Lagergeschichte auf verschiedenen analytischen Ebenen und aus unterschiedlichen Perspektiven. Während die Ausstellung *Das Konzentrationslager Mauthausen 1938–1945*[2] einen historischen Überblick bietet und die Lagergeschichte in den größeren politischen und gesellschaftlichen Rahmen einbettet, vertiefen die weiteren Ausstellungen einzelne zentrale Aspekte der KZ-Geschichte. Dazu sollen auch unterschiedliche ausstellungsdidaktische und -methodische Zugänge eingesetzt werden. Die einzelnen Vertiefungs-Ausstellungen verknüpfen ein Thema der Lagergeschichte jeweils mit einem konkreten historischen Ort. So befindet sich die im Kellergeschoß des ehemaligen Häftlingsreviers untergebrachte Ausstellung *Der Tatort Mauthausen – Eine Spurensuche* in unmittelbarer Nähe der Überreste der Gaskammer und Krematorien des Lagers; die weiteren Vertiefungs-Ausstellungen sollen im ehemaligen Stabsgebäude (Thema Lager-SS), im ehemaligen Steinbruch Wiener Graben (Thema Zwangsarbeit), in der ehemaligen Küchenbaracke (Thema Häftlinge) und im Besucherzentrum der KZ-Gedenkstätte (Themen Gedenkstättengeschichte/Rezeptionsgeschichte) realisiert werden.[3]

Der Tatort Mauthausen – Eine Spurensuche wurde allerdings anders als die erwähnten Ausstellungen weniger als optionales Angebot denn als integraler Bestandteil des neuen Rundganges über das historische Gelände konzipiert. Dem liegt die Beobachtung zugrunde, dass das Kellergeschoss des Reviergebäudes als ehemaliger Tötungsbereich auf viele BesucherInnen der Gedenkstätte eine besondere „Anziehungskraft" ausübt. Diese Räumlichkeiten waren Stätten des Massenmordes: Hier wurden Häftlinge des KZ Mauthausen erschossen, erhängt oder durch Giftgas ermordet, hier wurden ihre Leichen in Kühlräumen gelagert und schließlich in den Krematoriumsöfen verbrannt. Diese Räume sind seit der Befreiung des Konzentrationslagers Erinnerungsorte, an denen Hinterbliebene ihrer Angehörigen gedenken. Sozialwissenschaftliche Beobachtungen in der KZ-Gedenkstätte Mauthausen machten deutlich, dass die Räumlichkeiten der ehemaligen Tötungsvor-

information and guidance system, will incorporate a total of six new exhibitions. These decentralised exhibitions will allow visitors to approach the history of the camp from a range of perspectives and engage with it on different analytical levels. Whilst the exhibition *The Mauthausen Concentration Camp 1938-1945*[2] offers an overview of the camp's history and locates it within a wider political and social context, the other exhibitions will offer a more in-depth look at certain key aspects of concentration camp history. The aim is to use a variety of pedagogical and methodological approaches in the thematic exhibitions, each of which will connect a concrete historical site to a topic from the camp's history. Thus the exhibition *The Crime Scenes of Mauthausen – Searching for Traces*, housed in the basement of the former prisoner infirmary, is located in direct proximity to the remains of the gas chamber and the camp crematoria; the other thematic exhibitions will be installed in the former camp administration building (topic: the camp SS), the former Wiener Graben quarry (topic: forced labour), the former kitchen barracks (topic: prisoners) and in the visitor centre (topics: history of the memorial site / reception history).[3]

However, *The Crime Scenes of Mauthausen – Searching for Traces* – unlike the other exhibitions mentioned here – was conceived less as one option among many than as an integral part of the new tour around the historical site. Underlying this is the observation that as the former killing area, the basement of the infirmary building exerts a particular 'fascination' on many visitors to the memorial museum. These rooms were the site of mass murder; here prisoners of the Mauthausen concentration camp were shot, hanged or murdered by poison gas, here their corpses were stored in the mortuary and, finally, burned in the crematorium ovens. Since the liberation of the camp, these rooms have been places of remembrance where the bereaved remember their dead. Sociological studies carried out at the Mauthausen Memorial showed clearly that during visits to the memorial complex, the rooms housing the former killing facilities attracted the most interest and that, at

richtungen bei der Besichtigung der Gedenkstätte im Zentrum des Interesses standen und andere Orte und Aspekte der Lagergeschichte bisweilen wenig oder gar nicht beachtet wurden.[4] Das starke Augenmerk, das die BesucherInnen auf den ehemaligen Tötungsbereich richteten, führte folglich auch zu einem verzerrten Bild des Konzentrationslagers Mauthausen. Viele bringen ein vorgefasstes Bild vom Konzentrationslager als Ort, an dem die Gefangenen ausschließlich in der Gaskammer ermordet wurden mit. Im Zuge eines Gedenkstättenbesuchs, der sich auf diesen Bereich beschränkt, kann dieses Stereotyp nur sehr eingeschränkt aufgebrochen und in Einklang mit den historischen Fakten gebracht werden.[5]

Angesichts dieser Befunde wurde entschieden, dass der Besichtigung der baulichen Überreste des Tötungsbereiches zukünftig ein Informationsangebot vorangestellt werden müsse. Aus diesem Grund hatte die Realisierung der Ausstellung *Der Tatort Mauthausen – Eine Spurensuche* Vorrang vor der Erarbeitung der übrigen Vertiefungs-Ausstellungen.

Eng mit der Konzeptionierung der eigentlichen Ausstellung verbunden war die Frage, auf welche Weise zukünftig das Kellergeschoss zugänglich sein und erschlossen werden sollte. Das realisierte Leitsystem in Form eines Stegs hat zunächst die Funktion, den Lärmpegel und ein mögliches Gedränge zu reduzieren und damit eine den Gedenkbereich respektierende Atmosphäre zu schaffen.[6] In den Steg sind Informationstafeln integriert, auf denen die historische Funktion der zentralen Räumlichkeiten benannt wird und die in manchen Fällen in sehr knapper Form weitere Erläuterungen liefern. Die Zugangsmöglichkeiten zum Kellergeschoss wurden bewusst reduziert: Während früher der Kellerbereich von drei Richtungen her betreten wurde – vom Bunkerhof, direkt vom Appellplatz oder über die ehemalige Dauerausstellung im Reviergebäude –, gibt es nun nur noch einen ausgewiesenen und empfohlenen Zugang, der über die Ausstellung *Der Tatort Mauthausen* erfolgt.

Mit Hilfe dieser Wegführung und der Kombination von Steg und Ausstellung wird den BesucherInnen nun Wissen mitgegeben, mit dem sich die Räume

times, little or no attention had been paid to other sites or aspects of the camp's history.[4] Visitors' pronounced focus on the former killing area has led, in consequence, to a distorted image of the Mauthausen concentration camp. Many people bring with them a preconceived image of the concentration camp as a place where prisoners were murdered exclusively in the gas chamber. During a visit to the memorial site that is limited to this area, there is a limit to the extent to which this stereotype can be addressed and brought into line with the historical facts.[5]

In light of these findings, the decision was taken that, in future, visitors must be offered information before they go on to view the structural remains of the killing area. For this reason, the creation of the exhibition *The Crime Scenes of Mauthausen – Searching for Traces* took priority over the development of the other thematic exhibitions.

Closely connected to the concept for the exhibition itself was the question of how the basement area was to be accessed and navigated in future. The guidance system created in the form of a walkway serves, to start with, to reduce noise levels and prevent possible overcrowding, therefore engendering a respectful atmosphere befitting a memorial area.[6] Information panels are integrated into the walkway, giving the historical function of the main rooms and, in some cases, further explanation in succinct form. There was a deliberate reduction in the number of access points to the basement: whilst before the cellar area could be entered from any one of three directions – from the camp prison courtyard, directly from the roll call area or via the previous permanent exhibition in the infirmary building – there is now only one signposted and recommended entrance by way of the exhibition *The Crime Scenes of Mauthausen*.

With the help of this guidance system and the combination of the walkway and the exhibition, visitors are now given the knowledge they need to make sense of the rooms and the structural remains. This prevents too abrupt a confrontation

und Überreste entschlüsseln lassen. Dies verhindert eine unvermittelte Konfrontation mit den historisch stark belasteten Orten. Da die Ausstellung einen Großteil der historischen Information vermittelt, können die Orte selbst davon weitgehend frei gehalten werden. Einer ihrem Charakter als frühere Sterbe- und heutige Gedenkorte entsprechenden pietätvollen Begegnung wird dadurch der notwendige Raum gegeben.

Die Ausstellung *Der Tatort Mauthausen – Eine Spurensuche* weist allerdings über den Gebäudeabschnitt hinaus, dem sie unmittelbar vorgelagert ist. Das kuratorische Ziel ist es, der häufig von den BesucherInnen mitgebrachten Fokussierung auf die Tötungsorte Gaskammer oder Hinrichtungsraum entgegenzuwirken und den Blick auf andere Orte im Konzentrationslager zu lenken, an denen KZ-Häftlinge ebenfalls gezielt und massenhaft ermordet wurden. Die Tötungsräumlichkeiten im Kellergeschoss des Reviergebäudes werden in den Gesamtzusammenhang des systematischen Massenmords im KZ Mauthausen eingeordnet, den die SS abseits des bewusst in Kauf genommenen alltäglichen Sterbens in Folge permanenten Mangels verübt hat, um sich gezielt bestimmter Personengruppen zu entledigen, die ihr aus politischen, rassistischen oder pragmatischen Gründen „missliebig" waren. Diese Tötungsaktionen führte die SS an vielen Orten im Lager und unter Rückgriff auf vielfältige Methoden durch. Ziel der Ausstellung *Der Tatort Mauthausen – Eine Spurensuche* ist es, Umfang des Mordens und Vielfalt der Vernichtungspraktiken begreiflich zu machen.

Die zentrale Frage bei der Konzeptionierung der Ausstellung war, wie ein solches Thema in eine verständliche und nachvollziehbare Ausstellungsgliederung umgesetzt werden kann. Bei der Arbeit am Feinkonzept, welches das KuratorInnenteam in enger Zusammenarbeit mit den wissenschaftlichen Leitern des Ausstellungsprojektes Bertrand Perz und Jörg Skriebeleit erstellte, wurde bald deutlich, dass eine Strukturierung der Ausstellung weder allein über Opfergruppen, Tötungsmethoden, Tat-Motive noch über Quellenarten zielführend ist, da diese Aspekte inhaltlich zu eng miteinander verschränkt sind, als dass man sie auf sinnvolle Art und Weise getrennt voneinander darstellen könnte. Das Aus-

with places that carry a heavy historical burden. Since the exhibition covers the majority of the historical information, this is largely absent from the rooms themselves. In this way, a respectful encounter befitting a place shaped by past deaths and present remembrances is given the space it needs.

However, the exhibition *The Crime Scenes of Mauthausen – Searching for Traces* extends beyond the section of building it is located in front of. The curators' aim is to counteract visitors' all too frequent focus on the gas chamber or the execution room as killing sites and direct their attention to other sites in the concentration camp where prisoners were likewise murdered, deliberately and in large numbers. The killing area in the basement of the infirmary building is placed in the context of systematic mass murder at the Mauthausen concentration camp as a whole which, quite apart from the readily accepted deaths resulting on a daily basis from permanent deprivation, was perpetrated by the SS in order to target and dispose of particular groups of people whom it considered 'undesirable' for political, racial or pragmatic reasons. The SS carried out these killing actions in several places in the camp and with recourse to a variety of methods. The aim of the exhibition *The Crime Scenes of Mauthausen – Searching for Traces* is to shed light on the scale of the murder and the variety of the extermination practices.

The central question during the exhibition's conceptualisation was how such a topic could be transformed into a coherent and comprehensible exhibition structure. During work on the detailed concept, which was drawn up by the curators in close cooperation with the project's academic directors, Bertrand Perz and Jörg Skriebeleit, it soon became clear that structuring the exhibition solely by victim group, killing method, criminal motive or by source type was not an option, since these themes were too closely interwoven to allow them to be presented separately in any meaningful way. The narrative for the exhibition was finally reached via the definition of the Mauthausen camp as 'the scene of many crime scenes'. A total of six of

stellungsnarrativ ergab sich schließlich über die Definition des Lagers Mauthausen als „Ort voller Tatorte". Insgesamt sechs dieser Tatorte werden in der Ausstellung als Ausgangspunkt für die Darstellung zentraler *Tat-Komplexe* gewählt.

Das Leitmotiv „Tat-Ort" wird beim Betreten des Ausstellungsraums sogleich durch ein starkes visuelles Signal deutlich: Die BesucherInnen werden von großformatigen Farbfotografien des Gedenkstättengeländes im aktuellen Zustand empfangen, die an den Fronten der sechs im Raum verteilten Themenstationen angebracht sind. Diese Aufnahmen des Fotokünstlers Tal Adler rufen die eben noch beim Gedenkstättenrundgang gewonnenen Eindrücke in Erinnerung und setzen sie zugleich in einen neuen Zusammenhang. Erst auf der Rückseite der Ausstellungsstationen wird dieser Zusammenhang ersichtlich: Jeder gezeigte Ort steht als Tat-Ort in engem Bezug zu einem spezifischen Tat-Komplex, der in der jeweiligen Ausstellungsstation thematisiert wird. Dabei sind die Fotomotive in einigen Fällen Stellvertreter oder beispielhafte Orte für die beschriebenen Tötungsverbrechen. So führt die Fotografie des Appellplatzes hin zum Thema der alltäglichen, von SS und Funktionshäftlingen ausgeübten Gewaltexzesse, die das Leben der KZ-Häftlinge immerzu und in allen Bereichen des Lagers bedrohten (Station 1). Das Areal der ehemaligen Hinrichtungsstätte – heute eine Wiese außerhalb des ehemaligen Häftlingslagers, die in keiner Weise als historischer Tatort zu erkennen ist – steht beispielhaft für jene Orte im Konzentrationslager, an denen Exekutionen durchgeführt wurden (Station 2). Das Großfoto des Lagerzauns thematisiert die Lagergrenze als Ort gezielter Tötungen, wo Bewacher Gefangene in den mit Starkstrom geladenen Stacheldraht trieben oder erschossen, was nachträglich als vorgeblicher Selbstmord beziehungsweise Fluchtversuch getarnt wurde (Station 3). Eine Fotografie des Steinbruchs im Wiener Graben leitet zur Thematisierung der „Vernichtung durch Arbeit", in deren Rahmen die KZ-Häftlinge programmatisch durch die rücksichtslose Ausbeutung ihrer Arbeitskraft zu Tode geschunden wurden (Station 4). Das Areal des heute nicht mehr sichtbaren Sanitätslagers, wo tausende der medizinischen Hilfe Bedürftige zu Tode kamen, steht symbolhaft für den Mord unter Aufsicht und Anleitung von SS-Ärzten

these crime scenes were selected as starting points for illustrating the key *crime-complexes* in the exhibition.

On entering the exhibition space, the leitmotif of the 'crime-scene' immediately becomes clear through the use of a strong, visual signal: visitors are greeted by large-format colour photographs of the grounds of the memorial site in its current state, which are mounted to the front of the six thematic stations arranged around the room. These pictures by the photographer Tal Adler both call to mind the impressions just formed on the tour of the site and, at the same time, place them in a new context. It is only on the other side of the station that it becomes clear what that context is: each location depicted stands as a crime-scene in close connection to a specific crime-complex, which is thematised by the station in question. In some cases the subject of the photograph is representative of or an example of a location for the murders described. Thus the photograph of the roll call area leads to the topic of the everyday violent excesses practised by the SS and prisoner functionaries, which threatened the lives of the concentration camp prisoners at all times and in all areas of the camp (station 1). The area of the former execution site – today a meadow outside the former prisoners' camp, unrecognisable as a historical crime scene in any way – stands for those places in the concentration camp where executions were carried out (station 2). The picture of the camp fence thematises the camp perimeter as a site of targeted killings, where guards shot prisoners or forced them into the heavily electrified barbed wire fence, occurrences that were later covered up as alleged escape attempts or suicide (station 3). A photograph of the quarry in the Wiener Graben leads to the theme of 'annihilation through work', a framework in which, through the reckless exploitation of their labour, the concentration camp prisoners were systematically worked to death (station 4). The grounds of the now invisible infirmary camp, where thousands of those in need of medical care perished, symbolise the murders committed under the supervision and instruction of SS doctors (station

(Station 5). Einer aktuellen Aufnahme der Gaskammer folgt schließlich eine Darstellung der Massentötungen durch Giftgas (Station 6).

Während die Überblicks-Ausstellung das massenhafte Morden im Kontext der Gesamtgeschichte des Lagerkomplexes Mauthausen/Gusen darstellt, geht die Ausstellung methodisch anders vor: Sie nimmt einer Beweisaufnahme gleich die BesucherInnen – wie im Untertitel der Ausstellung angekündigt – mit auf eine *Spurensuche*. Durch die präsentierten Exponate wird ihnen die Möglichkeit geboten, an der Rekonstruktion historischer Ereignisse teilzuhaben. Die Suche führt über sehr unterschiedliche und oft nur bruchstückhaft überlieferte Indizien. Auf vielfache Weise haben die Täter versucht, ihre Morde geheim zu halten und zu verschleiern; kurz vor Kriegsende haben sie gezielt Tötungseinrichtungen und schriftliche Zeugnisse beseitigt und Augenzeugen ermordet. Dennoch sind Spuren erhalten geblieben und haben Zeugen überlebt. Die Ausstellung *Der Tatort Mauthausen – Eine Spurensuche* setzt einzelne Splitter zu Belegen zusammen und zeigt beispielhaft, woraus

5). A contemporary photograph of the gas chamber is followed by a display, finally, on mass murder by poison gas (station 6).

Whilst the overview exhibition places the mass murder of prisoners in the context of the history of the Mauthausen/Gusen camp complex as a whole, this exhibition takes a different methodological approach. As in an evidentiary hearing, it takes visitors – as advertised in the exhibition's title – *searching for traces*. Through the exhibits on show, visitors are given the opportunity to participate in the reconstruction of historical events. The search takes in very different forms of evidence, which have often survived as fragments. The perpetrators employed different tactics to keep their murders a secret and to disguise them; shortly before the end of the war they deliberately disposed of killing facilities and written evidence and murdered eyewitnesses. In spite of this, traces remained and witnesses survived. The exhibition *The Crime Scenes of Mauthausen – Searching for Traces* pieces these fragments together into evidence and gives

In jeder Themenstation findet sich ein Leitobjekt, das als Scharnier zwischen der Rekonstruktion der Geschehnisse und der Thematisierung der Nachgeschichte fungiert.
Foto: Tal Adler

Each thematic station has a main object that acts as a hinge between the reconstruction of events and the 'post-history' of the crimes.
Photograph: Tal Adler

das heutige Wissen über Tathergänge resultiert. Damit werden einerseits die Geheimhaltungs- und Verschleierungsstrategien der SS veranschaulicht, andererseits kann auf diese Weise auch den darauf beruhenden revisionistischen Geschichtsleugnungen entgegnet werden.

Die Ausstellung präsentiert Dokumente der SS-Lagerverwaltung ebenso wie heimlich von Häftlingen während der Lagerzeit angefertigte Zeugnisse, dingliche Überreste aus der NS-Zeit, später getätigte Aussagen von Augenzeugen sowie mit Hilfe naturwissenschaftlicher Analysetechniken erhobene Daten oder bei archäologischen Ausgrabungen geborgene Objekte.[7] Im Rahmen der Ausstellung kann die gewissermaßen als forensisch zu bezeichnende Vorgehensweise, aus verschiedenen Quellen Informationen zu gewinnen und diese zueinander in Beziehung zu setzen, nur exemplarisch vorgeführt werden. Trotzdem arbeitet die Ausstellung gezielt damit, den BesucherInnen einzelne Originalquellen, die oft nur schwer zu dechiffrieren sind, nicht nur durch kurze kommentierende Texte, sondern auch über die Kom-

examples of where today's knowledge of how the crimes were committed comes from. On the one hand, this illustrates the strategies of secrecy and concealment employed by the SS, whilst on the other it counters the revisionist denial of history based on these very strategies.

The exhibition presents documents from the SS camp administration but also testimonies produced in secret by prisoners during their time in the camp, material remains dating from the National Socialist era, statements given later by eye-witnesses, as well as data resulting from scientific analytical techniques and objects salvaged during archaeological excavations.[7] Within the scope of the exhibition, this what might be described as somewhat forensic approach of taking information from different sources and linking it together can only be carried out on a few examples. Nevertheless, the aim of the exhibition to make the individual original sources, which are often difficult to decipher, accessible to visitors not only through short explanatory texts but also through combining

Eines der Ziele der Ausstellungskonzeption bestand darin, jene Orte als Tatorte zu zeigen, die oft nicht mit Massentötungen und Massensterben assoziiert werden.
Foto: Tal Adler

One of the aims of the exhibition was to show as crime scenes those locations that are often not associated with mass killings and mass death.
Photograph: Tal Adler

bination mit anderen Quellen zu erschließen. Dies sei am Beispiel der Ausstellungsstation „Alltägliche Gewalt" (Station 1) erläutert: Dort wird ein aus dem Kontext der Lagerverwaltung stammendes Dokument gezeigt, in dem der Tod des italienischen Häftlings Danilo Veronesi im Außenlager Ebensee vermerkt ist.[8] Hinter dem Todesdatum wurde in der entsprechenden Meldung der Todesfälle aus dem Außenlager Ebensee vom 15. Mai 1944[9] als Todesursache „Freitod (Elektrizität)" vermerkt, womit Selbstmord durch Berühren des mit Starkstrom geladenen Lagerzauns vorgetäuscht wurde. Dieses Dokument wird in der Ausstellung zusammen mit einem Auszug aus den heimlich im Lager Ebensee angefertigten Notizen des tschechischen Häftlings Drahomír Bárta präsentiert. Darin beschrieb er, wie Lagerführer Otto Riemer und Blockführer Hans Bühner den Italiener Danilo Veronesi nach einem gescheiterten Fluchtversuch misshandelten und von der Dogge des Lagerführers zu Tode beißen hatten lassen.[10] Bárta, der in der Lagerschreibstube eingesetzt war, hielt zudem fest, dass die SS den Mord als Selbstmord am Lagerzaun verzeichnete. Die Notizen Bártas liefern damit nicht nur ein eindrückliches Beispiel für die exzessive Gewalt von SS-Angehörigen gegenüber Häftlingen, sondern in Kombination mit dem Dokument der Lagerverwaltung auch einen Nachweis für die Methoden der SS, Gewaltakte zu verschleiern. Das Thema der Vertuschung wird auch in den weiteren Stationen der Ausstellung wieder aufgenommen.

Im Zentrum der Themenstationen wird jeweils ein dreidimensionales Originalobjekt präsentiert, etwa der Abluftventilator aus der Gaskammer oder die zu einem Mordinstrument umfunktionierte Injektionsspritze eines KZ-Arztes. Diese zentralen Leitobjekte werden als gegenständliches Indiz für die Delikte im Konzentrationslager Mauthausen ausgestellt. Darüber hinaus fungieren sie in der Mitte der pultartigen Themenstationen aber auch als inhaltliches „Scharnier" zwischen den beiden an sie anschließenden Erzählsträngen: Während auf der einen Seite des Leitobjekts ein historischer Tat-Komplex anhand weitgehend lagerzeitlicher Quellen dargestellt wird, wird auf der anderen Seite einem Aspekt der „Nachgeschichte" dieser Tötungsverbrechen nachgegangen. Bereits durch den Einstieg der Ausstellung über

them with other sources. This can be explained using the topic of 'Everyday Violence' as an example (station 1). Here a document produced in the context of the camp administration is displayed in which the death in the Ebensee subcamp of the Italian prisoner Danilo Veronesi is recorded.[8] Under the date of death, the corresponding report on the deaths in the Ebensee subcamp on 15 May 1944[9] gives 'suicide (electricity)' as the cause of death, thereby fabricating a suicide through contact with the camp's high-voltage electric fence. In the exhibition, this document is presented together with an extract from a diary written in secret in the Ebensee camp by the Czech prisoner Drahomír Bárta. In this he describes how, after a failed escape attempt, the Italian Danilo Veronesi was mistreated by the head of the camp, Otto Riemer, and the block leader Hans Bühner, who allowed him to be mauled to death by the mastiff belonging to the head of camp.[10] Bárta, who was assigned to the camp clerk's office, also noted that the SS had recorded the murder as a suicide at the camp fence. Bárta's diary therefore not only provides a striking example of the excessive violence of members of the SS towards prisoners but, when combined with the camp administration's report, it also provides proof of the methods used by the SS to cover up their acts of violence. The topic of the cover-up is also addressed in other areas of the exhibition.

In the centre of each thematic display, an original, three-dimensional object is presented, for example the extractor fan from the gas chamber or a concentration camp doctor's syringe that has become an instrument of murder. These central objects are exhibited as material evidence of the crimes committed in the Mauthausen concentration camp. Furthermore, positioned in the centre of the desk-like display cases they also function as a thematic 'hinge' between the two narratives they are linked to. Whilst on one side of the object a historical crime-complex is presented on the basis of sources dating primarily from the time of the camp, on the other side one aspect of these murderous crimes' 'post-history' is investigated. Simply making the exhibition's starting point the scene of the crime in its current state and using

den heutigen Zustand der Tatorte und durch den methodischen Zugang der Spurensuche werden Fragen nach dem Umgang mit den historischen Orten und nach den vielfältigen Wegen der Überlieferung von Beweisen sowie deren Zerstörung aufgeworfen. Angesichts der Dimensionen der Verbrechen werden zudem Fragen nach der juristischen Ahndung und nach Erinnerungs- und Verdrängungsstrategien gestellt. Jede Themenstation greift einen der vielfältigen Aspekte der Nachgeschichte auf. So thematisiert die Ausstellungsstation „Hinrichtungen" beispielsweise Gründe für das „Verschwinden" von Tat-Orten sowie die aufwendige Rekonstruktion des Wissens über Orte, die physisch nicht mehr existieren. Der Klapptisch des Galgens aus dem Hinrichtungsraum ist das Leitobjekt dieser Themenstation. Mit ihm wird einerseits ein historisches Objekt, mit dem Exekutionen in Mauthausen durchgeführt wurden, als Beweismittel präsentiert. Andererseits ist der von tschechischen Überlebenden nach der Befreiung in ihre Heimat mitgenommene Klapptisch, die Geschichte seines Verschwindens und Wiederauftauchens, der Anlass, auf die zweite Seite der Themenstation überzuleiten und die Suche nach dinglichen oder baulichen Spuren von Exekutionen mit Hilfe von Zeugenaussagen sowie von Boden- und Bauarchäologie zu thematisieren. Diese Darstellung legt dem Ausstellungspublikum die Frage nach der Authentizität historischer Orte im heutigen Zustand dar und ermöglicht so ein kritisches Bewusstsein für die Begegnung mit diesen vielfach stark veränderten Orten.

Eine siebente Themenstation, die sich von den vorangegangenen sowohl inhaltlich wie gestalterisch unterscheidet, beschließt die Ausstellung. Sie bildet zugleich den Übergang zu den nachfolgenden Räumlichkeiten der ehemaligen Krematorien. Ihr Gegenstand ist der Umgang der Täter mit den Körpern der Toten. Mit der restlosen Beseitigung der Leichen in den Verbrennungsöfen vernichtete die SS zugleich sichtbare Spuren ihres Massenmords.

Gräber als konkrete Orte, um der Toten zu gedenken, gibt es in der Regel keine. In den Jahren nach dem Krieg übernahmen daher vermehrt die Krematorien diese Funktion und entwickelten sich zu zentralen Orten des Gedenkens an die Opfer des Lagers. Davon zeugen

a search for the traces as the methodological approach already raises questions about how historical sites are dealt with and about the manifold ways in which evidence is secured, as well as destroyed. Given the dimensions of the crime, questions about juridical punishment and strategies of commemoration or suppression are also relevant. Each thematic display takes up one of the many aspects of this post-history. For example, the display on 'Executions' looks at examples of why crime scenes 'disappear', as well as at the painstaking reconstruction of knowledge about places that no longer exist physically. The collapsible table for the gallows from the execution room is the central object in this display. On the one hand, the historical object with which executions in Mauthausen were carried out is presented as a piece of evidence. On the other hand, the collapsible table, with its history of disappearance – after liberation it was taken by Czech survivors to their home country – and reappearance provides the link to the other side of the display, which thematises the search for material or structural traces of executions with the help of witness statements, archaeological investigations and building archaeology. This display presents the exhibition public with the question of the authenticity of a historical site in its current state and thus helps to foster a critical awareness when encountering these places that have undergone several large-scale changes.

A seventh thematic display, which is different from what has gone before both in terms of content and design, ends the exhibition. At the same time it forms the bridge to the rooms of the former crematoria that follow. Its subject is how the perpetrators dealt with the bodies of the dead. With the complete and utter disposal of the corpses in the incinerators, the SS also destroyed the visible traces of its mass murder.

Graves as concrete places to commemorate the dead are, as a rule, nonexistent. In the years after the war, the crematoria therefore increasingly took on this function and developed into the central sites for commemorating the victims of

nicht nur die bei den erhaltenen Verbrennungsöfen niedergelegten Grablichter und Trauerkränze sondern auch zahlreiche Gedenktafeln, die Angehörige im ehemaligen Tötungsbereich anbrachten. Diese Tafeln zeigen in der Regel die biographischen Daten der Toten und auch Portraitfotografien. Sie leisten dadurch eine Individualisierung des Gedenkens und lassen jenseits von Denkmälern, die das Gedenken meist in einen nationalen oder gruppenspezifischen Kontext stellen,[11] die sonst nur schwer fassbaren Einzelschicksale sichtbar werden.

the camp. This is seen not only in the candles and wreaths laid by the remaining incinerators, but also in the many memorial plaques mounted by relatives in the former killing area. These plaques usually show the biographical dates of the dead along with a portrait. Through this, memory is individualised and, beyond memorials that tend to place remembrance in national or group-specific contexts,[11] the often elusive fate of the individual becomes visible again.

---

1. Bundesministerium für Inneres (Hg.): mauthausen memorial neu gestalten. Rahmenkonzept für die Neugestaltung der KZ-Gedenkstätte Mauthausen (Wien 2009). Mitglieder der Arbeitsgruppe waren Christian Dürr, Florian Freund, Harald Hutterberger, Yariv Lapid, Ralf Lechner, Stephan Matyus, Bertrand Perz, Barbara Glück, Jörg Skriebeleit, Franz Sonnenberger, Heidemarie Uhl und Robert Vorberg.

2. Der Katalog zu dieser Ausstellung wurde im Dezember 2013 veröffentlicht und enthält u.a. einen Artikel zur Ausstellungskonzeption – vgl. Christian Dürr/Ralf Lechner/Niko Wahl/Johanna Wensch: „Das Konzentrationslager Mauthausen 1938–1945". Zu Konzept und Erarbeitung der Ausstellung, in: Verein für Gedenken und Geschichtsforschung in österreichischen KZ-Gedenkstätten (Hg.): Das Konzentrationslager Mauthausen 1938–1945. Katalog zur Ausstellung in der KZ-Gedenkstätte Mauthausen (Wien 2013), S. 295–302.

3. Zum „dezentralen Ausstellungskonzept" siehe Bundesministerium für Inneres (Hg.): mauthausen memorial neu gestalten, S. 24–42.

4. Es war zu beobachten, dass BesucherInnen mit geringem Zeitbudget beim Personal der KZ-Gedenkstätte oftmals den schnellsten Weg zum ehemaligen Tötungsbereich erfragten. Die Wahrnehmung des ausgeprägten Interesses an diesen Räumlichkeiten wurde durch zwei von der KZ-Gedenkstätte Mauthausen in Auftrag gegebene Studien bestätigt, vgl. Das sozialwissenschaftliche Forschungsbüro: BesucherInnen-Erhebung, Querschnittanalyse. Unveröffentlichtes Manuskript (Wien 2009), S. 9, sowie dass.: BesucherInnen-Erhebung, Längsschnittanalyse. Unveröffentlichtes Manuskript (Wien 2011), S. 13, S. 34 und S. 62.
Eine zusammenfassende Darstellung dieser Studien publizierten Andreas Baumgartner/Isabella Girstmair: „… weil ich das einmal sehen wollte." Die Mauthausen-BesucherInnen-Studie im Zuge der Neugestaltung der KZ-Gedenkstätte, in: Bundesministerium für Inneres (Hg.): KZ-Gedenkstätte Mauthausen | Mauthausen Memorial 2010. Forschung, Dokumentation, Information. Jahrbuch der KZ-Gedenkstätte Mauthausen (Wien 2011), S. 43–53.

5. Hingegen zeigte die Erhebung, dass mit der längeren Besichtigungsdauer eine differenzierte Wahrnehmung der Geschichte des Konzentrationslagers einherging. Vgl. Das sozialwissenschaftliche Forschungsbüro: BesucherInnen-Erhebung, Längsschnittanalyse (Wien 2011), S. 62–64.

---

1. Federal Ministry of the Interior (ed.): Mauthausen Memorial redesign. Framework concept for the redesign of the Mauthausen Memorial (Vienna 2009). The members of the working group were Christian Dürr, Florian Freund, Harald Hutterberger, Yariv Lapid, Ralf Lechner, Stephan Matyus, Bertrand Perz, Barbara Glück, Jörg Skriebeleit, Franz Sonnenberger, Heidemarie Uhl and Robert Vorberg.

2. The catalogue to this exhibition was published in December 2013 and contains, amongst others, an article on the concept behind the exhibition – cf. Christian Dürr/Ralf Lechner/Niko Wahl/Johanna Wensch: 'The Mauthausen Concentration Camp 1938-1945'. On the concept and development of the exhibition, in: Association for the Remembrance and Historical Research in Austrian Concentration Camp Memorials (ed.): The Mauthausen Concentration Camp 1938–1945. Catalogue to the Exhibition at the Mauthausen Memorial. Vienna 2013, p. 295–302.

3. On the 'decentralised exhibition concept' see Federal Ministry of the Interior (ed.): Mauthausen Memorial redesign, p. 24–42.

4. It has been observed that visitors with only a short amount of time at their disposal often asked staff at the memorial complex the quickest way to get to the former killing area. The sense of the marked interest in these rooms was confirmed by two studies commissioned by the Mauthausen Memorial, cf. Das sozialwissenschaftliche Forschungsbüro: BesucherInnen-Erhebung, Querschnittanalyse. Unpublished manuscript (Vienna 2009), p. 9, as well as, Das sozialwissenschaftliche Forschungsbüro: BesucherInnen-Erhebung, Längsschnittanalyse. Unpublished manuscript (Vienna 2011), p. 13, p. 34 and p. 62.
A summary of these studies was published by Andreas Baumgartner/Isabella Girstmair: „… weil ich das einmal sehen wollte." Die Mauthausen-BesucherInnen-Studie im Zuge der Neugestaltung der KZ-Gedenkstätte, in: Bundesministerium für Inneres (ed.): KZ-Gedenkstätte Mauthausen | Mauthausen Memorial 2010. Forschung, Dokumentation, Information. Jahrbuch der KZ-Gedenkstätte Mauthausen (Vienna 2011), p. 43–53.

5. In contrast, the study showed that a longer visit went hand in hand with a more differentiated understanding of the history of the concentration camp. Cf. Das sozialwissenschaftliche Forschungsbüro: BesucherInnen-Erhebung, Längsschnittanalyse. Unpublished manuscript (Vienna 2011), p. 62–64.

6 Siehe dazu den Beitrag von Manuel Schilcher in diesem Band.

7 Begleitend zu den Arbeiten an den neuen Ausstellungen wurden ab 2009 unter der Leitung von Claudia Theune vom Institut für Ur- und Frühgeschichte der Universität Wien archäologische Untersuchen am Gelände der KZ-Gedenkstätte Mauthausen durchgeführt. Vgl.: Claudia Theune: Zeitschichten. Archäologische Untersuchungen in der Gedenkstätte Mauthausen, in: Bundesministerium für Inneres (Hg.): KZ-Gedenkstätte Mauthausen | Mauthausen Memorial 2009. Forschung, Dokumentation, Information. Jahrbuch der KZ-Gedenkstätte Mauthausen (Wien 2010), S. 25–30.

8 Siehe S. 21 in diesem Band.

9 Meldung der Todesfälle im Außenlager Ebensee an das Hauptlager, 15. Mai 1944, Hrvatski povijesni muzej, Zagreb, ur. broj: 3-18-1/13. Im Totenbuch des SS-Standortarztes Mauthausen ist als Todesursache „Freitod durch Elektrozaun" bzw. „Freitod durch Starkstrom" vermerkt – vgl. National Archives and Records Administration (NARA), RG 238, World War II War Crimes Records, International Military Tribunal, Prosecution Exhibit USA 251, Mikrofilmkopie im Archiv der KZ-Gedenkstätte Mauthausen (AMM), Y/46.

10 Drahomír Bárta: Tagebuch aus dem KZ Ebensee. Herausgegeben von Verena Pawlowsky und Florian Freund (Wien 2005), S. 61. Zur Ermordung Veronesis siehe auch: Florian Freund: Arbeitslager Zement. Das Konzentrationslager Ebensee und die Raketenindustrie (Wien 1989), S. 354–356.

11 Die in Form der Denkmäler erfolgte Zuschreibung von Toten zu Nationen sowie zu bestimmten Opfergruppen und der damit einhergehende Ausschluss zahlreicher Opfer aus dem Gedenken, war ein wesentlicher Beweggrund, einen „Raum der Namen" zu realisieren, in dem alle namentlich bekannten Toten frei von Hierarchisierungen repräsentiert werden. Die Publikation eines Gedenkbuches mit den Namen der Toten ist für das Jahr 2015 projektiert. Vgl. Andreas Kranebitter: Die Toten des KZ Mauthausen/Gusen. Gedenkbuch und „Raum der Namen", in: Bundesministerium für Inneres (Hg.): bulletin Mauthausen 01/2013 (Wien 2013), S. 61–65.

6 On this topic see the article by Manuel Schilcher in this volume.

7 Alongside work on the new exhibitions, from 2009 onwards archaeological investigations led by Claudia Theune of the Institute of Prehistory and Early History at the University of Vienna were carried out on the grounds of the Mauthausen Memorial. Cf.: Claudia Theune: Zeitschichten. Archäologische Untersuchungen in der Gedenkstätte Mauthausen, in: Bundesministerium für Inneres (ed.): KZ-Gedenkstätte Mauthausen | Mauthausen Memorial 2009. Forschung, Dokumentation, Information. Jahrbuch der KZ-Gedenkstätte Mauthausen (Vienna 2010), p. 25–30

8 See p. 21 in this volume.

9 Notification of deaths in the Ebensee subcamp sent to the main camp administration, 15 May 1944, Hrvatski Povijesni Muzej, Zagreb, Ur. broj: 3-18-1/13. In the death register of the Mauthausen SS camp doctor the cause of death is noted as 'suicide by electric fence' or 'suicide by high-voltage current' – cf. National Archives and Records Administration (NARA), RG 238, World War II War Crimes Records, International Military Tribunal, Prosecution Exhibit USA 251, Mikrofilmkopie im Archiv der KZ-Gedenkstätte Mauthausen (AMM), Y/46.

10 Drahomír Bárta: Tagebuch aus dem KZ Ebensee. Edited by Verena Pawlowsky and Florian Freund (Vienna 2005), p. 61. On Veronesi's murder, see also: Florian Freund: Arbeitslager Zement. Das Konzentrationslager Ebensee und die Rakentenindustrie (Vienna 1989), p. 354–356.

11 The allocation of the dead to nations or particular victim groups through memorials, and the exclusion of many victims that went with this, was one of the deciding factors in the creation of the 'Room of Names', in which all the known names of the dead are listed in a non-hierarchical manner. The publication of a memorial book with the names of the dead is planned for 2015. Cf. Andreas Kranebitter: The Dead of the Mauthausen/Gusen Concentration Camp. Memorial Book and 'Room of Names', in: Federal Ministry of the Interior (ed.): bulletin Mauthausen 01/2013 (Vienna 2013), p. 61–65.

Paul Mitchell

Building Archaeology at the Mauthausen Memorial

Building archaeology – also often called buildings research – is the scientific and analytical survey of a historical building with the aim of determining the age of its individual parts and thus reconstructing its construction history. Building archaeology's findings are important for the building industry, for conservation staff and for architects seeking to maintain and renovate a building as sensitively as possible – i.e. without, as a rule, destroying features of historical significance. Furthermore, the data that building archaeology delivers can expand the current state of research, or even lead to its revision.

A building archaeology team made up of specialists from different disciplines such as archaeology, history, art history and architecture will research as many written and pictorial sources as possible

Tunnel between the infirmary building and camp prison. Pencil markings made by the men working on the building site, around 1941.

Photograph: Stephan Matyus

lichst alle Schrift- und Bildquellen zu einem Gebäude – wobei historische Pläne und Bauzeichnungen besonders wertvoll sind – und analysiert diese zusammen mit aktuellen Baubestandsplänen. Bauarchäologie bedeutet, sich exakt mit dem Baubestand auseinanderzusetzen – also unter anderem mit der Bautechnik und den verwendeten Baustoffen, deren Einsatz den technischen Entwicklungen gemäß ständigen Veränderungen unterliegt. Die Bauarchäologie arbeitet auch eng mit der „Bodenarchäologie" zusammen, die in den vergangenen Jahren bereits an vielen Stellen in der KZ-Gedenkstätte Mauthausen zum Einsatz kam.[1]

Die Arbeit des Bauarchäologen beginnt mit der genauen Beobachtung und Protokollierung von Gebäuden und ihren Räumen. Oft ist ältere Bausubstanz sogar frei sichtbar, aber nie dokumentiert worden. Dort, wo einst beispielsweise ein Fenster vorhanden war, kann dies noch durch Fugen und Unterschiede im Mauermörtel erkennbar sein. Zwei Mauern, die sich etwa durch die Verwendung verschiedener Ziegel oder den Versatz der verwendeten Steine unterscheiden, sind wahrscheinlich in zwei verschiedenen baulichen Phasen entstanden. Ein historisches Gebäude ist in der Regel nicht in einem Zuge entstanden, sondern weist viele Umbauphasen und Sanierungskampagnen auf. Alte Mauern können abgebrochen worden und neue Zwischenwände entstanden, Bodenniveaus und Raumgestaltungen verändert worden sein.

BauarchäologInnen müssen die Bauabfolge, d.h. die „Bauphasen" nachvollziehen. Manchmal werden zu diesem Zweck kleine „Sondagen" angelegt, um die Oberflächenaufträge auf einer Mauer, wie Putz, Anstriche oder Tapeten, Schicht für Schicht freizulegen und zu analysieren. Dabei können zum Beispiel Risse, Fugen, verschiedene Farbfassungen oder die älteste Oberfläche festgestellt werden.

Alle Bauteile werden detailliert beschrieben. Dabei wird bestimmt, an welchen Stellen welche Baustoffe verwendet worden sind. Hilfreich ist dabei die seit rund zweihundert Jahren geläufige Praxis, Ziegel und Fliesen, aber auch metallene Teile mit Firmennamen oder Seriennummern zu kennzeichnen. Seit einigen Jahren stehen auch naturwissenschaftliche

about a building – historic plans and architectural drawings are of particular value here – and analyse them alongside current plans of the existing building stock. Building archaeology means conducting a rigorous analysis of the building stock – including, amongst other things, the construction methods and building materials used, since these are subject to constant change as technologies develop. Building archaeology also works together closely with 'historical archaeology', which has already been employed at several sites around the Mauthausen Memorial in recent years.[1]

The work of a building archaeologist begins with a thorough examination and precise record of the buildings and their rooms. Often the older structures are still clearly visible but have never been documented. The place where, for example, there was once a window can still be identified from the joints and differences in mortar. Two walls which differ in the bricks used, for instance, or where the stonework does not match up were probably erected in two different periods of construction. As a rule, historic buildings were not built in one go, but rather exhibit several phases of modification and restoration campaigns. Old walls might have been knocked down and new partition walls erected, or floor levels changed and interior decoration altered.

Building archaeologists have to be able to understand the building sequence, i.e. the 'construction phases' or the order in which construction took place. For this purpose, small 'sondages' or test patches are sometimes used in order to reveal and then analyse, layer by layer, wall coverings such as plaster, paint or wallpaper. This makes it possible to identify things like cracks, joints, different paint colours or determine the oldest layer.

All parts of the building are described in detail. As part of this process, it is necessary to determine which building materials were used where. This is helped by the common practice, started around two hundred years ago, of marking bricks and tiles, but also metal parts, with company marks or serial numbers. Scientific research methods such as

Untersuchungsmethoden wie die „Dendrochronologie" zur Verfügung, bei der mittels vergleichender Analyse von Baumringen das Fälljahr eines Baumes bestimmt werden kann und Hölzer damit allgemein datiert werden können. Geophysikalische Methoden wie das „Georadar" ermöglichen Einblicke in den inneren Aufbau einer Mauer.

Alle verwendeten bauarchäologischen Methoden werden schließlich in einem Bericht zusammengefasst, der die Baugeschichte eines Gebäudes samt Fotodokumentation und verschiedenen Plänen dokumentiert. Besondere Bedeutung kommt dabei dem – zumeist im Grundriss gezeichneten – Baualters- oder Bauphasenplan zu, in dem das Alter jedes Bauteils kartiert ist.

Bauarchäologie in der KZ-Gedenkstätte

Seit 2009 sind Bauarchäologen in der KZ-Gedenkstätte Mauthausen aktiv.[2] Es mag überraschen, dass SpezialistInnen, die normalerweise in mittelalterlichen Häusern oder Renaissanceschlössern arbeiten, in einem Baukomplex zu tun haben, der weniger als hundert Jahre alt ist. Dafür gibt es zwei Gründe: Erstens ist ein Großteil der SS-Unterlagen über den Ausbau des Lagers zerstört worden oder verloren gegangen. Obwohl die Baugeschichte des Lagers in groben Zügen bekannt ist, gibt es noch viele offene Fragen und – wie sich gezeigt hat – noch sehr viel herauszufinden. In den weitläufigen Kellern, Bunkern und Tunneln der Gedenkstätte liegt buchstäblich noch vieles im Dunkeln. Zweitens machen Vergänglichkeit und Veränderungen auch nicht vor der KZ-Gedenkstätte halt. Daher mussten immer wieder Bauten saniert oder für den laufenden Betrieb adaptiert werden. Seit der Befreiung vom Nationalsozialismus hat es drei große Sanierungsphasen gegeben (1948/1949, 1968/1969 und seit 2002), die zur „Verunklärung" der historischen Zustände beigetragen haben und leider oft nicht ausreichend dokumentiert worden sind. So ist nicht immer sofort ersichtlich, ob eine Zwischenwand oder Farbschicht eine Erneuerung der Nachkriegszeit darstellt oder noch während der NS-Herrschaft entstanden ist.

Die bauarchäologischen Untersuchungen haben zahlreiche neue Erkenntnisse und interessante De-

'dendochronology' have also been available for a number of years. This uses the comparative analysis of tree rings to establish the year a tree was felled and thus date lumber. Geo-physical methods such as 'geo-radar' can provide information about the internal structure of a wall.

Finally, all the building archaeological approaches used are brought together in a report that documents the building's construction history complete with photographic documentation and various plans. Special significance is given to the building age or building phase plan – usually given as part of the floor plan – which maps the age of each part of the building.

Building archaeology at the concentration camp memorial site

Building archaeologists have been active at the Mauthausen Memorial since 2009.[2] It might come as a surprise that specialists who normally work in medieval houses or renaissance palaces are concerned with a building complex that is not yet a hundred years old. There are two reasons for this: Firstly the majority of the SS documents on the expansion of the camp were destroyed or have been lost. Although it is possible to sketch a rough outline of the camp's construction history, many questions remain open and – as has been shown – new discoveries are still being made. In the extensive cellars, bunkers and tunnels of the memorial site, there is much that we are literally still in the dark about. Secondly, memorial sites are not immune from time and change. Hence the buildings frequently had to undergo renovation or be adapted for their then current uses. Since liberation from National Socialism, there have been three major periods of renovation (1948/1949, 1968/1969 and post-2002) which have contributed to the 'de-clarification' of the historic situation and which, unfortunately, were often inadequately documented. It is therefore not always immediately obvious whether a partition wall or a coat of paint represents a post-war renovation or dates from the period of National Socialist rule.

The building archaeological investigations have brought numerous new findings and interesting

tails ans Licht gebracht. Fast jedes Gebäude wurde noch zur NS-Zeit erweitert oder adaptiert, um mit der Vergrößerung des gesamten Lagers oder neuen Forderungen der SS Schritt zu halten. Es konnte zum Beispiel gezeigt werden, dass das während des Winters von 1940/1941 begonnene sogenannte „Reviergebäude", in dem heute das Museum untergebracht ist, ursprünglich genau die Länge der anderen Funktionsgebäude am Appellplatz haben sollte (52,5 Meter). Eine Planänderung um 1941/1942 führte jedoch zur Verlängerung des Gebäudes auf die heutigen 115 Meter.[3]

An einigen Stellen ist es gelungen, unmittelbare Spuren zu finden, die von den Männern – großteils Häftlinge – stammen, die das Lager bauten. Bleistiftkritzeleien, mit denen Poliere ihren „Mitarbeitern" den Arbeitsablauf erklärten, oder Vermessungszeichen, an die sich die Betonbauer und Fliesenleger halten sollten. Dem versierten Blick des Bauarchäologen sind auch nicht die Standortspuren von Geräten entgangen, die nach dem Krieg abgebaut und wohl zur Weiterverwendung an andere Orte transferiert wurden. Dazu gehören Abdrücke sowohl der Kochkessel, der Dampfkessel im Boden des Heizraumes sowie Spuren von Waschmaschinen in der Mitte des Bodens der ehemaligen Wäscherei.

Das „Dritte Reich" war nicht nur ein politischmilitärisches Gebilde, sondern auch ein großer wirtschaftlicher Binnenraum. Das zeigt sich an den verwendeten Baustoffen, die aus dem ganzen Imperium stammten. So kamen Wandfliesen aus Wien – mit der Herkunftsangabe auf Englisch „MADE IN GERMANY" –, feuerfeste Ziegel aus der Steiermark, aber auch Bodenfliesen aus Böhmen und Dachziegel aus Sachsen und Schlesien. Weiters kamen die Heizungsrohre aus Köln, viele Fensterbeschläge aus dem Ruhrgebiet, sogenannte Fettabscheider der Küchenbaracke aus Hessen – und die Krematorienöfen aus Erfurt und Berlin.

Für die Lager-SS bestand kein Grund, ihren „Arbeitsplatz" in düsteren oder nüchternen Farben zu halten. Nichtsdestotrotz überrascht es, dass Innenwände im ganzen Lager bunte Farben trugen, die manchmal in Streifen und geometrischen Mustern angeordnet

details to light. During the National Socialist era itself nearly every building was expanded or adapted to keep up with the enlargement of the camp as a whole or meet the needs of the SS. It could be shown, for example, that the so-called infirmary building, which was begun during the winter of 1940/1941 and today houses the museum, was originally planned with the same length as the other functional buildings on the roll call area (52.5m). However, a change to the plans around 1941/1942 led to the extension of the building to its current 115m.[3]

In some places it has been possible to find direct traces left by the men – mainly prisoners – who built the camp; pencil scribblings made by the foremen to explain the work to their 'staff', or measurement marks for the concrete workers and tile layers. The practised eye of the building archaeologist also sees the marks left by pieces of equipment that were removed after the war and probably taken elsewhere for further use. This includes the impressions left by the cauldrons in the kitchen and the boilers in the heating room, as well as the marks in the middle of the floor in the former laundry left by the washing machines.

The 'Third Reich' was not only a political and military entity but also a large internal market. This can be seen from the building materials used, which came from all over the Reich. There were wall tiles from Vienna – with the country of origin on the back in English: 'MADE IN GERMANY' – fireproof bricks from Styria, as well as floor tiles from Bohemia and roof tiles from Saxony and Silesia. In addition, the heating pipes came from Cologne, many of the window fittings from the Ruhr region, the so-called grease traps in the kitchen barracks from Hessen – and the crematorium ovens from Erfurt and Berlin.

For the SS there was no reason to decorate their 'place of work' in gloomy or sober colours. Nonetheless it comes as a surprise that throughout the camp, the interior walls were painted in bright colours, sometimes with stripes or geometric patterns. This applies not only to rooms in the brothel (Block 1), but also to the SS office in the

Negativabdruck einer Wandfliese in der Gaskammer mit dem Schriftzug „VIENNA MADE IN GERMANY".
Foto: Stephan Matyus

Negative imprint left by a wall tile in the gas chamber with the words 'VIENNA MADE IN GERMANY'.
Photograph: Stephan Matyus

waren. Das gilt nicht nur für die Bordellzimmer (Block 1), sondern auch für das SS-Dienstzimmer im Krematorium, dessen Wände in einer hellblauen Farbe angestrichen wurden, sowie für das Wachzimmer des Arrestgebäudes, in dem ein kitschig wirkendes Blumenmuster vorgefunden wurde. Während der Nachkriegszeit hatte man offenbar kein Verständnis für solche Farbschemen: Fast überall wurden sie mit weißen, gelben oder graugrünen Deckschichten übertüncht. Abgesehen vom Abbau von Geräten und Rohrleitungen wurden die heute noch erhaltenen Funktionsgebäude am Appellplatz im Zuge der Einrichtung der Gedenkstätte 1948/1949 meist rücksichtsvoll saniert. Fenster und Türen wurden damals mit ursprünglichen Beschlägen restauriert, die von abgebrochenen Lagerbauten stammten, so dass man heute nicht mehr entscheiden kann, ob sie aus der NS-Zeit oder von der Sanierung 1948 stammen. Umso umfangreicher waren 1968 die Eingriffe in das Häftlings-Reviergebäude, das heute das Museum beherbergt.

crematorium, whose walls were painted in a light blue colour, as well as to the guard room in the detention building, where a kitschy floral pattern was found. In the post-war period there was clearly little appreciation for such colour schemes: nearly all the walls were painted over with a top coat of white, yellow or grey-green. With the exception of the removal of equipment and pipes, the functional buildings that stand on the roll call area today were, for the most part, sensitively renovated when the memorial was created in 1948/1949. Windows and doors were restored using original fittings that had been taken from torn-down parts of the camp, making it impossible to know today whether they date from the National Socialist era or from the renovations in 1948. The alterations made in 1968 to the prisoners' infirmary building, which now houses the museum, were all the more comprehensive.

Das ehemalige Reviergebäude

Nachdem das Reviergebäude 2009 vom Bauforschungsteam untersucht worden war, wurde auch die Sanierung des Gebäudes 2010/2011 durch die Bauarchäologie betreut. Jeder bauliche Eingriff wurde im Voraus mit dem Bundesdenkmalamt Österreich und der Bauarchäologie abgesprochen, um den Charakter des Gebäudes möglichst authentisch zu bewahren und daher die notwendigen Reparaturen und Ergänzungen gering zu halten. Die Baustelle wurde regelmäßig aufgesucht und die laufend zum Vorschein kommenden Überreste dokumentiert. Wie auch im Arrestgebäude und in der Kommandantur, erfolgte die Erschließung des Erdgeschosses des Reviers durch einen zentralen Gang, von dem Räume beiderseits abgingen. An der Seite zur Lagermauer lagen die Krankenräume, zum Platz hin die übrigen Räume wie Kanzlei, Operationssaal, Wachzimmer, Sanitär- und Abstellräume. Im Untergeschoss gab es weitere Krankenräume, ein Laboratorium und unweit der Gaskammer eine große, erst 1945 fertiggestellte Krematoriumsanlage. Als man 1968 das Museum einrichtete, wurden viele Zwischenwände entfernt, um ausreichend Platz für die Ausstellung zu schaffen. Gleichzeitig wurden auch die bis dahin noch teilweise erhaltenen bunten Farbschichten an den Wänden weiß übertüncht.

Während der jüngsten Sanierung von 2010/2011 sind die Abdrücke und die letzten Reste der 1968 ausgerissenen Wände im Boden und in den Wandflächen entdeckt worden. Der einstige Verlauf dieser Wände wurde nun überall im Boden und an den Wänden nachgezogen, um die ehemalige Raumaufteilung sichtbar zu machen. Auch das NS-zeitliche Farbschema wurde wieder entdeckt und in einem in seinen ursprünglichen Dimensionen erhaltenen Krankenraum sogar vollständig freigelegt. Interessant waren an mehreren Stellen auch die Schuhabdrücke, die die auf der Baustelle arbeitenden Häftlinge vermutlich im Jahr 1941 im noch feuchten Beton hinterlassen haben. Diese sind ebenfalls an einer Stelle sichtbar gelassen worden.

The former infirmary building

Having surveyed the infirmary building in 2009, building archaeologists also monitored the renovations to it in 2010/2011. Every structural intervention was discussed beforehand with the Austrian Federal Monuments Office and the building archaeology team in order to retain as much as possible of the authentic character of the building. Necessary repairs and additions were therefore kept to a minimum. The site was visited regularly and the new findings that were continually coming to light were documented. As in the detention and camp administration buildings, the ground floor of the infirmary was structured around a central corridor, with rooms leading off it to either side. The sickrooms were on the side by the camp wall, while rooms such as the office, operating room, guard room, washrooms and storage rooms were on the side facing the roll call area. There were more sickrooms and a laboratory in the basement, as well as a large crematorium installation near the gas chamber that was only completed in 1945. When the museum was set up in 1968, many of the internal partition walls were removed to create space for the exhibition. At the same time, any walls which still had coloured paint on them were painted over in white.

During the most recent renovations in 2010/2011, the impressions and remains of the walls ripped out in 1968 were discovered in the floors and walls. The positions of these walls have now been traced back onto the walls and floors in order to make the former layout visible again. The National Socialist era colour scheme was also rediscovered and has been exposed in full in one of the sickrooms that had survived in its original dimensions. Another interesting finding were the footprints, found in several places, that were left in the wet concrete by the prisoners working on the building site, presumably in 1941. As with the colour scheme, these have also been left on show in one area.

Der ehemalige Tötungsbereich – die wichtigsten Spuren

Das Bauforschungsteam hat sich auch mit den am meisten belasteten Stellen der Gedenkstätte auseinandergesetzt. So konnte an Ort und Stelle nachvollzogen werden, dass die Räumlichkeiten der Tötungsmaschinerie (Bereich der Gaskammer und der Krematorien) viermal erweitert wurden, um die Eskalation der Vernichtung zu ermöglichen.

Nach der Einrichtung eines Krematoriums im Kellergeschoss des Arrestgebäudes („Bunker") im Jahr 1940 wurde im Keller des Reviergebäudes mit dem Bau eines zweiten Krematoriums begonnen.[4] Noch vor dessen Fertigstellung wurde der sogenannte „Sonderbau" – Gaskammer und Exekutionsstätte – zwischen Arrest und Revier gebaut.

Vom Raum der „Tatortausstellung" betritt man das zuletzt gebaute Krematorium (1) mit dem Doppelofen der Firma Topf („Krematorium 3"), deren Firmenmarke an mehreren Stellen sichtbar angebracht und erst 1945 in Betrieb genommen wurde. Der Ofen und die Fliesen des Bodens sind im Originalzustand erhalten. An einer Seite des Ofens ist noch heute ein Rohr zu sehen, durch das ein Gebläse Luft zur Entfachung der Flammen blies. Vom Ofen führte unter dem Boden ein mit dunklen Klinkersteinen abgedeckter Rauchkanal zum Schornstein. Hinter dem Krematorium befindet sich ein Zwischenraum (2), von dem links Toiletten (3/4) und ein Waschraum (5) des Krematoriumskommandos abgehen. Auf der rechten Seite ist an einer Fensterlaibung ein schräger Abdruck erkennbar, der möglicherweise von einer Transportrutsche stammte, mit der vermutlich Koks oder gar Leichen „geliefert" wurden. Am Ende eines langen Gangs (6) ist eine Türöffnung, die 1941/1942 verschlossen wurde, um an dieser Stelle die Gaskammer einzubauen.

Der heute als „Raum der Namen" genutzte Raum (7) wurde von der SS als zweite Leichenhalle geplant, jedoch nie fertig gestellt. Sie blieb unverfließt und ohne befestigten Boden. Ihre geplante Funktion ist an ihrer Fensterlosigkeit und an Standortsvorkehrungen für das Aufstellen eines Kühlgeräts ablesbar.

The former killing area – the most important traces

The buildings research team also had to deal with the most sensitive area of the memorial site. It could be shown in situ that the killing facilities (the area of the gas chamber and crematoria) had been expanded four times in order to make the escalation of extermination possible.

Following the installation of the crematorium in the basement of the detention building ('Bunker') in 1940, construction then began on a second crematorium in the basement of the infirmary building.[4] Even before its completion, the so-called *Sonderbau* (special building), comprising gas chamber and execution room, had been built between the camp prison and the infirmary.

The first room on entering from the *Crime Scenes* exhibition is the final crematorium to be built (1), which contains a double oven manufactured by the firm Topf ('Crematorium 3'); the company's trademark is still visible in several places on the oven, which only came into use in 1945. The oven and the floor tiles have been preserved in their original form. On one side of the oven a pipe can still be seen through which air was blown in to fan the flames. From the oven a smoke duct covered with dark clinker bricks led under the floor to the chimney. Behind the crematorium there is a space (2) leading to toilets on the left (3/4) and a washroom on the right (5), which were used by the crematorium work detachment. On the right-hand side, a sloping indentation can be seen in the inner part of a window frame that was possibly made by a chute, via which coke, presumably, or even corpses would have been 'delivered'. At the end of a long passageway (6) there is a doorway that was closed up in 1941/1942 in order to create the gas chamber in that area.

The room used today as the 'Room of Names' (7) was planned by the SS as a second mortuary but was never finished. It was never tiled and remained without fixed flooring. Its intended function can be ascertained from the absence of windows and in the provisions made for the installation of a cooling

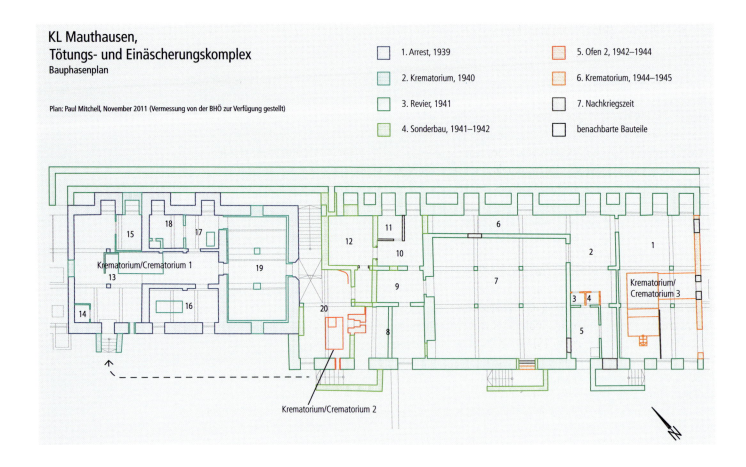

Bauphasenplan des ehemaligen Tötungsbereiches im KZ Mauthausen. Die farbigen Unterschiede weisen auf die unterschiedliche Entstehungszeit der jeweiligen Bereiche hin.
Grafik: Paul Mitchell

Building phase plan of the former killing area of the Mauthausen concentration camp. The different colours denote the different construction periods of each area.
Graphics: Paul Mitchell

In der Mauer links ist um 1942 eine Türöffnung geschaffen worden, damit der Keller zwischendurch als Lager verwendet werden konnte, die 1944 wieder verschlossen wurde, als das neue Krematorium gebaut wurde.

Hinter dem „Raum der Namen" betritt man den Gaskammerbereich. Den ersten der kleinteiligen Räume (8) mussten die Opfer vom Arresthof aus betreten, um sich auszukleiden. Daran schließt der Vorraum der Gaskammer an (9/10), von dem aus je eine Tür zur „Gaszelle" (11) und in die Gaskammer (12) führte. An der Wand neben der Gaskammertür wurde nach einer Vergasung mit einem Hebel der Lüftungsdeckel geöffnet, der heute noch zu sehen ist, und nach der Entfernung der Leichen Duschbrausen eingeschaltet – um den Raum zu reinigen.

Vom „Bunkerhof" aus gesehen befindet sich vor dem älteren Krematorium aus dem Jahr 1940 ein

device. In around 1942 a doorway was created in the left-hand wall so that the cellar could be used as a storeroom for a while. This was closed up again in 1944 when the new crematorium was built.

The area containing the gas chamber is located behind the 'Room of Names'. Victims entered the first of the small, compartmentalised rooms (8) from the camp prison courtyard and were made to undress there. This adjoined the anteroom to the gas chamber (9/10), from which doors led to the 'gas cell' (11) and the gas chamber (12). A lever mounted on the wall next to the door to the gas chamber was pulled after a gassing to open the extractor fan cover, which can still be seen today, and to turn on the showers – in order to clean out the room after the corpses had been removed.

Coming from the 'Bunkerhof' ('camp prison courtyard'), and before reaching the older

Aufenthaltsbereich (13) für die dort beschäftigten Häftlinge, für die ein WC (14) und ein Waschraum mit Fliesenboden (15) eingebaut wurden. An der Wand sind vier Haken erhalten, an denen das Werkzeug für die Bedienung der Ofenkammer hing, sowie Halterung und Schacht eines Ventilators. Der von der Firma Kori in Berlin hergestellte Krematoriumsofen („Krematorium 1") ist aus Ziegeln gemauert, wobei dieses Mauerwerk zusätzlich durch entsprechende Bemalung betont wurde. Obwohl diese Bemalung nach der Befreiung aufgefrischt wurde, ist der NS-zeitliche Anstrich darunter zum Teil noch sichtbar. Hinter dem Ofen liegt gegenüber des Sezierraums (16) ein kleiner Raum (17), in dem das Betonfundament für ein Aggregat erhalten ist, das ein Kühlgerät in der Leichenhalle angetrieben hat. Von dort geht das ursprünglich hellblau gestrichene Dienstzimmer des verantwortlichen SS-Kommandoführers Martin Roth ab (18). Der nächste Raum (19) ist die Leichenhalle. Viele der Wandfliesen weisen „Abplatzungen" auf, die auf große Temperaturschwankungen zurückzuführen sind. Das bereits erwähnte Kühlgerät ist noch erhalten und befindet sich in einer Ecke des Raums.

Die Exekutionsstätte (20) ist heute nur zum Teil begehbar. Hier befand sich der Galgen. In diesem Raum sind lediglich Betonfundamente des heute nicht mehr vorhandenen, ölgefeuerten Krematoriumsofens („Krematorium 2") und neben dem Eingang zur Gaskammer der vier Zentimeter breite, halbkreisförmige Abdruck des „Kugelfangs" erhalten, vor dem die Opfer vor ihrer Exekution stehen mussten. Da nur wenige Spuren erhalten sind, wurde der Zugang für BesucherInnen eingeschränkt, um die bauliche Substanz zu schonen.

Kurz vor der Befreiung wurden der Kugelfang und andere Teile der Tötungsmaschinerie auf Befehl der SS abgebaut, um ihre Spuren zu verwischen. Dazu gehört der Apparat, mit dem das Giftgas in die Gaskammer eingeleitet wurde und der in der „Gaszelle" stand, einem kleinen Raum neben der Gaskammer. Die Wände dieser Gaszelle wurden ebenfalls entfernt, um 1948 aber an derselben Stelle wieder aufgebaut – allerdings schmaler, wie am Boden zu erkennen ist. Die Stelle, an der der sogenannte Gaseinfüllapparat montiert war,

crematorium that dates from 1940, there is a room (13) that was used by the prisoners working there for whom a toilet (14) and a washroom with tiled floor (15) were installed. Four hooks for hanging up the instruments used in operating the ovens are still on the wall, as are the mountings and hole for an extractor fan. The crematorium oven made by the firm Kori in Berlin ('Crematorium 1') is a brick construction, with red and white paint imitating the brickwork underneath. Although this paintwork was reapplied after liberation, in places the National Socialist era paint is still visible underneath. Behind the oven and opposite the autopsy room (16) is a small room (17) in which the concrete foundations can still be seen for the device used to power a cooling unit in the mortuary. Off this room is the office of the head of the SS crematorium unit Martin Roth (18), which was originally painted a light blue colour. The next room (19) is the mortuary. Many of the wall tiles display signs of cracking or 'spalling', which can be attributed to large changes in temperature. The above-mentioned cooling device has survived and is located in a corner of the room.

The execution room (20) is only partially accessible today. This is where the gallows were located. All that remains in this room are the concrete foundations of the now non-existent oil-fired crematorium oven ('Crematorium 2') and, next to the entrance to the gas chamber, the semicircular mark, four centimetres wide, left by the 'bullet trap'; prisoners were executed standing in front of this. Since only these few traces have survived, access to visitors has been limited in order to preserve the physical remains.

Shortly before the liberation the SS ordered the dismantling of the bullet trap and other parts of the killing facilities in order to cover their tracks. This also included the apparatus used to feed poison gas into the gas chamber, which stood in a small room next to the gas chamber known as the 'gas cell'. The walls of this 'gas cell' were also removed but were rebuilt in the same position in around 1948 – albeit narrower, as an examination of the floor revealed. The place where the gas filling

Deckel der Entlüftungsanlage in der Gaskammer. .
Foto: Paul Mitchell

Cover of the extractor fan in the gas chamber.
Photograph: Paul Mitchell

fällt heute an der Wand zur Gaskammer in der Ecke der Gaszelle neben dem Fenster durch weiße Wandfliesen auf. Wie gezeigt werden konnte, ließ die SS den Apparat abbauen, das Loch verputzen und mit neun Fliesen schließen. Nach der Befreiung wurde dieses Loch zunächst wieder aufgemacht, später jedoch – nachdem die Umgebung inzwischen weiter beschädigt war – mit sechzehn Fliesen erneut geschlossen. Die mutmaßliche Lage des Gasrohrs konnte mittels Georadar bestätigt werden. In der Gaskammer selbst stammen die leicht gelblichen, eher rissigen Wandfliesen aus der NS-Zeit und die weißen Fliesen aus einer nachkriegszeitlichen Sanierung. In der Ecke zur Gaszelle jedoch zeigen Fehlstellen und gelbe Fliesen – eingesetzt im April 1945 – jene Stelle an, wo das Gasrohr durch die Mauer geführt wurde. An zwei ähnlichen Stellen daneben wurde das Rohr zusätzlich verankert.

Nach jeder Vergasung musste die Gaskammer entlüftet werden. Der Deckel der Lüftung ist an der Decke neben der Tür zur Exekutionsstätte zu sehen. Lange Zeit war der weitere Verlauf der Lüftung unklar. Durch eine Ausgrabung der Universität

apparatus was mounted is conspicuous today for its white wall tiles. As could be shown, the SS had the apparatus removed and the hole plastered over and covered with nine tiles. After liberation this hole was initially opened up again, later however – the surrounding area had suffered further deterioration in the meantime – it was closed again with sixteen tiles. The assumed location of the gas pipe was confirmed using geo-radar. In the gas chamber itself, the slightly yellowed, somewhat cracked wall tiles date from the National Socialist era and the white tiles from a post-war renovation. In the corner adjoining the gas cell however, gaps and yellow tiles – put up in April 1945 – point to the place where the gas pipe went through the wall. Two similar places show where the pipe was additionally anchored.

After every gassing the gas chamber had to be ventilated. The cover of the extractor fan can be seen in the ceiling next to the door to the execution room. For a long time it was unclear how the ventilation worked after that. However, during

Wien unter der Leitung von Claudia Theune wurde im Jahr 2011 allerdings das Dach der Tötungsstätte freigelegt. Oberhalb des Deckels wurde die Halterung gefunden, in der ein Sauger zur Entfernung des Gases und das an ihn angeschlossene, mehrere Meter lange Entlüftungsrohr fixiert waren. In wenigen Metern Entfernung liegt die Stelle, an dem das „Krematorium 2" entlüftet wurde. Nachdem das erste Entlüftungsrohr des Ofens nicht adäquat funktionierte, musste – wie festgestellt wurde – die erste Öffnung geschlossen und daneben der jetzige Schornstein errichtet werden. Beide freigelegte Stellen sind jetzt sichtbar.

Bauarchäologische Analyse und Dokumentation stellen nicht nur einen wichtigen Beitrag zu einer möglichst genauen Rekonstruktion der historischen Ereignisse dar, sondern liefern auch wesentliche Informationen in Bezug auf die Baugeschichte des jeweiligen historischen Bauwerks. Im Fall der KZ-Gedenkstätte Mauthausen werden mit diesen Ergebnissen Kenntnislücken gefüllt, die sowohl für die historische Forschung relevant sind, als auch dazu dienen, das allgemeine Wissen über das System der Konzentrationslager zu vertiefen. Die Bauarchäologie leistet außerdem einen entscheidenden Beitrag zur Denkmalpflege: Zwar kann der langsame Verfall eines Tatorts letztlich nicht aufgehalten werden – auch durch jede Sanierung wird der Ort zwangsweise (wenn auch nur minimal) verändert – aber eine sorgsame bauarchäologische Untersuchung auch der kleinsten Spuren führt dazu, dass kaum etwas übersehen wird und somit die sichtbaren Überreste des NS-Terrors noch so lange wie möglich besichtigt werden können.

excavations carried out in 2011 by the University of Vienna under the supervision of Claudia Theune, the roof of the killing area was exposed. Above where the extractor fan cover is located, a mounting was found to which the extractor fan itself and the ventilation pipe this was attached to – measuring several metres – would have been fixed. The ventilation point for 'Crematorium 2' was located a few metres away. When the oven's first ventilation pipe failed to function properly, the first opening – as has been found – had to be closed and the current chimney built next to it. Both uncovered sections are now visible.

Building archaeological analyses and documentation represent not only a significant contribution to as exact a reconstruction as possible of historical events, they also provide crucial information regarding the construction history of the historical structure in question. In the case of the Mauthausen Memorial, these results fill some of the gaps in our knowledge, proving relevant for historical research as well as contributing to and deepening general knowledge about the concentration camp system. Furthermore, building archaeology makes a valuable contribution to the preservation of historical monuments: whilst the slow deterioration of a crime scene cannot ultimately be prevented – every renovation will necessarily (albeit minimally) alter the site – a building archaeological investigation attentive to even the smallest of traces will mean that virtually nothing is overlooked and thus that the traces of National Socialist terror will remain visible for as long as possible.

1 Bodenarchäologische Untersuchungen und geo-magnetische Prospektionen werden in der KZ-Gedenkstätte seit 2009 durchgeführt, so unter anderem im Bereich des ehemaligen Sanitätslagers, des „Bunkerhofs" und des so genannten Zeltlagers des KZ Mauthausen. Vgl. dazu z.B. Claudia Theune: Zeitschichten. Archäologische Untersuchungen in der Gedenkstätte Mauthausen, in: Bundesministerium für Inneres (Hg.): KZ-Gedenkstätte Mauthausen | Mauthausen Memorial 2009. Forschung, Dokumentation, Information. Jahrbuch der KZ-Gedenkstätte Mauthausen (Wien 2010), S. 25–30 sowie Paul Mitchell: Bauarchäologie in der KZ-Gedenkstätte Mauthausen, in: Bundesministerium für Inneres (Hg.): bulletin Mauthausen 01/2013 (Wien 2013), S. 47–50. Zu den in der KZ-Gedenkstätte Gusen durchgeführten diesbezüglichen Maßnahmen vgl. Roman Ilg/Paul Mitchell: Memorial Gusen. Die bauhistorische und bodenarchäologische Untersuchung des Krematoriumsofens im Vorfeld seiner Restaurierung, in: Bundesministerium für Inneres (Hg.): KZ-Gedenkstätte Mauthausen | Mauthausen Memorial 2013. Forschung, Dokumentation, Information. Jahrbuch der KZ-Gedenkstätte Mauthausen (Wien 2014), S. 59–70.

2 Das Bauforschungskernteam in der Gedenkstätte besteht aus vier Mitarbeitern: Der Verfasser (Paul Mitchell) ist für die Untersuchung und Dokumentation des Baubestandes vor Ort zuständig. Er bereitet auch die Baualterspläne vor. Ein zweiter Kollege (Karl Scherzer) ist auf die Untersuchung und Dokumentation der Putz- und Farbschichten spezialisiert. Ein Dritter (Günther Buchinger) ist für die Erhebung der schriftlichen und bildlichen Quellen und ein Vierter (Michael Grabner) für die Dendrochronologie zuständig. Zurzeit (Frühjahr 2014) liegen Berichte und Pläne für alle Gebäude innerhalb der Lagermauer vor.

3 Die 80 Zentimeter starke Mauer, die den Ostabschluss des Reviergebäudes hätte bilden sollen, ist heute noch im Keller neben der Treppe zu sehen.

4 Vgl. zur Geschichte der Krematorien im KZ Mauthausen auch Bertrand Perz/Christian Dürr/Ralf Lechner/Robert Vorberg: Die Krematorien von Mauthausen. Katalog zur Ausstellung in der KZ-Gedenkstätte Mauthausen (Wien 2008); dies.: Die Krematorien von Mauthausen. In: Bundesministerium für Inneres (Hg.): KZ-Gedenkstätte Mauthausen | Mauthausen Memorial 2008. Forschung, Dokumentation, Information (Wien 2009), S. 12–23.

1 Historical archaeological investigations and geo-magnetic surveys have been ongoing at the memorial site since 2009, for example in the area of the former infirmary camp, the 'Bunkerhof' ('camp prison courtyard') and the so-called tent camp of the Mauthausen concentration camp. Cf. Claudia Theune: Zeitschichten. Archäologische Untersuchungen in der Gedenkstätte Mauthausen, in: Bundesministerium für Inneres (ed.): KZ-Gedenkstätte Mauthausen | Mauthausen Memorial 2009. Forschung, Dokumentation, Information. Jahrbuch der KZ-Gedenkstätte Mauthausen (Vienna 2010), p. 25–30, as well as Paul Mitchell: Building Archaeology at the Mauthausen Memorial Site, in Federal Ministry of the Interior (ed.): bulletin Mauthausen 01/2013 (Vienna 2013), p. 47–50. On the archaeological measures carried out at the Memorial Gusen, cf. Roman Ilg/ Paul Mitchell: Memorial Gusen. Die bauhistorische und bodenarchäologische Untersuchung des Krematoriumsofens im Vorfeld seiner Restaurierung, in: Bundesministerium für Inneres (ed.): KZ-Gedenkstätte Mauthausen | Mauthausen Memorial 2013. Forschung, Dokumentation, Information. Jahrbuch der KZ-Gedenkstätte Mauthausen (Vienna 2014), p. 59–70.

2 The core buildings research team working at the memorial site was composed of four members: The author (Paul Mitchell) was responsible for surveying and documenting the buildings on site. He also drew up the plans showing the age of the buildings. A second colleague (Karl Scherzer) specialised in examining and documenting the layers of plaster and paint. A third (Günther Buchinger) was responsible for finding written and pictorial sources and a fourth (Michael Grabner) for the comparative analysis of tree-rings (dendochronology).

3 The 80cm thick wall, which should have formed the eastern boundary of the infirmary building, is still visible today next to the stairs in the basement.

4 On the history of the crematoria in the Mauthausen concentration camp, cf. Bertrand Perz/Christian Dürr/Ralf Lechner/Robert Vorberg: Die Krematorien von Mauthausen. Katalog zur Ausstellung in der KZ-Gedenkstätte Mauthausen (Vienna 2008); Bertrand Perz/Christian Dürr/Ralf Lechner/Robert Vorberg: Die Krematorien von Mauthausen. In: Bundesministerium für Inneres (ed.): KZ-Gedenkstätte Mauthausen | Mauthausen Memorial 2008. Forschung, Dokumentation, Information (Vienna 2009), p. 12–23.

Robert Vorberg

Vom Reviergebäude zum Museum. Zur Nutzungsgeschichte eines Gebäudes

Robert Vorberg

From Infirmary to Museum. On the history of a building and its uses

Die Errichtung des zweigeschossigen Häftlingskrankenhauses am Appellplatz des Konzentrationslagers Mauthausen begann am 1. September 1940.[1] Bis dahin war der meist als „Revier" bezeichnete Bereich an mehreren Orten des Lagers untergebracht. Erst im Sommer 1944 wurde ein Teil des Gebäudes in Verwendung genommen. Die Einrichtung entsprach dem damaligen Standard eines Krankenhauses, jedoch hatte nur ein Bruchteil der Häftlinge des KZ Mauthausen – vermutlich meist deutsche Häftlinge und Funktionshäftlinge – Zugang zu diesem Bereich.[2] Die Mehrheit der kranken Häftlinge wurde in das so genannte „Sanitätslager" gebracht und unter katastrophalen medizinischen und hygienischen Bedingungen weitgehend sich selbst überlassen.

Construction work on the two-storey prisoners' hospital on the roll call area of the Mauthausen concentration camp began on 1 September 1940.[1] Until then, the area generally termed the 'infirmary' had been located at several sites across the camp. Not until summer 1944 did parts of the building come into use. The facility met standards for a hospital at that time; however, only a fraction of the prisoners of the Mauthausen concentration camp – in the main probably German prisoners and prisoner functionaries – had access to this area.[2] The majority of sick prisoners were taken to the so-called 'infirmary camp' where, under catastrophic conditions in terms of medical care and hygiene, they were largely left to their own devices.

Befreite Häftlinge vor dem Reviergebäude, Mai 1945. Die Aufnahme stammt von Mae Lopatin, die als Krankenpflegerin für die US Army arbeitete.
Foto: Mae Lopatin
Tauber Holocaust Library – JFCS Holocaust Center, San Francisco, Mae Lopatin papers, 1988.1128

Liberated prisoners in front of the infirmary building, May 1945. The picture was taken by Mae Lopatin, who worked as a nurse in the US Army.
Photograph: Mae Lopatin
Tauber Holocaust Library – JFCS Holocaust Center, San Francisco, Mae Lopatin papers, 1988.1128

Aufnahme aus dem Jahr 1946, die den historischen, unverputzten Zustand des Gebäudes zeigt.
Fotograf unbekannt Fotoarchiv der KZ-Gedenkstätte Mauthausen, Sammlung BHÖ

Picture taken in 1946 showing the building in its historical, unrendered condition.
Unknown photographer Fotoarchiv der KZ-Gedenkstätte Mauthausen, BHÖ Collection

Bis zur Befreiung wurde das Gebäude nicht fertiggestellt: Teile blieben ungenutzt und auch der Außenputz wurde nicht mehr angebracht. Nach der Befreiung des Lagers wurden die meisten Einrichtungsgegenstände des Gebäudes – wie auch in anderen Teilen des Lagers – durch die Rote Armee, die das Lager als Kaserne nutzte, entfernt oder später durch die Bevölkerung der Umgebung abmontiert und für eigene Zwecke verwendet.[3]

Im Zuge der Einrichtung der KZ-Gedenkstätte Mauthausen wurde im Rahmen eines Forderungskatalogs unter anderem das Gesamtensemble der Baracken und Steingebäude um den Appellplatz, zu dem auch das ehemalige Reviergebäude gehörte, als erhaltenswert erachtet.[4] Zwischen 1948 und 1951 erfolgten

The building was still unfinished by the time the camp was liberated: sections remained unused and the exterior rendering had not yet been applied. After the liberation of the camp, most of the building's fixtures and fittings were removed – as were those in other parts of the camp – by the Red Army, which used the camp as a barracks, or later dismantled by people from the surrounding area and taken away for their own use.[3]

A requirement brief drawn up during the establishment of the Mauthausen Memorial listed, amongst others, the ensemble consisting of the barracks and the stone buildings around the roll call area, which included the former infirmary building, as deemed worthy of preservation.[4] Initial

erste Sanierungsmaßnahmen, nachdem das Bundesdenkmalamt Österreich Empfehlungen für den Erhalt und zur Restaurierung des ehemaligen Lagers abgebeben hatte und sich damit erstmals mit Fragen des Denkmalschutzes im Zusammenhang mit einem ehemaligen Konzentrationslager befasst hatte.[5] Durch aktuelle bauarchäologische Untersuchungen konnte festgestellt werden, dass diese ersten Bauarbeiten nach Kriegsende insofern bereits durch einen bewussten Umgang mit der erst wenige Jahre alten und als bedeutsam erachteten Bausubstanz gekennzeichnet waren.[6] Die fehlenden Fenster im Erdgeschoss wurden durch neue im selben Stil ersetzt; die Außenmauern wurden aus bauphysikalischen Gründen verputzt.

Der Umbau zum Museumsgebäude und die Einrichtung einer neuen Ausstellung

Im Juli 1964 fasste der Ministerrat der Republik Österreich den Beschluss, in den noch vorhandenen Gebäuden der KZ-Gedenkstätte ein Museum einzurichten. Damit wurde einer Forderung des Internationalen Mauthausen-Komitees und österreichischer Widerstandsorganisationen entsprochen.[7] Den Planungen über die Einrichtung eines Museums zufolge sollten ursprünglich sowohl die Küchenbaracke, als auch das Reviergebäude als Ausstellungsorte genutzt werden. Die Hauptausstellung sollte demnach in der ehemaligen Küchenbaracke untergebracht werden, während das Reviergebäude als Ort für nationale Ausstellungen genutzt werden sollte.[8] Als Ergebnis dieses Beschlusses beauftragte das Bundesministerium für Inneres auf Vorschlag des KZ-Verbandes den ehemaligen Häftling und damaligen Polizeirat Hans Maršálek als Koordinator für das neue Museum, wofür er vom Polizeidienst beurlaubt wurde.[9] Auf Basis seiner Arbeiten sollte der architektonische Entwurf der Adaptionsarbeiten und Ausstellungsgestaltung erfolgen. Damit begann auch erstmals die systematische Sammlung von Quellenmaterial zur Geschichte des Konzentrationslagers Mauthausen. Auf Grund der bis dahin nur in begrenztem Ausmaß durchgeführten historischen Forschung konnte die Beschaffung der notwendigen Ausstellungsobjekte erst 1967 abgeschlossen werden.[10]

Auf Basis des gesammelten Materials wurde ein Konzept erstellt, das die Küchenbaracke als zentra-

renovation works were carried out between 1948 and 1951 following recommendations issued by the Austrian Federal Monuments Office concerning the upkeep and restoration of the former camp, thereby leading it to consider questions of historical preservation with regard to a former concentration camp for the first time.[5] Through recent building archaeological investigations it has been possible to determine that these first construction works carried out after the end of the war were already characterised by a sensitive approach to building stock that, whilst only a few years old, was deemed significant.[6] Windows missing on the ground floor were replaced by new ones in the same style; the exterior walls were rendered to maintain the building's physical condition.

Conversion to a museum building and the creation of a new exhibition

In July 1964 the federal cabinet of the Republic of Austria passed a resolution to establish a museum in the remaining buildings at the Mauthausen Memorial, thereby meeting a demand from the *Internationale Mauthausen Komittee* (International Mauthausen Committee) and Austrian resistance organisations.[7] The main exhibition was to be located in the former kitchen barracks, whilst the infirmary building was to be used to house national exhibitions.[8] The resolution also led the Federal Ministry of the Interior to appoint, at the suggestion of the *KZ-Verband* (Concentration Camp Association), the former prisoner and now police official Hans Maršálek as the co-ordinator of the new museum, for which task he was released from his police duties.[9] The architectural design for the structural adaptations and exhibition layout were to follow on the basis of his work. It was also the beginning of the first systematic collection of source materials on the history of the Mauthausen concentration camp. Because historical research up to that point had been rather limited, it took until 1967 to acquire the necessary exhibition objects.[10]

Based on the collected materials, a concept was drawn up that designated the kitchen barracks as the central exhibition location. For this purpose, several walls were to be erected to divide the

len Ausstellungsort auswies. Zu diesem Zweck sollte die Baracke durch die Errichtung mehrerer Mauern in fünf Räume unterteilt werden, die jeweils einem inhaltlichen Thema zugeordnet würden.[11] Nicht berücksichtigt wurde in diesem Konzept jedoch der bauliche Zustand der noch erhalten gebliebenen Gebäude der KZ-Gedenkstätte. Im Zuge einer Besprechung über das neue Museum wurde im April 1967 die Küchenbaracke besichtigt und massive Schäden durch Regen und Schmelzwasser festgestellt, die als derart gravierend eingestuft wurden, dass sie vorübergehend für Besucher gesperrt werden musste.[12] Somit rückte das ehemalige Reviergebäude aus pragmatischen Gründen ins Zentrum der Überlegungen bezüglich eines Ausstellungsortes in der KZ-Gedenkstätte. Um den endgültigen Ort für das neue Museum festzulegen, wurde ein Gutachten in Auftrag gegeben, das zu dem Ergebnis kam, dass ein Neubau gegenüber einer baulichen Adaptierung des Krankenreviers erhebliche Mehrkosten mit sich bringen würde.[13] Ausschlaggebend für die Wahl des Reviergebäudes war laut Gutachten schlussendlich der gute bauliche Zustand auf Grund der Ziegelbauweise gegenüber der reparaturanfälligeren Holzbauweise der Küchenbaracke. Im Juli 1967 beauftragte das für die baulichen Maßnahmen an der KZ-Gedenkstätte Mauthausen zuständige Amt der Oberösterreichischen Landesregierung die Architektin Irmgard Nobel mit der Ausarbeitung der Planungen für das Museum.[14] Nobel legte noch im selben Monat ein Konzept mit Entwurfsplänen vor, das – wie heutige bauarchäologische Untersuchungen bestätigen – weitgehend der Plangrundlage entsprechend umgesetzt wurde.[15] Die Einrichtung des Museums machte wesentliche Eingriffe in die historische Bausubstanz notwendig. So wurde – um das Erd- und Kellergeschoss besser zu verbinden – der Fußboden an zwei Stellen durchbrochen und zwei breite Treppen eingebaut. Ein Teil des Kellers wurde bis auf die aus statischen Gründen notwendigen Mauerteile vollständig entkernt, um großflächige Ausstellungsräumlichkeiten zu schaffen. Auch das Erdgeschoss wurde in weiten Teilen umgestaltet, jedoch beschränkte man sich hier weitgehend auf die Zusammenlegung von Räumen, um mehrere durch Wände getrennte Ausstellungsbereiche zu erhalten. Äußerlich wurde das Erscheinungsbild des

barracks into five rooms, each of which would be assigned thematic content.[11] However, this concept did not take into account the structural condition of the memorial site's surviving buildings. During a meeting about the new museum in April 1967, a visit was made to the kitchen barracks where large-scale damage due to rain and meltwater was observed; it was considered so serious that the barracks had to be closed temporarily to visitors.[12] Thus pragmatic considerations meant that the former infirmary building became the focus of discussions regarding an exhibition space at the memorial site. In order to determine the final location for the new museum, a report was commissioned which came to the conclusion that a new building would involve considerably higher costs in comparison with structural adaptations to the infirmary building.[13] According to the report, the crucial factor in favour of the infirmary building was, ultimately, its good structural condition on account of its brick construction, as opposed to the wooden construction of the kitchen building, which was more prone to repair. In July 1967 the Upper Austrian government department responsible for construction work at the Mauthausen Memorial commissioned the architect Irmgard Nobel to develop plans for the museum.[14] Within the month Nobel had presented the design plans for her concept, which – as recent building archaeological investigations confirm – was largely implemented in accordance with her plans.[15] The museum's creation necessitated substantial alterations to the historical building. In order to better connect the ground floor with the basement, the floor was broken through in two places and two wide staircases were installed. Leaving only the load-bearing walls, a section of the basement was completely gutted in order to create an extensive exhibition space. Large parts of the ground floor were also modified, although here measures were generally limited to joining rooms together in order to create several exhibition areas divided by walls. The building's external appearance was less heavily altered. The rendering from the 1940s was renewed and, bar two exceptions, the windows installed in this period were replaced with more up-to-date double glazing.[16]

Gebäudes weniger stark verändert. Der Putz der 1940er-Jahre wurde weitgehend erneuert und die ebenfalls in diesem Zeitraum eingebauten Fenster bis auf zwei Ausnahmen durch zeitgemäße Doppelglasfenster ersetzt.[16]

Trotz des bereits damals bestehenden Denkmalschutzes in Bezug auf die KZ-Gedenkstätte Mauthausen geht eine Einbeziehung des zuständigen Denkmalamtes über die teilweise massiven Veränderungen im Inneren des Gebäudes aus den vorliegenden Quellen nicht hervor. Dennoch dürften denkmalpflegerische Aspekte vermutlich hinsichtlich des äußerlichen Erscheinungsbildes des Gebäudes eine Rolle gespielt haben. Die Österreichische Lagergemeinschaft Mauthausen betonte schon im Juli 1966 in einem Schreiben an das Bundesministerium für Inneres, dass sie mit den notwendigen Maßnahmen einverstanden sei, da dadurch das Gesamterscheinungsbild des Appellplatzes nicht beeinträchtigt werde.[17] Dieses Schreiben bezog sich noch auf die Adaption der Küchenbaracke – es ist jedoch anzunehmen, dass hinsichtlich der Baumaßnahmen am Reviergebäude ähnliche Grundsätze gegolten haben.

Die Sanierungs- und Adaptionsarbeiten für die 1970 eröffnete erste Dauerausstellung bildeten bis zum im Jahr 2009 gestarteten Neugestaltungsprozess die letzten wesentlichen baulichen Maßnahmen im ehemaligen Reviergebäude, das damit als zentrales Museumsgebäude der Gedenkstätte fungierte.

Im Rahmen der ersten Umsetzungsschritte zur Neugestaltung der KZ-Gedenkstätte Mauthausen wurden mit der Einrichtung eines neuen Museumsgebäudes die nötigen infrastrukturellen Voraussetzungen dafür geschaffen, die Gedenkstätte auch als Bildungsort neu zu gestalten.

Nach einem intensiven Diskussionsprozess wurde entschieden, die in der ersten Phase der Neugestaltung zu erarbeitenden Ausstellungen *Das Konzentrationslager Mauthausen 1938–1945* und *Der Tatort Mauthausen – Eine Spurensuche* sowie den sogenannten „Raum der Namen" im Erd- und Kellergeschoss des Reviergebäudes einzurichten. Dabei

Despite the fact that the Mauthausen Memorial was already listed as a historical preservation site, the available sources do not indicate any involvement on the part of the relevant monuments' office regarding what were, in some cases, substantial changes to the interior of the building. Nevertheless, it appears that aspects of historical preservation probably did play a role with regard to the external appearance of the building. In a letter to the Federal Ministry of the Interior in 1966, the *Österreichische Lagergemeinschaft Mauthausen* (Austrian Camp Association Mauthausen) had already stressed that they had no objections to the necessary measures since they would not detract from the appearance of the roll call area as a whole.[17] This letter still referred to the adaptation of the kitchen barracks – but it can be assumed that similar principles applied with regard to the building measures proposed for the infirmary building.

Until the redesign process started in 2009, the renovation and adaptation works for the first permanent exhibition that opened in 1970 constituted the last significant building measures to be carried out in the former infirmary building, which then served as the memorial site's central museum building.

The establishment of a new museum building, as part of the first phase of the Mauthausen Memorial redesign, also created the necessary infrastructural prerequisites for redesigning the memorial site as a place of learning as well.

Following a period of intense discussion, the decision was taken to locate those exhibitions to be created as part of the first phase of the redesign – *The Mauthausen Concentration Camp 1938-1945* and *The Crime Scenes of Mauthausen – Searching for Traces* as well as the so-called 'Room of Names' – on the ground floor and in the basement of the infirmary building. In the process it was agreed that structural changes to such a sensitive place as the Mauthausen Memorial needed to be carried out as part of an overall concept. Alongside infrastructural requirements, the concept also had to take

Die Architektur der Ausstellung fügt sich in den bauhistorisch weitgehend unveränderten Zustand des Reviergebäude-Untergeschosses ein.
Foto: Tal Adler

The exhibition architecture slots into the largely unaltered historical structure of the basement of the infirmary building.
Photograph: Tal Adler

wurde festgelegt, dass bauliche Veränderungen an einem derart sensiblen Ort wie der KZ-Gedenkstätte Mauthausen eines umfassenden Konzepts bedürfen. Neben den infrastrukturellen Notwendigkeiten war auch der Denkmalschutz zu berücksichtigen, in dessen Blickpunkt vermehrt Bauten aus der NS-Zeit gerückt waren. Neben der jahrzehntelangen Nutzungstradition des Gebäudes als Museum spielte für die Wahl des Gebäudes vor allem eine Rolle, dass das ehemalige Reviergebäude wie beschrieben nur zu einem Teil in Verwendung gewesen war und als vergleichsweise neutraler Ort angesehen werden kann. Für die neuen Ausstellungen war eine neuerliche Sanierung und Adaption des ehemaligen Reviergebäudes nötig. Die durch die Burghauptmannschaft Österreich (BHÖ) beauftragten Baumaßnahmen sollten jedoch nicht nur die Voraussetzungen für ein zeitgemäßes Museumsgebäude schaffen, sondern auch das ursprüngliche, in der Nachkriegszeit

into account ideas of heritage and monument preservation, something that National Socialist era buildings had increasingly come to the attention of. Besides the decades-long tradition of using the building for exhibitions, one of the main factors in the choice of the former infirmary building was the fact that, as described above, it was only ever partly in use and can be viewed as a comparatively neutral site. Further renovations to and adaptations of the former infirmary building were necessary for the new exhibitions. However, the building work commissioned by the *Burghauptmannschaft Österreich* (*BHÖ* – Austrian Buildings Commission) aimed not only to put in place what was needed for a contemporary museum but also to make the building's original appearance, altered in the postwar period, visible again as far as possible. This sense of the building's original character was to be achieved through the use of particular design

überbaute Erscheinungsbild des Gebäudes so weit wie möglich sichtbar machen. Durch besondere gestalterische Maßnahmen sollte eine Vorstellung von der ursprünglichen Gebäudebeschaffenheit gegeben werden. Zu diesem Zweck wurden in der Planungsphase umfangreiche bauarchäologische Untersuchungen durchgeführt.[18] Auf Basis der dadurch gewonnenen Informationen wurden gemeinsam mit dem zuständigen Architekten Helmut Neumayer und in Absprache mit dem Bundesdenkmalamt Österreich, welches sich seit 2006 intensiv mit Fragen des Umgangs mit NS-zeitlicher Bausubstanz auseinandersetze,[19] Überlegungen angestellt, wie mit der vorhandenen Bausubstanz umzugehen sei. Wichtig in diesem Zusammenhang waren auch die durch die vom Innenministerium eingesetzte Arbeitsgruppe formulierten Leitlinien für die Neugestaltung.[20]

Dabei wurde es als notwendig erachtet, dass alle baulichen und gestalterischen Maßnahmen, die den BesucherInnen den Zustand aus dem Jahr 1945, aber auch später durchgeführte Eingriffe andeuten sollen, selbsterklärend sind. Beispielsweise wurden die ursprünglichen historischen Wandstellungen durch Markierungen an Boden, Wänden und Decke angedeutet. An ausgewählten Stellen, deren Bausubstanz 1945 noch gut erhalten war, in späteren Sanierungsmaßnahmen allerdings verändert wurde, machte man diese wieder sichtbar. So wurden in einem vermutlich als Krankenzimmer genutzten Raum die Wandfarben freigelegt, um den BesucherInnen einen Eindruck der ursprünglichen Innenraumgestaltung geben zu können. Ebenso entfernte man an einer Ecke des Gebäudes die Fassade, um den im Jahr 1945 vorhandenen unverputzten Zustand sichtbar zu machen.

Um die Voraussetzungen für ein zeitgemäßes Museumsgebäude zu schaffen, waren zudem neue bauliche Veränderungen notwendig. Dabei wurde versucht, die Eingriffe so gering wie möglich zu halten und als nachträgliche Veränderungen kenntlich zu machen. Um die Funktion als Ausstellungsort erfüllen zu können, wurde im Mitteltrakt des Gebäudes eine neue Stahlstiege eingerichtet, ein Teil der Räume wurde als neuer Sanitärbereich für BesucherInnen sowie als Personalbereich adaptiert. Ein wei-

strategies. To assist this, comprehensive building archaeological investigations were carried out during the planning stages.[18] On the basis of the information gained from these, and together with the architect responsible, Helmut Neumayer, as well as in consultation with the Austrian Federal Monuments Office – which has been conducting intense discussions on the question of how to deal with National Socialist era building stock since 2006[19] – consideration was given to how best to deal with the existing structures. The guidelines for the redesign developed by the working group set up by the Ministry of the Interior were also important in this regard.[20]

It was felt that any structural and design measures intended to indicate to visitors the building's condition in 1945, but also any later changes, must be self-explanatory. For example, the original position of the walls has been indicated by markings on the floors, walls and ceilings. In selected places where the underlying structure from 1945 was in good condition but had been altered by later renovations, these structures have been made visible again. For example, in a room probably used as a sickroom, the wall paint has been stripped back to in order to give visitors an impression of the original interior decoration. Similarly, the external facing has been removed from a corner of the building in order to show its unrendered state in 1945.

The need to meet the requirements of a modern museum building also made new structural changes necessary. However, these interventions were kept to a minimum and, as changes from a later period, were made recognisable as such. In order for the building to be able to fulfil its function as an exhibition space, a new steel stairway was installed in the central tract and some of the rooms were adapted to create new visitor washrooms and areas for staff. A major aim of the construction work was also to make the building itself, as well as the adjoining memorial room in the basement by the crematoria and gas chamber, accessible to visitors with mobility needs. To this end both a lift inside the building and a ramp in the courtyard

teres wesentliches Ziel der Baumaßnahmen war es, sowohl das Gebäude selbst als auch den im Keller angrenzenden Gedenkraum im Bereich der Krematorien und der ehemaligen Gaskammer barrierefrei zugänglich zu machen. Zu diesem Zweck wurde ein Lift eingebaut sowie im Hof des ehemaligen Lagergefängnisses eine barrierefreie Rampe errichtet. Diese Eingriffe in die historische Bausubstanz waren nicht unumstritten, wurden allerdings als notwendig erachtet, um den Besuch des Museumsgebäudes und des neuen Gedenkraums einer großen Zahl von BesucherInnen ermöglichen zu können. Die von der BHÖ durchgeführten Baumaßnahmen dauerten von Sommer 2010 bis Herbst 2011.

Mit der neuerlichen Adaption und Sanierung des ehemaligen Reviergebäudes und der Eröffnung der neuen Ausstellungen steht der KZ-Gedenkstätte nun ein Museumsgebäude zur Verfügung, das den zeitgemäßen Erfordernissen einer Gedenkstätte entspricht.

of the former camp prison were installed. These interventions in the historical structure were not without controversy but were nevertheless considered necessary in order to enable a large number of visitors to visit the museum building and the new memorial room. The construction measures carried out by the *BHÖ* lasted from August 2010 until autumn 2011.

With the latest adaptation and renovation of the former infirmary building and the opening of the new exhibitions, the Mauthausen Memorial now has a museum building at its disposal that meets the needs of a contemporary memorial site.

---

1 Vgl. Bericht der SS-Bauleitung 1944, AMM A/3/1.
2 Vgl. Hans Maršálek: Die Geschichte des Konzentrationslagers Mauthausen. Dokumentation. Wien 2006, S. 201f.
3 Vgl. Bertrand Perz: Die KZ-Gedenkstätte Mauthausen. 1945 bis zur Gegenwart, Innsbruck 2006, S. 51f.
4 Vgl. ebd., S. 89f.
5 Vgl. ebd., S. 100, sowie Paul Mahringer: Der Alterswert als Narrativ für traumatische Erfahrungen des 20. Jahrhunderts, Denkmalkultus, lebendige Geisteswissenschaft, Postmoderne und neue Zugänge in Theorie und Praxis der Denkmalpflege, in: Österreichische Zeitschrift für Kunst und Denkmalpflege, Heft 1/2 2013, Wien 2014, S. 15.
6 Vgl. Paul Mitchell/Günther Buchinger: Die Baugeschichte des neuen Reviergebäudes KL Mauthausen, unveröffentlichter Projektbericht, Wien 2010, S. 17.
7 Vgl. Memorandum, Öffentliches Denkmal Mauthausen, S. 12.
8 Vgl. Öffentliches Denkmal Mauthausen; Umbau des ehem. Krankenreviergebäudes für ein Museum, AMM 1.6.1., Box 20, BMI GZ. 273.633 -33/67. Das Konzept entsprach jenem des Museums Auschwitz-Birkenau. Vgl. Bertrand Perz: Das Konzentrationslager darstellen. Alte und neue historische Ausstellungen in Mauthausen, in: Verein für Gedenken und Geschichtsforschung in österreichischen KZ-Gedenkstätten (Hg.): Das Konzentrationslager Mauthausen 1938–1945. Katalog zur Ausstellung in der KZ-Gedenkstätte Mauthausen. Wien 2013, S. 287–294.
9 Vgl. Memorandum, Öffentliches Denkmal Mauthausen, S. 12.
10 Vgl. Ministerratsvortrag Oktober 1967, AMM 1.6.1., Box 20, BMI GZ. 276.928-33/67.

1 Cf. Bericht der SS-Bauleitung 1944 [Report of the SS Head of Construction 1944], AMM A/3/1
2 Cf. Hans Maršálek: Die Geschichte des Konzentrationslagers Mauthausen. Dokumentation. Vienna 2006, p. 201f.
3 Cf. Bertrand Perz: Die KZ-Gedenkstätte Mauthausen. 1945 bis zur Gegenwart, Innsbruck 2006, p. 51f.
4 Cf. ibid., p. 89f.
5 Cf. ibid., p. 100, also Paul Mahringer: Der Alterswert als Narrativ für traumatische Erfahrungen des 20. Jahrhunderts, Denkmalkultus, lebendige Geisteswissenschaft, Postmoderne und neue Zugänge in Theorie und Praxis der Denkmalpflege, in: Österreichische Zeitschrift für Kunst und Denkmalpflege, vol. 1/2 2013, Vienna 2014, p. 15.
6 Cf. Paul Mitchell/Günther Buchinger: Die Baugeschichte des neuen Reviergebäudes KL Mauthausen, unpublished project report, Vienna 2010, p. 17.
7 Cf. Memorandum, Öffentliches Denkmal Mauthausen [Mauthausen Public Memorial], p. 12.
8 Cf. Öffentliches Denkmal Mauthausen; Umbau des ehem. Krankenreviergebäudes für ein Museum [Mauthausen Public Memorial; Adaptation of the former infirmary building as a museum], AMM 1.6.1., Box 20, BMI GZ. 273.633 -33/67. This concept corresponded to that at the Auschwitz-Birkenau Museum. Cf. Bertrand Perz: Exhibiting the Concentration Camp. Old and new historical exhibitions at Mauthausen, in: Association for the Remembrance and Historical Research in Austrian Concentration Camp Memorials (ed.): The Mauthausen Concentration Camp 1938-1945. Catalogue to the Exhibition at the Mauthausen Memorial. Vienna 2013, p. 287–294.

11 Vgl. Technisches Szenarium Museum Mauthausen, Planbeilage, AMM 1.6.1., Box 20, BMI GZ. 273.079-33/67.

12 Vgl. Öffentliches Denkmal Mauthausen; Einrichtung eines Museums. Vorbereitungsarbeiten – Besprechung, AMM 1.6.1., Box 20, BMI GZ. 272.728/67. Auch die ehemaligen Häftlingsbaracken auf der gegenüberliegenden Seite des Appellplatzes wurden im Zuge dieser Besichtigung für BesucherInnen gesperrt.

13 Vgl. Öffentliches Denkmal Mauthausen; Umbau des ehem. Krankenreviergebäudes für ein Museum, AMM 1.6.1., Box 20, BMI GZ. 273.633-33/67.

14 Vgl., Öffentliches Denkmal Mauthausen; Vorbereitungsarbeiten für die Einrichtung eines Museums, AMM 1.6.1., Box 19, BMI GZ. 278.316-33/67.

15 Vgl. Öffentliches Denkmal Mauthausen, Einrichtung eines Museums, AMM 1.6.1., Box 20, BMI GZ. 276.928-33/67, sowie Paul Mitchell/Günther Buchinger: Die Baugeschichte des neuen Reviergebäudes KL Mauthausen, unveröffentlichter Projektbericht, Wien 2010, S. 19.

16 Vgl. ebd., S. 21f.

17 Vgl. Öffentliches Denkmal Mauthausen; Einrichtung eines Museums. Instandsetzung der Türen und Fenster der ehemaligen Küchenbaracke, AMM 1.6.1., Box 20, BMI GZ. 248.119-33/66.

18 Siehe dazu den Beitrag von Paul Mitchell in diesem Band.

19 Ausführlich dazu: Eva-Maria Höhle: Staatlicher Schutz für NS-Bauten – Ein österreichisches Dilemma?; in: Österreichische Zeitschrift für Kunst und Denkmalpflege, Heft 1, 2007, Wien 2007, sowie Paul Mahringer: Der Alterswert als Narrativ für traumatische Erfahrungen des 20. Jahrhunderts, Denkmalkultus, lebendige Geisteswissenschaft, Postmoderne und neue Zugänge in Theorie und Praxis der Denkmalpflege, in: Österreichische Zeitschrift für Kunst und Denkmalpflege, Heft 1/2, 2013, Wien 2014.

20 Die Leitlinien wurden im Zuge der Erstellung eines Rahmenkonzepts durch die Arbeitsgruppe zur Neugestaltung der KZ-Gedenkstätte Mauthausen erarbeitet. Die Arbeitsgruppe setzte sich aus externen ExpertInnen und internen wissenschaftlichen MitarbeiterInnen zusammen und wurde 2008 durch den damaligen Bundesminister Günter Platter eingesetzt. Siehe auch: Rahmenkonzept für die Neugestaltung der KZ-Gedenkstätte Mauthausen, Wien 2009 (Hg. vom Bundesministerium für Inneres, Abteilung IV/7), S. 14.

9 Cf. Memorandum, Öffentliches Denkmal Mauthausen, p. 12.

10 Cf. Ministerratsvortrag Oktober 1967 [Federal Cabinet Address October 1967], AMM 1.6.1., Box 20, BMI GZ. 276.928-33/67.

11 Cf. Technisches Szenarium Museum Mauthausen, Planbeilage [Technical scenario for the Mauthausen Museum, enclosed plans], AMM 1.6.1., Box 20, BMI GZ. 273.079-33/67.

12 Cf. Öffentliches Denkmal Mauthausen; Einrichtung eines Museums. Vorbereitungsarbeiten – Besprechung [Mauthausen Public Memorial; Establishment of a museum. Preparatory plans – consultation], AMM 1.6.1., Box 20, BMI GZ. 272.728/67. The prisoners' barracks on the opposite side of the roll call area were also closed to visitors as a result of this visit.

13 Cf. Öffentliches Denkmal Mauthausen; Umbau des ehem. Krankenreviergebäudes für ein Museum [Mauthausen Public Memorial; Adaptation of the former infirmary building as a museum], AMM 1.6.1., Box 20, BMI GZ. 273.633-33/67.

14 Cf. Öffentliches Denkmal Mauthausen; Vorbereitungsarbeiten für die Einrichtung eines Museums [Mauthausen Public Memorial; Preparatory plans for the establishment of a museum], AMM 1.6.1., Box 19, BMI GZ. 278.316-33/67.

15 Cf. Öffentliches Denkmal Mauthausen, Einrichtung eines Museums [Mauthausen Public Memorial, Establishment of a museum], AMM 1.6.1., Box 20, BMI GZ. 276.928-33/67, also Paul Mitchell/Günther Buchinger: Die Baugeschichte des neuen Reviergebäudes KL Mauthausen, unpublished project report, Vienna 2010, p. 19.

16 Cf. ibid., p. 21f.

17 Cf. Öffentliches Denkmal Mauthausen; Einrichtung eines Museums. Instandsetzung der Türen und Fenster der ehemaligen Küchenbaracke [Mauthausen Public Memorial; Establishment of a museum. Overhaul of the doors and windows in the former kitchen barracks], AMM 1.6.1., Box 20, BMI GZ. 248.119-33/66.

18 See the article by Paul Mitchell in this volume.

19 In more detail see: Eva-Maria Höhle: Staatlicher Schutz für NS-Bauten – Ein österreichisches Dilemma?; in: Österreichische Zeitschrift für Kunst und Denkmalpflege, vol. 1, 2007, Vienna 2007, also Paul Mahringer: Der Alterswert als Narrativ für traumatische Erfahrungen des 20. Jahrhunderts, Denkmalkultus, lebendige Geisteswissenschaft, Postmoderne und neue Zugänge in Theorie und Praxis der Denkmalpflege, in: Österreichische Zeitschrift für Kunst und Denkmalpflege, vol. 1/2, 2013, Vienna 2014.

20 The guidelines were developed by the working group for the redesign of the Mauthausen Memorial as part of the creation of a framework concept. The working group was composed of external experts and in-house academic staff and was appointed by the then Minister of the Interior Günter Platter. See also: Framework concept for the redesign of the Mauthausen Memorial, Vienna 2009 (ed. by Bundesministeriem für Inneres, Abteilung IV/7), p. 14.

Manuel Schilcher

Die architektonische Gestaltung der Ausstellung

Ausstellungen sind Orte der erlebbaren Dreidimensionalität, Heterotopien im Sinne des französischen Philosophen Michel Foucault. Wenn eine Gedenkstätte wie Mauthausen als Ort der Nichtalltäglichkeit besucht wird, wird nicht nur Geschichte betrachtet, sondern ein vom alltäglichen Umfeld gravierend unterscheidbarer Ort besucht. Als Ort dieser Begegnung mit seiner Historie, den gezeigten Objekten, seinen nachvollziehbaren Spuren hat der räumliche Kontext, in dem eine Ausstellung stattfindet, einen entscheidenden Einfluss auf die Wahrnehmung des Besuchenden. Die ausgebildete Raumgestaltung erzeugt spezifische Atmosphären, stimuliert und löst Verhalten aus, fördert Kommunikation und weckt Assoziationen, sie versetzt BesucherInnen in Stimmungen und sensibilisiert sie für Wahrnehmungen. Unser Verständnis von Ausstellungen ist jene von der Konstruktion von Räumen. Bei der Neugestaltung der KZ-Gedenkstäte Mauthausen kam den erhaltenen historischen Räumen eine zentrale Rolle zu.

Im Untergeschoss, in dem sich die Ausstellung *Der Tatort Mauthausen – Eine Spurensuche* befindet, fanden wir einen relativ „ursprünglichen" bauhistorischen Zustand vor. In den weitgehend unveränderten Originalräumlichkeiten wurden die unterschiedlich rohen und teilweise unverputzten Oberflächen durch ein Schlämmverfahren optisch vereinheitlicht. Diese Maßnahme lässt die ursprünglichen Texturen noch klar spüren, dennoch bildet die einheitliche Tönung eine homogenisierende Klammer. Dies schafft eine neutralere Grundstimmung für die Ausstellung, ohne die archaische Expressivität der Raumsituation zu schwächen.

Die grundsätzliche architektonische Idee war es, die zentrale Säulensituation mit ihren drei parallelen Zonen weiterhin offen und damit erlebbar zu lassen. Der gesamte Raum ist auf einen Blick zu erfassen. Um diese Ursprünglichkeit des Raumes zu gewährleisten, wurden diesem Konzept zufolge keine Einbauten in Augenhöhe implementiert, um den Blick nicht unnötig zu

Manuel Schilcher

The Exhibition's Architectural Design

Exhibitions are places where three-dimensionality is experienced, heterotopias in the sense of the French philosopher Michel Foucault. When a memorial site such as Mauthausen is visited as a place outside of the everyday, not only is history contemplated, but a visit is made to a place which is profoundly set apart from the everyday world. As a place of this encounter with history, with the objects on display, with visible traces, the spatial context in which an exhibition takes place has a powerful effect on visitors' perceptions. The interior design engenders specific atmospheres, stimulates and provokes certain behaviours, encourages communication and evokes associations, it affects visitors' moods and raises their perceptual awareness. Our understanding of an exhibition is that of the construction of space. In the redesign of the Mauthausen Memorial, the preserved historical spaces took on a central role.

In the basement in which the exhibition *The Crime Scenes of Mauthausen – Searching for Traces* is located, we were faced with a structure in a relatively 'original' historical condition. The different raw and partially unplastered surfaces in these largely unaltered original spaces were treated with whitewash to give a unified optical appearance. This process allows the original textures to remain tangible yet the unified hue creates a homogenising frame. This builds a neutral basis for the exhibition without detracting from the archaic expressivity of the space.

The basic architectural idea was to leave the layout formed by the columns with their three parallel zones open and therefore perceptible. The entire room can be taken in at a glance. It followed that, in order to guarantee the original nature of the room, nothing was to be installed at eye-level so as not to disturb the line of sight unnecessarily. From the top of the stairs, which are positioned at a right-angle to the exhibition, visitors are met with a large illuminated

brechen. Vom Stiegenabgang aus, der in rechtem Winkel zur Ausstellung steht, werden die BesucherInnen von einem großen Leuchtbild empfangen, das in die Thematik einführt. Unten angelangt, behaupten sich zunächst sechs monolithische Körper. Diese pultartigen Ausstellungselemente zeigen auf der Bildseite je ein hinterleuchtetes zeitgenössisches Foto des jeweiligen Tatortes, der in dieser Themenstation behandelt wird. Ihre versetzte Aufstellung erzwingt ein mäanderndes Durchschreiten des Raumes und bricht mit der Möglichkeit, geradlinig zum ehemaligen Krematoriumsbereich zu gelangen. Erst die jeweiligen Rückseiten der Elemente enthalten textliche und audiovisuelle Inhalte.

Die frei auskragenden Körper aus Glas und Corian bilden in ihrer klaren Form einen eindeutigen Kontrast zu den rauen Oberflächen von Wand und Decke. Die vorherrschende Farbe ist weiß, wobei Grüngelb die „Schmuckfarbe" bildet. Die Materialität der Elemente hat eine verhaltene Transparenz und wird von innen hinterleuchtet.

Am Ende der Ausstellung wird ein siebtes Thema dargestellt, das die Beseitigung der Leichen darlegt. Das betreffende Ausstellungselement nimmt die Formensprache der Pulte auf, ist jedoch an der Wand als Winkel positioniert. Mit diesem Themenblock werden die BesucherInnen auf den folgenden Pietätsbereich vorbereitet.

Der Wegführung im Pietätsbereich wird mittels Steg gelöst. Dieser Steg ist unterleuchtet und führt – wenige Zentimeter vom originalen Boden abgehoben – durch die verwinkelten Raumabfolgen. Schräge Keile, die aus dem Steg hervorragen, benennen die einzelnen historischen Objekte und Räume und dienen als Leitsystem. Zweck des Steges ist es, einerseits den historischen Raum architektonisch auch aus konservatorischen Gründen nicht weiter zu beeinflussen, anderseits den sehr in Mitleidenschaft gekommenen Boden zu schonen und die BesucherInnen behutsam davon abzuhalten, Spuren zu hinterlassen. Der Steg führt am Krematoriumsofen und den Votivtafeln vorbei durch den Raum der Namen in den Bunkerhof. Ein Hochzug des Steges, obwohl nur etwa kniehoch, verhindert es, die Gaskammer wie auch andere Räume zu betreten. Die Wegführung gibt eine klare Gehrichtung vor und erlaubt auch größeren Gruppen einen gut orientierten Ablauf.

photograph that draws them into the topic. Having reached the bottom, six monolithic display cases form the initial impression. The fronts of these desk-like blocks each show a back-lit, contemporary photo of the crime scene to be dealt with at the thematic station in question. Their offset placement forces the visitor to take a meandering path through the room and breaks with the possibility of heading in a straight line for the former crematorium area. Only the reverse side of each block contains text and audiovisual content.

With their clear and simple form, the free-standing, overhanging blocks made of glass and Corian stand in clear contrast to the rough surfaces of the walls and ceiling. The dominant colour is white, with greeny-yellow forming the 'spot colour'. The blocks' materiality is one of muted transparency and they are lit from within.

At the end of the exhibition a seventh topic is presented that deals with the disposal of the corpses. Here the exhibition furniture takes up the design vocabulary of the desk-like blocks but is positioned on the wall to form a corner. This thematic block prepares visitors for the historically sensitive area to follow.

The path through the historically sensitive area is determined by a walkway. This walkway is lit from below and – raised a few centimetres above the original ground level – leads through the winding sequence of rooms. Diagonal wedges rising up out of the walkway are labelled for the individual historical objects and rooms and serve as a guidance system. The purpose of the walkway is, on the one hand, to prevent further architectural interference to the historical space, also for reasons of historical preservation, whilst on the other hand it protects the already very dilapidated floor and gently deters visitors from leaving any traces of their own. The walkway leads past the crematorium oven and the remembrance plaques, through the Room of Names to the prison courtyard. Pulling the end of the walkway up to create a vertical barrier, albeit only to knee height, prevents access to the gas chamber and other rooms. The walkway sets out a clear path and the easy orientation it provides also facilitates the flow of larger groups.

Konzentrationslager Mauthausen 1938–1945
The Mauthausen Concentration Camp 1938–1945

Der Tatort Mauthausen – Eine Spurensuche
The Crime Scenes of Mauthausen – Searching for Traces

Raum der Namen
Room of Names

Impressum
© 2013

Gesamtleitung
Director
Barbara Glück

Projektkoordination und -abwicklung
Project organisation and management
Robert Vorberg, Jochen Wollner

Kuratierung der Ausstellung *Konzentrationslager Mauthausen 1938–1945*
Curators *The Mauthausen Concentration Camp 1938–1945*
Christian Dürr, Ralf Lechner, Niko Wahl, Johanna Wensch
mit Gregor Holzinger und Andreas Kranebitter

Kuratierung der Ausstellung *Der Tatort Mauthausen – Eine Spurensuche*
Curators *The Crime Scenes of Mauthausen – Searching for Traces*
Christian Dürr, Ralf Lechner, Niko Wahl, Johanna Wensch

Kuratierung Raum der Namen
Curators Room of Names
Andreas Kranebitter, Niko Wahl

Wissenschaftliche Leitung, Co-Leitung
Academic director, Co-director
Bertrand Perz, Jörg Skriebeleit

Ausstellungsgestaltung, -architektur und -umsetzung
Exhibition design, architecture and coordination
argeMarie – architektur, szenografie, linz
Siegfried Miedl
Manuel Schilcher

Recherchen
Researchers
Alfons Adam, Ute Bauer, Benito Bermejo, Katharina Czachor, Christian Dürr, Isolde Füsselberger, Nicole Hördler, Stefan Hördler, Gregor Holzinger, Matthias Kaltenbrunner, Ralf Lechner, Marion Krammer, Andreas Kranebitter, Dagmar Lieske, Stephan Matyus, Gerlinde Schmidt, Johannes Schwartz, Robert Vorberg, Niko Wahl, Doris Warlitsch, Johanna Wensch, Barbara Wiesinger, Veronika Zangl

Begleitende Forschungsprojekte
Associated research projects
Ilsen About / Thomas Fontaine / Adeline Lee (Archivalien und Artefakte in französischen Archiven / Archival material and artifacts in French archives), Alfons Adam (Artefakte aus dem KZ-Mauthausen in tschechischen Archiven / Artefacts from the Mauthausen concentration camp in Czech archives), Helga Amesberger / Brigitte Halbmayer (Weibliche Häftlinge des KZ Mauthausen / Female prisoners of the Mauthausen concentration camp), Veronika Brandt / Maria Hörtner / Juliane Zeiser (Statistische Auswertungen / Statistical analyses), Regina Fritz (Auswertung von Überlebenden-Interviews / Assessment of survivor interviews), Stefan Hördler / Magdalena Frühmann / Christian Rabl (Dachauer Mauthausen-Prozesse / Dachau Mauthausen Trials), Bernhard Mühleder / Franz Pötscher (Interviewprojekt „regionales Umfeld" / 'Regional surroundings' interview project), Reinhard Otto / Tatiana Szekely / Sabrina Auböck (Sowjetische Häftlinge im KZ Mauthausen / Soviet prisoners in the Mauthausen concentration camp), Alexander Prenninger (Evakuierungstransporte und Todesmärsche / Evacuation transports and death marches), Alexander Salzmann (Ungarisch-jüdische ZwangsarbeiterInnen / Hungarian Jewish forced labourers), Marlene Schütze / Isolde Füsselberger (Auswertung Artefakte-Sammlung der KZ-Gedenkstätte Mauthausen / Assessment of the Mauthausen Memorial Artefact Collection), Claudia Theune / Paul Mitchell / Günther Buchinger (Archäologische Untersuchungen am Gedenkstättengelände / Archaeological investigations at the memorial site), Stefan Wolfinger (Bestände in oberösterreichischen Archiven / Collections in Upper Austrian archives)

Konzeptgruppe Neugestaltung
Redesign concept working group
Christian Dürr, Florian Freund, Barbara Glück, Harald Hutterberger, Yariv Lapid, Ralf Lechner, Stephan Matyus, Bertrand Perz, Jörg Skriebeleit, Franz Sonnenberger, Heidemarie Uhl, Robert Vorberg, Jochen Wollner

Jury Gestaltungswettbewerb
Design competition jury
Barbara Glück, Hermann Dikowitsch, Eva-Maria Höhle, Bertrand Perz, Jörg Skriebeleit, Szabolcs Szita

Begleitende Baukontrolle
Construction monitoring
Johannes Hofmeister

Beschaffung Reproduktionen, Leihverkehr, Produktionsbetreuung
Reproductions acquisition, loan agreements, coordination object transport and handling
Karin Gschwandtner
Katharina Czachor (Artefakte-Sammlung der KZ-Gedenkstätte Mauthausen / Artefact Collection of the Mauthausen Memorial)

Restauratorische Expertise
Conservation expertise
Bettina Dräxler

Objekteinbringung
Object handling
Bettina Dräxler
vienna arthandling

Objektrestaurierung
Object conservation
Paulina Bittschi-Matysik, Sigrid Eyb-Green, Andrea Friedl, Elisabeth Macho-Biegler, Katherina Mergl, Murat Yaşar

Lektorat
Copy-editing
Verena Pawlowsky / Harald Wendelin (Forschungsbüro, Wien)

Englische Übersetzungen
Translation into English
Joanna White
Mitarbeit Ausstellung *Konzentrationslager Mauthausen 1938–1945* / Additional English translation *The Mauthausen Concentration Camp 1938–1945*: Brenda Black

Raum der Namen
Room of Names
Redaktionelle Mitarbeit / Editorial assistance: Maria Hörtner, Juliane Zeiser
Mitarbeit / Assistance: Baris Alakus, Sabrina Auböck, Yasmina Beciragic, Suzanne de Bekker, Jan Benda, Benito Bermejo, Ionne Biffi, Veronika Brandt, Elżbieta Byrdziak, Egin Ceka, Sandra Checa, Jakub Deka, Paul Dostert, Florian Freund, Vladimir Geiger, Julius Höck, Merethe Jensen, Matthias Kaltenbrunner, Sonia Kamenova, Monika Kokalj Kočevar, Hilda Kolevska, Alexej Konopatschenkow, Ilja Kruglow, Neven Kulenović, Adeline Lee, Gianfranco Maris, Giovanna Massariello, Andrea Mayr, Hazir Mehmeti, Irene Müller, Marica Karakaš Obradov, Reinhard Otto, Monika Pekova, Aikaterini Petraki, Markus Rachbauer, Martina Grahek Ravančić, Armin Rockenschaub, Jakob Rosenberg, Nicole Schneider, Oula Silvennoinen, Dušan Stefančič, Vojtěch Šustek, Tatiana Szekely, Réka Tercza, Sofie Van Wassenhove
Grafik / Graphic design: Walter Stromberger (kest), Claudia Offner (kest)

Animationen/Visualisierungen
Animations/Visualisations
Konzeption / Concept: Gregor Holzinger, Andreas Kranebitter, Niko Wahl
Technische Umsetzung / Technical production: Christine Pilsl / Stefan Schilcher (contraire)

Außenlagerterminal
Subcamp terminal
Konzeption / Concept: Woeishi Lean, Ralf Lechner
Ausarbeitung / Development and content: Isolde Füsselberger, Ralf Lechner
Technische Umsetzung / Technical production: Woeishi Lean

Vertiefungselement Biografien SS-Kommandanturstab
Additional biographies SS camp administration
Konzeption und Ausarbeitung / Concept, Development and content: Gregor Holzinger

Video- und Audioproduktion
Video and audio production
Wolfgang Schober
Sprecher Deutsch / Voiceover German: Rudolf Otahal, Sprecher Englisch / Voiceover English: Andrew Golder

Fotografien Ausstellung *Der Tatort Mauthausen – Eine Spurensuche*
Photographs for the exhibition *The Crimes Scenes of Mauthausen – Searching for Traces*
Tal Adler

Ausstellungsbau *Konzentrationslager Mauthausen 1938–1945* und *Der Tatort Mauthausen – Eine Spurensuche*
Exhibition construction *The Mauthausen Concentration Camp 1938-1945* and *The Crimes Scenes of Mauthausen – Searching for Traces*
Tischlerei Pucher, St. Marienkirchen

Bau *Raum der Namen* und Steg
Construction *Room of Names* and walkway
Bruckschwaiger, Langenzersdorf

Ausstellungsgrafik
Exhibition graphics
Jochen Kern / Manuel Schilcher (argeMarie)

Lichteinrichtung
Lighting design
CG-Technik

Druck
Printing
DigiCut Rubmer GesmBH, Langenstein
Lang + Lang GesmBH, Leonding

Medien Hardware
Multimedia hardware
Roland Babl
Gerd Thaler

Wir danken folgenden Archiven, Institutionen und Privatpersonen für Leihgaben und Reproduktionen
We are grateful to the following archives, institutions and private individuals for loans and reproductions
Amicale française de Mauthausen, Paris
Archeo Prospections®, Wien
Archiv der Barmherzigen Schwestern vom Heiligen Kreuz, Linz
Archiv der Stadt Linz
Archiv der Zeugen Jehovas, Selters
Archiv Granitwerke Poschacher, Mauthausen
Archiv Heimatverein Katsdorf
Archives du Comité International de la Croix-Rouge, Genf
Archives Nationales, Paris
Archiv Verein Lila Winkel, Empersdorf
Association des Amis du Centre d'Histoire de la Résistance et de la Déportation, Lyon
Bayerische Staatsbibliothek, München
Familie Belgiojoso, Mailand
Hana Berger-Moran, Orinda/Kalifornien
Bruno Biermann, Tübingen
bpk – Bildagentur für Kunst, Kultur und Geschichte, Berlin
Nancy Bowman, Lake Panasoffkee
Adolf Brunnthaler, Weyer
Bundesarchiv, Berlin
Bundesarchiv, Koblenz
Bundeskriminalamt Österreich, Wien

Burghauptmannschaft Österreich, Wien
Centralnyi Archiv Ministerstva Oborony Rossijskoj Federacii, Moskau
Centre d'Histoire de Sciences Po, Archives d'histoire contemporaine, fonds Charles Dubost, Paris
Walter Dall-Asen, Landl
Deutsche Dienststelle (WASt), Berlin
Deutsche Nationalbibliothek, Leipzig
Deutsches Historisches Museum, Berlin
Dokumentationsarchiv des österreichischen Widerstandes, Wien
Dokumentationsstelle Hartheim des Oberösterreichischen Landesarchivs, Alkoven
Pater Jeremia Karl Eisenbauer, Melk
Fédération Nationale des Déportés et Internés, Résistants et Patriotes, Paris
Emanuel Fernandez, Langenstein
Filmarchiv Austria, Wien
Fondation pour la Mémoire de la Déportation, Paris
Fortunoff Video Archive of Holocaust Testimonies, Yale University Library
Fotoarchiv des Engineering Center Steyr-Magna Powertrain, St. Valentin
Florian Freund, Wien
Gemeindeamt Bachmanning
Geschichteclub Stahl, Linz
Ghetto Fighters' House archives, Westgaliläa
Gosudarstvennyj archiv Rossijskoj Federazii, Moskau
Franz Hackl, Mauthausen
Heimo Halbrainer, Graz
Rudolf A. Haunschmied, St. Martin/Traun
Hrvatski Povijesni Muzej, Zagreb
L'Humanité, Paris
Institut für Zeitgeschichte, Wien
Institut für Zeitgeschichte der Universität Wien, Sammlung Bertrand Perz
Instituut voor Oorlogs-, Holocaust- en Genocidestudies (NIOD), Amsterdam
Instytut Pamięci Narodowej, Warschau
International Tracing Service, Bad Arolsen
Istituto per la Storia della Resistenza e della Società Contemporanea in Provincia di Asti
Istituto piemontese per la storia della Resistenza e della società contemporanea "Giorgio Agosti" (Istoreto), Turin
Paul Jiménez, Eggersdorf
KZ-Gedenkstätte Ebensee
Landesarchiv NRW – Abteilung Rheinland, Düsseldorf
Lenzing AG, Lenzing
Luftbilddatenbank Dr. Carls, Esterwegen/WienRosa Lina Marafante, Selvino/Bergamo
Rosa Lina Marafante
Marktgemeinde Mauthausen
Mauthausen Survivors Documentation Project
Musée National d'Histoire et d'Art, Luxemburg
Museu d'Història de Catalunya, Barcelona
Museum der Moderne Salzburg
Muzeum Powstania Warszawskiego, Warschau
Muzeum Stutthof
Národní archiv, Prag
Wilhelm Nowy, Mauthausen
Oberösterreichisches Landesarchiv, Linz
Oberösterreichisches Landesmuseum, Linz
Simone Odierna, Hannover

Ennio Giuseppe Odino, Brüssel
Österreichische Nationalbibliothek, Wien
Österreichisches Staatsarchiv, Wien
Památník Terezín
Państwowe Muzeum Auschwitz-Birkenau, Oświęcim
Nicolas Piquée-Audrain, Poitiers
Aurelia Płotkowiak, Poznán
Thomas Punkenhofer und Claudia Schatz, Mauthausen
Christian Rabl, Wilhelmsburg
Ralph Edwards Productions
Franz Rampold, Bachmanning
Rossijskij Gosudarstvennyj Voennyj Archiv, Moskau
Karl Sänftl, Niederaichbach
Service Historique de la Défense, Archives Iconographiques, Vincennes
Service Historique de la Défense, Bureau des Archives des Victimes des Conflits Contemporains, Caen
Simon Wiesenthal Center, Los Angeles
SPÖ Mauthausen
Staatsarchiv Nürnberg
Staatsarchiv Würzburg
Stadtarchiv Amstetten
Stadtarchiv der Ortsbürgergemeinde St. Gallen
Stadtarchiv Passau
Státní okresní archiv Mělník
Barbara Stickler, Wien
Erich Strobl, Hirtenberg
Tauber Holocaust Library – JFCS Holocaust Center, San Francisco
Thüringisches Hauptstaatsarchiv Weimar
ullstein bild, Berlin
United States Air Force Historical Research Agency, Maxwell, AL
United States Holocaust Memorial Museum, Washington, DC
United States National Archives and Records Administration
Unternehmensmuseum der Hirtenberger AG, Hirtenberg
USC Shoah Foundation Institute, Los Angeles
Joaquín Valsells Casasús, Barcelona
Verein für die Geschichte der Arbeiterbewegung, Wien
Verzetsmuseum Amsterdam
Vojenský historický archiv, Prag
Walter Frentz Collection, Berlin
Wienbibliothek
Wiener Stadt- und Landesarchiv
Wien Museum
Yad Vashem, The Holocaust Martyrs' and Heroes' Remembrance Authority, Jerusalem
Yale University, Manuscripts & Archives, New Haven
ZF Friedrichshafen AG, Konzernarchiv, Friedrichshafen

Dank für die Unterstützung des Projekts „Raum der Namen" gilt folgenden Botschaften und Institutionen
Our thanks for their support of the 'Room of Names' project go to the following embassies and institutions

Botschaften der Länder / Embassies of the following countries: Albanien, Armenien, Aserbaidschan, Belarus, Belgien, Bosnien-Herzegowina, Estland, Frankreich, Georgien, Griechenland, Italien, Kasachstan, Kosovo, Kroatien, Lettland, Litauen, Luxemburg, Mazedonien, Moldau, Niederlande, Polen, Rumänien, Russische Föderation, Serbien, Slowenien, Slowakei, Spanien, Tschechien, Ungarn.

Institutionen / Institutions
Amicale des déportés, familles et amis de Mauthausen, Associazione nazionale ex deportati nei campi nazisti, Centre de Documentation et de Recherche sur la Résistance, Comité International de Mauthausen, Dokumentationsarchiv des österreichischen Widerstands, Fundacja Polsko-Niemieckie Pojednanie, Gedenkstätte Bergen-Belsen, Holokauszt Emlékközpont Budapest, Hrvatski institut za povijest, International Tracing Service, Bad Arolsen, Institut für Konfliktforschung, KZ-Gedenkstätte Dachau, KZ-Gedenkstätte Ebensee, KZ-Gedenkstätte Flossenbürg, Lern- und Gedenkort Schloss Hartheim, Lietuvos gyventojų genocido ir rezistencijos tyrimo centras, Ministerstvo obrany České republiky, Ministarstvo rada, zapošljavanja i socijalne politike Republike Srbije, Ministerstvo Vnútra Slovenskej Republiky, Państwowe Muzeum Auschwitz-Birkenau, Stichting Vriendenkring Mauthausen.

Dank für Hinweise, Unterstützung und Mitarbeit
With thanks for advice, support and assistance

Ilsen About, Michael Ahrer, Krzysztof Antonczyk, Andrea D'Arrigo, Andreas Baumgartner, Judith Benedix, Andreas Bilgeri, Anne Bonamy, Gerhard Botz, Elżbieta Brzóska, Günther Buchinger, Sandra Checa, Pierre Serge Choumoff (†), Madeleine Choumoff, Judith Cohen, Guy Dockendorf, France Filipič (†), Florian Freund, Oliver Fürnhammer, Martha Gammer, Iva Gaudesová, Sergio Gibellini, Martin Gilly, Patrick F. Greaney, Heide Gsell, Neal Guthrie, Rudolf A. Haunschmied, Walter Hofstätter, Regina Hönerlage, Michael Huemer, Rudolf Jeřábek, Sr. Klara Maria Katzensteiner, Josef Klat, Katharina Kniefacz, Albert Knoll, Karsten Kühnel, Paul LeCaër, Margret Lehner-Wessely, Franka Lechner, Nedina Malinović, Hans Maršálek (†), Hilde Maršálek, Gianfranco Maris, Josef Mötz, Bernhard Mühleder, Norbert Obernhumer, Marco Odino, Thomas Punkenhofer, Wolfgang Quatember, Ines Rieder, Heike Rührig, Christine Schindler, Amy Schmidt, Florian Schwanninger, Elisabeth Schwarz, Ursula Schwarz, Bernhard Seyringer, Agnieszka Sieradzka, Daniel Simon, Wilhelm Stadler, Jana Starek, Anatol Steck, Dušan Stefančič, Richard Steger, Frits van Suchtelen, Vojtěch Šustek, Tilman Taube, Gerhard Ungar, Susanne Urban, Günter Vielhaber, Franz Walzer, Rüdiger Weibold, Tony West, Barbara Wiesinger, Michael Winninger, Ernst Ziegler, Joanna Ziemska

Allen Mitgliedern des Internationalen Forum Mauthausen
All the members of the International Forum Mauthausen

Allen MitarbeiterInnen und Zivildienstleistenden der KZ-Gedenkstätte Mauthausen
All the staff and those performing their civilian service at the Mauthausen Memorial

Allen involvierten Organisationseinheiten des Bundesministeriums für Inneres.
All the departments involved at the Federal Ministry of the Interior

Im Besonderen bedanken wir uns bei Frau Bundesministerin Johanna Mikl-Leitner und Sektionschef Hermann Feiner.
In particular we would like to thank Federal Minister Johanna Mikl-Leiter and Department Head Hermann Feiner.

Sollte trotz sorgfältiger Zusammenstellung jemand vergessen worden sein, bitten wir um Nachsicht. Allen Beteiligten sei sehr herzlich für ihre Hilfe und Unterstützung gedankt.
We extend our deepest gratitude to all who provided this invaluable support, and our apologies to anyone who may have escaped acknowledgement.

Die Ausstellungen wurden durch Mittel des Bundesministeriums für Inneres der Republik Österreich realisiert.
The exhibitions were funded by the Federal Ministry of the Interior of the Republic of Austria.

Der Zukunftsfonds der Republik Österreich hat begleitende Forschungsprojekte unterstützt, die vom Verein für Gedenken und Geschichtsforschung in österreichischen KZ-Gedenkstätten dankenswerterweise administrativ betreut wurden.
The Future Fund of the Republic of Austria provided funding for the associated research projects, which were kindly administrated by the Association for Remembrance and Historical Research in Austrian Concentration Camp Memorials.

Die Sanierung des Museumsgebäudes wurde in Kooperation mit dem Bundesdenkmalamt realisiert und aus Mitteln der Burghauptmannschaft Österreich finanziert.
The renovations to the museum building were carried out in co-operation with the Federal Monuments Office and funded by the Austrian Buildings Commission.